THE ELEMENTARY SCHOOL HANDBOOK

OTHER TITLES IN THIS SERIES

THE PRESCHOOL HANDBOOK
by Barbara Brenner

**OTHER BANK STREET COLLEGE OF
EDUCATION BOOKS**

RAISING A CONFIDENT CHILD
*by Joanne Oppenheim, Barbara Brenner, and
Betty D. Boegehold*

BUY ME! BUY ME!:
THE BANK STREET GUIDE TO CHOOSING
TOYS FOR CHILDREN
by Joanne Oppenheim

CHOOSING BOOKS FOR KIDS
*by Joanne Oppenheim, Barbara Brenner,
and Betty D. Boegehold*

BANK STREET'S COMPLETE PARENT GUIDE TO K-6

THE ELEMENTARY SCHOOL HANDBOOK

MAKING THE MOST OF YOUR CHILD'S EDUCATION

BY JOANNE OPPENHEIM

PANTHEON BOOKS
NEW YORK

Library of Congress Cataloging-in-Publication Data
Oppenheim, Joanne.
The elementary school handbook.
"A Bank Street College of Education Book."
Includes index.
1. School, Choice of—United States.   2. Elementary schools—
United States—Evaluation.   3. Education—United States—
Parent participation.   4. Home and school—United States
I. Title.
LB1027.9.067   1989   371'.00973   89-42554

Book Design by Jan Melchior

Manufactured in the United States of America'

First Edition

TO MY MOTHER

CONTENTS

CHAPTER 3

CHAPTER 4

CHAPTER 9

CHAPTER 10

ACKNOWLEDGMENTS

So many people have been helpful in the preparation of this book. I am especially grateful to Joan Cenedella, dean of Children's Programs at Bank Street College, who shared her ideas and expertise from first draft to last.

My thanks to many Bank Street colleagues, who allowed me to observe in their classrooms or graciously answered my many questions. Thanks go to Joan Auclair, Lesley Bell, Dr. Bernice Berk, Barbara Brenner, Christine Burns, George Burns, Rosemarie Buzzeo, Rob Caramella, Judith Gold, Mark Greenwald, Rebecca Kesler, Dr. Leah Levinger, Anne Marie Mott, Beth Norford, Sandra Pezzella, Ann Schaefer, Amy Waterbury, and Pearl Zeitz. Grateful acknowledgment is made to Margaret Peet, who prepared the many drafts of this manuscript, and to Jeanette Stanziano, who was my link to the staff of the Bank Street School for Children. Thanks also to Lourdes L. Andre, president of the Bank Street Parents Association.

Many thanks to James Levine, president of the Media Group, who supported this project, and to William Hooks, my editor, who, as always, gave me encouragement and insightful suggestions.

Outside the Bank Street community, I am indebted to Dr. John Savidge, principal of the Pocono Elementary Center, and the parents of that school, who graciously answered a lengthy questionnaire about their experiences. Thanks also to Dr. Carol Seefeldt of the University of Maryland, Dr. Jessica Cohen, coordinator of Effective School Planning of the Onondaga-Cortland-Madison

B.O.C.E.S., and Selma Field, member of the Board of S.U.N.Y., New Paltz, all personal friends who listened and raised questions during the early gestation of this book.

Special thanks to Tom Engelhardt, my editor at Pantheon, for his patience and for adding so many important ideas as the book grew.

My thanks to the dozens of children, parents, teachers, and administrators with whom I worked and whose lives touched my own and that of my family.

Finally, my thanks to my husband, Stephen L. Oppenheim, who remains my captive listener, constructive critic, and most loyal fan.

THE
ELEMENTARY
SCHOOL
HANDBOOK

I N T R O D U C T · I O N

Few things are of greater concern to parents than the education of their children. In fact, in the earliest years, whether they realize it or not, they have probably been their children's main teachers. Yet when "real" school begins, parents often find that they, too, feel like beginners. Every question that comes up may seem unnerving: How do you choose the school where your child will feel most comfortable, the place most likely to foster learning, growth, and the values you care about? Or what do you do if you have no choice but a less than great school for your child? How do you talk with your child's teacher about your concerns? How (and how much) do you help your child with his or her reading, math, writing, and other schoolwork? How do you navigate the unknown realms of school testing? Parents want to be involved in their child's school experience, and they are likely to care deeply about what sort of education their child gets, but how can these feelings be translated into actions? Once the new sneakers, lunchbox, and back-to-school supplies have been bought, where does the parent fit into the educational process, and where does school fit into parenting?

Whatever confusion parents may feel, schools often add to it with well-meaning but contradictory messages. Educators frequently urge parents to work with them as partners. But what does that actually mean? Yes, they may say, "Get involved!" but no, they may also add, loud and clear, "Don't interfere!" In other words, help—but not too much and only in the "right" way.

3

Aside from baking cupcakes for the class party or going to the school fair (which you may or may not have either the time or the inclination to do), how should you as a parent get involved in the school experience in educationally meaningful ways? How can you tell where the parent's role ends and the school's role begins? How can you make that "partnership" something more than a pleasantly vague phrase?

Naturally enough, you want to help, and the truth is, you can. The purpose of this book is to give *you* ways, large and small, to do that: ways to deal with the problems school—any school—is guaranteed to bring into your life; ways, large and small, to help your child learn and grow through the school years; ways, large and small, to help you, too, get pleasure and enjoyment from the partnership you actually can create between your child, your school, and yourself.

PARENTS AS PARTNERS TO WHAT?

Interested as parents may be, they aren't sure what's happening in their child's school or when it should be happening. Yet, asking is not always easy. Questioning may be interpreted as criticism, and many parents are reluctant to offend the teacher's authority. Indeed, for some parents, school brings back the child inside their grown-up selves. Old feelings from their earlier experiences in the classroom come back to haunt them. So, otherwise totally competent adults can be reduced to that "whatever you say, ma'am" sense of powerlessness the moment they open the schoolhouse door again. Since most of us were sent off to school with new shoes, new pencils, and the admonition "The teacher is the boss," it is not easy to figure out how to play this new role in an ill-defined partnership.

Nor do all parents feel confident that their children are attending the best of all possible schools. Like our parents and grandparents, we send our children to school with the expectation that they are going to learn. But we no longer trust that the school will do the whole job or do it well. And reports in the media confirm our worst fears. Recent studies suggest the need for more tests, more homework, more discipline, tougher standards for promotion, a longer school day, a lengthened school year. This get-tough attitude, an outgrowth of the "Back to Basics" movement, is partially a reaction to the short-lived "open classroom" reforms of the seventies. It also reflects recurrent reports that our schools are not

4

preparing children for the increasingly complex and international world in which they will live. In the search for quick cures and perfect solutions educational trends tend to shift from one extreme to another. All educators do not agree on how children learn best, what they need to learn, or even when. As always there are conflicting philosophies and, all too frequently, no philosophy at all but only an ever-changing smorgasbord of "new programs." So, on whom should parents rely? If you have the luxury of choice, what kind of school should you select? Or if, like most of us, you must send your child to the "only show in town," what role do you play? How do you press school authorities for change? Can you make up for the school's deficiencies by what you do at home? How do you help your child get the most from these crucial learning years? With whom do you become partners?

A DUAL PERSPECTIVE

In my own experience as both a parent and a teacher I sat at both sides of the desk, and I believe that gives me a different kind of perspective than those who have done only one job or the other. Long before becoming a teacher I was an activist in school affairs and served as president of the Parent-Teacher Association. I have known the frustration of getting the school board to cut the size of my first-grade son's class from thirty-seven to twenty-five, only to find that they did so by increasing my fourth-grade son's class from twenty-eight to thirty-eight.

Similarly, after pressing for regular parent-teacher conferences and setting forth the how and why of instituting them, conferences were scheduled in the multipurpose room at seven-minute intervals, at which time parents were handed the same report card children otherwise would have brought home. Neither the amount of time nor the space invited any meaningful or personal exchange of ideas or concerns. As a parent I discovered that making changes in schools is often like wading through Jell-O. You think you've made progress, but when you look back, it's hard to see the laborious steps you've trudged through. This is not to say that parents cannot bring positive change about; it is rather an acknowledgment that in doing so, the reality often falls short of the mark.

In my teaching years I also had to come to terms with the frustration of working in a rigidly "traditional" school that was basically in conflict with my training, in what is generally known as a "progressive" school. This, too, I believe, gives this book a different perspective than books written by those who have only known one approach or the other. While it would have been easier—and a happier experience, no doubt—to have worked at and sent my three children to a "perfect" or at least "better" school, like many parents and teachers, there was no real choice. It was the only school where we lived and not very different from those we might have commuted to instead. All of these experiences, both in and out of the classroom, have helped to shape this book.

WHAT THIS BOOK IS ABOUT

The Elementary School Handbook will show you how to make the partnership between parents, school, and child into a meaningful relationship that works. At times that partnership will call for stepping in and acting as an advocate on behalf of your child's needs and rights. More often than not, it will involve dealing directly with your child; knowing when to help (and when not to); recognizing the difference between a problem that needs active attention and one that is normal and simply bears watchful concern. Very often parents are told that children's performance in school reflects parental expectations. However, parents who have unrealistically high expectations can do as much damage as those who expect too little. This book can help clarify what you should (and should not) realistically expect from your child. Studies show that parental involvement relates directly to children's success in school. Such involvement not only improves student achievement, it can improve the quality of schools themselves.

This book will give you a closeup look at schools as they are today. In a generally nonjudgmental way, it examines the differences between traditional and less traditional schools and how those differences affect what, when, and even how children are taught. While it is true that many traditional schools have borrowed and modified ideas from less traditional schools, essentially the basic differences become most apparent in how those ideas are translated into practice. Although all schools share the common goals of teaching children basic skills, we will look at the significant differences in how those goals are enacted.

To describe those differences, I have drawn on my own experience in the classroom; on interviews with dozens of parents and teachers; and on observations in a variety of classrooms, in both public and private schools in urban, suburban, and rural settings.

The Elementary School Handbook is not a manual for reforming the schools, yet it can help parents see the way schools are and how they could or should be. While parents and teachers may find ideas that they wish were at work in their children's schools, the focus here is on dealing with schools as they are. This doesn't mean that parents can do nothing to bring change about, nor that a multitude of changes are not needed in our schools today. In fact, we will look at how some parents have done exactly that. However, personal experience suggests that translating such ideas into reality takes time and the joint efforts of parents and school personnel.

While these efforts are worth striving for, such long-range goals seldom solve the immediate and individual needs of children who are going to school right now. In other words, change comes slowly, but children grow fast. For that reason, this book addresses the many ways that parents can best support their children's educational experiences in whatever school they are attending.

USING THIS BOOK

This is a book that you will use in multiple ways at different points in your child's school career. It is not a book you are likely to read from cover to cover, but rather a resource you can turn to as needs arise.

Even before your child enters a school, you'll find that chapter one, "What Are Your Choices? (Even If You Have None)," can give you some direction in selecting the school of your choice or evaluating the only school available. It will help you to see how schools differ philosophically and how those differences shape the climate of a school and its goals. You'll learn what to look for and what questions to ask yourself and others in order to evaluate how well a school is likely to fit your goals and your child's needs.

In making your choices it will also be helpful to read through the sections of this book that are age-appropriate for your child in order to think about what's important to *you* in a school. For example, if you're concerned about reading, you can turn to the section on reading in the kindergarten or primary grades. This will give you some sense of the issues you should consider, the things you might look for during your visit, and the questions you might want to ask of that school. Such evaluations can shape your final choices or help you to recognize where your active involvement may be needed to enrich your child's learning experiences.

You can use this book to prepare yourself more generally for what to expect in the upcoming elementary years. By reading through the age-appropriate sections, you'll get an overview of what to expect and when. It will tell you about the general issues for a particular age level, what problems you are likely to encounter, and matters you may need to consider. For example, months before your child enters kindergarten, you will find useful information about how to prepare for this major event. Or, as your child moves from third to fourth grade, you may find it helpful to read about the intermediate grades and how the emphasis shifts from learning the three Rs to using them in new ways.

You can also use this book for immediate problem solving. For example, suppose you and your second-grader are having a terrible time over homework, fighting about it every night. What can you do? You might start by reading the suggestions about dealing with homework in the primary chapter. In fact, you'll find age-appropriate sections about homework in the intermediate-grades and kindergarten chapters, as well. Or suppose the school notifies you that they want to test your child for learning disabilities. The sections on testing and learning disabilities will give you information about what to expect and what questions you should ask. If you're concerned about an upcoming conference or feel confused about test scores, you can use the index to find specific pages that will answer your questions.

Whether you're worried about your child's science, math, reading, or any other subject, you can use this book to come up with innumerable suggestions for ways in which you as a parent can be positively involved in your child's education inside of and—perhaps more importantly—outside of school. *The Elementary School Handbook* offers literally hundreds of ways you can work with your child and in some cases make up for deficiencies in his or her education. Instead of feeling totally passive or helpless about what's happening, you can use the appropriate "How Parent's Can Help" activities to support skills children are learning in school. You may also find it helpful to share portions of this book with those who share with you the responsibilities of caring for your child. In today's two-career families, parents frequently need to rely on other caregivers during afterschool hours. Whether it's a grandparent, housekeeper, or nanny, this book can be a resource they can use for practical suggestions.

However, keep in mind that no child needs or should be expected to do all of these activities. Indeed, if you helped your child in every area mentioned, the book would turn into a full-time occupation and your child's life into a drudgery of "fun" exercises at home. You, the parent, don't want to become just another nag, nor turn home into another school, in the negative sense. Consider which of these activities will be helpful, but be selective. Pick and choose only those activities that are enjoyable in an easy and relaxed way. The bottom line should be having fun with your child without adding pressure to perform. You also need to recognize your own strengths and weaknesses. As a child you may have had trouble with math, or, on the other hand, you may be a highly sophisticated mathematician. In either case, you may be the wrong person to help your child with math. You might be well advised to leave that subject to the teacher and others. Knowing when to stay out as a parent is often as important as knowing when to get involved. Trust your gut instincts if you have the feeling that getting involved in certain activities will lead to trouble.

In the final chapters of the book you'll find information that deals with testing, conferences, school personnel, special programs, and organizations that you should know about. You can also use the book for more general problem solving. You may feel, for example, that your child's school leaves a lot to be desired. But, you may wonder, what can I do about it? How can I help? You'll find a multitude of ideas in each chapter that you can act on as an individual or in concert with other concerned parents. You'll also find a section on parents' organizations (see pages 287–91) and how parents have joined together and brought about positive changes in their schools.

In dealing with the language of gender I recognize that teachers and students are neither all *he*s nor all *she*s. However, to avoid the cumbersome intrusion of *he/she* or *s/he*, teachers are frequently referred to as *she*. For variety's sake, students are sometimes referred to as *he*, sometimes as *she*. However, the pronouns do not indicate a gender-specific problem. The issues being discussed are applicable to both genders. These decisions were made for ease of reading.

While some parents may enjoy reading the entire book so that they have an overview of what's coming next, most will want to use it as a resource they can turn to as issues arise. By assuming the role of an active and informed partner in your child's education, you will be helping your child get the most from these early school years. Making that partnership work is not always easy—but it's elementary.

WHAT ARE YOUR CHOICES?

(EVEN IF YOU HAVE NONE)

EVALUATING THE CHOICES

Whether you as parents have multiple choices or virtually none in selecting a school for your child, it's important for you to know how to evaluate the schools in your community. That's what this chapter is about.

Informed parents are better able to help children get the most from whatever school their child attends. Knowing what to look for and what questions to ask can help you.

▲ Select wisely if there are choices
• Work harmoniously with your child and the school
▪ Lend extra support at home in areas that the school may not be addressing

▲ Become an articulate and active participant in school issues and your child's education

• Become an advocate for change where it is needed

KNOW YOUR CHOICES

There may be a neighborhood public school around the corner or a "magnet" school with a special art or science program that requires a half-hour bus ride each day. "Magnet" schools are those designed to attract (like a magnet) culturally diverse students from several neighborhoods who have special interests or talents. In some areas there may be a voucher system that allows you to pick and choose from a range of schools with very different philosophies and approaches. Then, too, your community may have a variety of private schools with differing philosophies. One may be a religious-based school that reflects your spiritual beliefs. Another may have a reputation for academic excellence. A third may be an experimental-lab school on a university campus. How do you go about sorting out the possibilities?

HOW SCHOOLS DIFFER

Driving from one rural community to another, it's often not hard to recognize the local elementary schools. Those sprawling, one-storied, flat-roofed, concrete-block buildings, their windows plastered with pumpkins or hearts (depending on the season), their playgrounds dotted with climbing bars and swings, all look pretty much alike. Built in the post–World War II years, they are architectural timepieces, as identifiable as the WPA two-story brick schoolhouses of the 1930s. Yet, what goes on inside those look-alike schools tends to be diverse.

In broad philosophical terms most schools fall roughly into one of three categories:

THE TEACHER-CENTERED SCHOOL: Here the driving force in the classroom is the teacher. It is from her that all knowledge flows. Even the arrangement of the room reflects her approach to children. Their desks lined up in orderly rows facing her desk at the front of the room. She spends her day actively teaching, drilling, testing, and reteaching what must be learned. It is the teacher who must fill the empty heads of her students. She controls the discipline as well as the questions, for which she is the arbiter of

12

correct answers. She may be cool and stern or kindly and even-handed, but clearly it is she alone who orchestrates the day and conducts the show. Students are expected to follow her lead. She is the active "giver" while children play the more passive role of "receivers."

THE SUBJECT-CENTERED SCHOOL: Here the driving force in the classroom is the curriculum. It is the subject matter that sets the timetable that both teacher and students are expected to follow. Often the choice of that curriculum is made by administrators who rely heavily on textbooks designed by experts. Often, too, there is an implied assumption that teachers need scripts from which to teach. So decisions are made from the top down, and learning is viewed as a series of premade lessons that can be taught on a sequential time line. Such schools are often run like businesses where the buzzwords are *efficiency* and *accountability*. Progress is tracked by flow charts and measured by test scores. Here the curriculum is the "giver" and both students and teachers are "receivers."

THE CHILD-CENTERED SCHOOL: Here the driving force comes from the children, and the curriculum is shaped to meet their developmental needs and interests. The teacher facilitates learning by providing an environment that invites questions, exploration, and experimentation. Rather than dictating or directing every step of the way, the teacher plays the role of initiator and sounding board. Instead of imposing a premade curriculum, she tailors instruction to children's individual needs. Here the students are at the center of their own learning. Children play a more active role and have a wider range of choices in what and how they will study. The motivation to learn is not imposed by others, but supported by taking cues from the child. Both teacher and child respond to each other in an atmosphere of give-and-take.

No schools are entirely teacher-, subject-, or child-centered. Many schools, both public and private, combine traits from all three models. All elementary schools share the common goal of teaching children the basic skills. How they do so differs.

Typically traditional schools lean more closely toward the

teacher- and subject-centered mode. Their focus is largely on academic skills. There are both public and private schools that follow this model. More recently many of these schools have identified themselves with the "Back to Basics" movement. Of course, good schools, traditional or not, have never given up the "basics."

However, basic academic skills in nontraditional schools, while viewed as important, are seen as only part of what children need to learn in the process of becoming educated individuals. Nontraditional schools tend to use a more child-centered approach. Their focus is more likely to be on the child's total development as a thinking, feeling, and social being.

At their worst, traditional schools can be arid and restrictive environments that impose an ill-fitting agenda. Similarly, at their worst, nontraditional schools can be chaotic environments that lack an agenda. Both models have inherent weaknesses and strengths. At their best, both traditional and experimental elementary schools can give children the foundations for a lifetime of learning.

THE STYLES OF GROUPING

Schools also differ in the way they organize classes for instruction. Your child may be placed in a *heterogeneous group*. Here students with varying levels of achievement are put together. Often academic achievement is the main factor in placement decisions, but social and behavioral issues may also be considered. There are many variations of heterogeneous grouping. Historically the old one-room schoolhouse was the precursor of this kind of grouping. In such classrooms today, children's ages as well as their academic achievements may vary. Within the classroom the teacher usually groups children by ability for instructional ease. She may also work at times with individual students. So, in fact, within the heterogeneous group there may be several groups of children with similar skills levels.

In some schools children are placed in *homogeneous groups*. Here students with similar academic achievement skills are placed together for instruction. While other factors, such as social and emotional issues, may be considered, placement is primarily made on the basis of academic skills. At one time such groupings were considered the most feasible way of meeting children's needs. Schools that favor homogeneous grouping usually have an "A" class for their ablest students and a "B" (and possibly a "C") class for less able children at each grade level. You may have attended such a school.

However, homogeneous grouping is less favored these days. Why? Because even within such a group there are likely to be broad variations. For example, one child may be terrific in reading but not in math, or academically a student might be years ahead of his peers but socially unable to hold his own. In other words, children as individuals are not homogeneous. Studies have also found that such labels often prove to be self-fulfilling prophecies by shaping the expectations of both students and teachers. When teachers are told their students are ''slow,'' they seem to expect less, and children seem to respond accordingly. This kind of grouping can be demoralizing for teachers as well as for students. The teacher of the ''best'' group may be perceived as the ''best'' and therefore most desirable teacher, whereas the teacher of a B or C group may be considered less able, even though her job calls for equal or greater talents.

In some instances homogeneous grouping really leads to de facto segregation. Since such groups are usually made on the basis of standardized tests, which are biased in favor of middle-class white students, it's no surprise that more minority students end up in the B or C groups. Such grouping not only separates rich from poor, it reinforces class differences by slotting children on separate ''tracks'' with significantly different programs and long-range outcomes. Enter most B or C classrooms and you are more likely to find a steady stream of workbooks, ditto sheets, and programmed instruction read from a script. It's as if it has been decided that the children of the poor only need to learn answers to questions that have right, wrong, or simplistic answers.

''Tracking'' not only puts children in programs that limit what they will learn and therefore what they will ultimately be able to do, it also makes no provision for those who might blossom on a slightly different time schedule. Indeed, it is most especially the children of the poor who are likely to have deficiencies in language as it is defined by those who rely on standardized tests for placement.

Although some schools continue to use homogeneous grouping, educators currently believe that children benefit more from working, playing, and living in a heterogeneous group. They feel this is especially important during the early years of school.

15

Keep in mind that in a heterogeneous group the child who is average in academic areas may be the best pitcher or singer in the class. The ablest reader may motivate or assist a classmate, and both will grow from the experience. Indeed, a lot of valuable peer teaching and learning can go on in heterogeneous groups. Recent studies indicate that when students of mixed abilities are put in cooperative learning situations, student achievement is increased for all. In such settings children have opportunities both to lead and to follow, to give as well as to take. There are some children who get off to a quick start and then plateau, while others flounder at first and then forge ahead. When young children are placed in ability groups, there is a real danger of prematurely judging and labeling them before they have had time to develop.

THE FIRST STEP IN CHOOSING A SCHOOL FOR YOUR CHILD

To begin with, you need to examine your own values and goals for your child. Of course, all of us want the best school we can find. Probably the word *excellence* comes to mind. But what if, by all accounts, the only excellent school in your community is a religious-based school and you are not an especially religious person. If the religious part of its program extends and harmonizes with your own beliefs, it may be a comfortable choice. But how will you respond if you are pressured by your child (or the school) to embrace rituals that you don't believe in? If you refuse, will your child be put in the position of being different to a fault? What if, in fact, you are a practicing agnostic? Chances are this "excellent" school would nevertheless be a poor choice.

In certain circumstances, however, compared with all other available choices it may seem like the only feasible one. For example, in Chicago 40 percent of the enrollment in Catholic parochial schools is made up of non-Catholic students. Faced with a choice of drugs, violence, and high dropout rates in inner-city public schools, parents feel less threatened by the idea of their children attending a few hours of religious classes.

Such conflicts are hardly limited to the issue of religion. You might feel that a school's approach to discipline is at variance with your own. A school may strike you as too permissive or too rigid and mean-spirited. In either case, the setting would be inappropriate for your child. There might be any number of other issues concerning a school's philosophy or methodology that clash with your own values.

A serious disparity between your personal beliefs and the school's is likely to lead to endless conflicts between home and school, with your child caught in the middle. While no home and school will ever always see eye to eye, choosing a school whose philosophy is fundamentally different from your own is an invitation to disaster.

What Are the School's Goals?

In considering a school, you'll want to find one that most closely reflects your value system and your philosophy of child rearing. The fact that a school has a great reputation for getting students into the best high school or teaches reading to five-year-olds does not automatically make it the best choice for your child. You'll need to consider how successful your child is apt to be in such a setting. Many bright children simply don't "fit" in schools that run on the fast track. Keep in mind, a school that focuses on high scores may be a pressure cooker that values the school's reputation more than its students' developmental needs.

While parents may wish to give children every opportunity, remember that one need not attend the "best" nursery school, grade school, or high school to be a happy and successful individual. Children who get caught up in such pursuits at five may burn out before they attain goals set by others. Indeed, they may go out of their way later on to reject such goals. In looking toward the future we need to be sure that what is done in the present is appropriate.

Does the School Meet Your Child's Needs?

In choosing a school you need to consider your child's individual style, talents, interests, and temperament. A school with rigorous academic demands may be fine for your eldest son and totally inappropriate for your youngest. One child may thrive in a setting where children have many choices and are expected to work with great independence. Another child may flounder with that much freedom and need a more tightly directed program.

That a school has limited physical-education facilities may make little difference for some children but be a major flaw for those who thrive on sports. Similarly, a child who is musically or artistically inclined may be perfectly miserable in a school that puts great emphasis on its chess or swim team. Ideally, during the elementary years, a school should offer a rich mix of activities so that children can test and explore a variety of interests. However, some schools are more clearly directed toward the arts or sports. Others are more focused on children's academic development at the expense of their emotional and social growth. Parents need to evaluate a school on the basis of each child's unique needs. They need to ask themselves, ''Is this the right school for this particular child?''

PUBLIC VERSUS PRIVATE SCHOOL

As you evaluate a school, it's easy to be impressed with an up-to-date physical plant, the trendiest programs and equipment, or the highest tuition. Remember, schools often use their equipment to impress parents. You need to get past the window dressing and price tag to evaluate a school's worth. It's how equipment is used and by whom that really counts.

Parents sometimes assume that because they pay more, their children will get more. As a result, those who can afford a pricey private school tend to vie for a coveted spot when there's an excellent public school just down the street that's free of charge. For some it's a status trip to be able to say, ''My child goes to———.'' It proves what good providers they are and puts them among the ''select'' few. To cover the fees, they may make sacrifices or take on extra work loads to buy the best. So, the gain may end up as a loss of energy and time to share directly with their child. Indeed, where budgets are extremely strained, the net result may be resentment for the parents and guilt for the child.

Before you decide that private school is a must, don't dismiss public school out of hand. Check your options carefully. You may be surprised to discover a gem of a public school that will not strain the budget and possibly relationships in the family. Even if money is no object, the high price of a school is no guarantee of its high quality.

If you are considering a private school, be sure to inquire about all the costs involved. Remember, the tuition is not likely to include the costs of transportation, lunch, trips, uniforms, books, and other possible surprises. Ask about these up front. Inquire, too, about the availability of full or partial scholarships. Some schools have such funds available, and you may qualify. Although we often think of private schools as the domain of the rich, many fine schools offer financial assistance to less affluent families so that their student bodies will better reflect the real world.

IS THIS SCHOOL NONRACIST?

As you visit a school ask yourself, does this school offer cultural diversity? Or is it a ghettoized school? There are rich ghettos as well as poor ones, and neither is an appropriate place for children to learn in the fullest sense. Ideally, during their formative years, children benefit from working and playing with others from various cultural and ethnic backgrounds. Their teachers, too, should reflect the multicultural society in which they are growing up. However, the reality is that in urban areas especially, ghettoized schools reflect ghettoized neighborhoods. Parents may have little or no choice in where they live or in the schools their children attend.

Many of today's parents were schoolchildren when the battle for desegregated schools was being waged. Ultimately change was mandated by law. However, the goal of integrated classrooms has yet to be achieved either in the South or the North. Rather than strengthening our schools, the aftermath of the sixties has brought with it an abundance of private academies and urban flight that reflect historic racist bias. Over the past several decades we have seen northern cities wrenched with anger and violence as leaders tried to break the pattern of de facto segregation by bussing children in and out of ghettoized schools and neighborhoods.

Although we like to think that we have come miles since those days in the sixties when federal marshals had to accompany black students into all-white classrooms, public schools of the late eighties remain essentially biased against the success of students from poor families. Schools in poor neighborhoods and communities generally have fewer dollars to spend per student and their performance reflects as much. More affluent families have the option of living in neighborhoods that can afford the tax dollars needed to buy more staff, textbooks, and equipment. They also have the option and money to send their children to private schools. The fact that students in poorer schools are less likely to achieve or that more of them will drop out before completing high school represents a tremendous failure of our society and a potential tragedy for our country's future.

Whether these issues affect your child directly or not today, they must ultimately affect all of us and our children's future in particular. It is not just our own child's education that we need to be concerned about, but the educational opportunities for all of our children. As a parent you may have no options or multiple choices. In either case, as a citizen you can work toward the ideals of better schools for everyone. You can do that by being well informed and supporting candidates who make schools and education a priority, not just campaign rhetoric. You can work as a school board member, as an activist in your parent organization, or as a volunteer in a school that needs your talents and interests.

Those who have the luxury of making choices often fear that exposure to other lifestyles and cultures will interfere with the values they are trying to convey. Yet in choosing schools that isolate children from those unlike themselves, we give children a limited view of the world that can have long-range effects on their understanding of themselves and others. It is from their interaction with all sorts of people that children can best find commonalities and appreciate, rather than fear, differences.

As you evaluate a school, keep in mind that a racially mixed student population does not in and of itself indicate a nonracist approach to education. Schools that label and group children by early test scores tip the scales against poorer students who, as pointed out earlier, traditionally score less well on standardized tests, which are culturally biased. They test with language and concepts that may be as unfamiliar and unfair to some students as say, taking a quiz in calculus would be for kindergartners. All too often such test scores are used to justify more limited programs and expectations for economically and socially disadvantaged students. So, from early on, many children are closed out of some programs and locked into others.

In evaluating a school, whether or not you are a minority parent, ask how students are grouped for instruction. Homogeneous (ability) grouping may indicate that students are essentially separated on fast and slow tracks. Note, too, if there are minority adults in leadership roles as teachers, administrators, school nurse or secretary. Or are the only minority adults in the school washing dishes or pushing a broom? There's nothing wrong with manual labor, but students should have multi-ethnic models in leadership positions as well.

Schools that are seriously committed to providing a non-racist environment do more than simply accept students who apply. Instead of children fitting into ability groups, flexible programs are fitted to children's abilities. Barriers are not put in the path by slotting children onto the fast or slow track. Testing and evaluation is used to give more individualized attention to students' needs rather than to score or judge children prematurely. Extra help is given where needed within mixed ability groups that allow for greater gains and higher expectations for all students, not just the quick starters. Such schools do not foster a mentality of second-class citizenship that separates the "haves" and "have-nots." They make free instruments available for those who would like to play in the band rather than saying, "None of our poor students seem to be interested." Private schools offer scholarships to students who would otherwise be unable to attend. They do not simply say, "No poor students applied." In short, a truly integrated school takes affirmative action to give all of its students opportunities to grow. Schools can take an active role in leadership by providing an environment that fosters the dignity, skills, and dreams of our democracy and all its citizens. Parents who are actively involved can press for such leadership and responsibility.

Look for Yourself!

The newest trend in evaluating schools is a movement to grade schools with report cards. California, Illinois, West Virginia, and New Jersey are publishing report cards that compare each school's test scores against those of other schools in a community and against the state average. Of course, the fallacy here is that education can be reduced to number crunching—like batting averages. Given the nature of (and inherent weakness of) standardized tests (see pages 221–26), this kind of score card can lead to building curriculum around testing. That's like letting the tail wag the dog.

Those who have several choices will want to take the time to visit the schools they are considering. A school may have a fine reputation and still be the wrong choice for your child. Valuable as word-of-mouth reports may be, recommendations from others are of less value than a firsthand evaluation of your own. Your neighbor may have different expectations than you do. Furthermore, her child may have very different needs than yours.

Call the schools you want to visit early enough in the year so that you can see them in session. Avoid making decisions about a school without looking for yourself. Private schools often begin interviews and visits in the fall. Arrange to visit on days when schools are in session. Although a school may have a marvelous physical plant, the real story unfolds when it comes alive with people. Surprisingly enough, you can often get a gut-level "reading" just by spending a few hours in a place.

EVALUATING WHAT YOU SEE

A school can be new or old, but its physical condition goes beyond the date it was built. As you walk through the building consider the following:

▲ Are the classrooms stuffy or well ventilated?
• Is there good lighting?
▪ How are the rooms furnished? Do children's desks and chairs fit them comfortably?
▲ Are books, puzzles, art supplies, and other learning materials organized for easy access by the children?
• Is equipment attractively organized? Is the room pristinely neat or a jumble of clutter? Either extreme would be undesirable. A pristine setting may indicate that materials are not really being used. A jumbled room may indicate a chaotic or disorganized environment.
▪ Are the bathrooms clean and well ventilated?
▲ What are the conditions of the hallways and rooms? Do students seem to take responsibility and pride in the building, or are walls marked with graffiti and floors littered with debris?
• What kind of equipment is on the playground? Is there space to run and climb? Are the grounds attractive and safe?
▪ What is the lunchroom like? Is it chaotic, or is there an unrealistic expectation for silence? Neither would be conducive to a pleasant mealtime.

As you visit classrooms, you can discover a great deal about the school's approach to children. If possible, visit more than one classroom so that you see more than one teacher's approach. Ask yourself:

▲ How do teachers and children interact? Is the teacher talk-ing *at* the class or talking *with* them?

• Does she seem to value opinions and original ideas, or is the main object of her questions right and wrong answers?

■ Is there silence in the rooms and hallways, or is there a great deal of chaos and unruly behavior? Either extreme may tell you that things are amiss.

▲ Is it a friendly place where respect flows two ways between children and teacher? Or is the atmosphere restrictive and cold?

• Are children expected to sit still for prolonged periods of time, or is the day scheduled with a reasonable mix of active and quiet times? The younger the children, the more urgent the need for active scheduling breaks.

Age 6.

■ Is there children's art and writing on the walls in class-rooms and hallways? Or are bulletin boards covered with teacher-made or store-bought materials? Schools that value children's work opt for the former.

▲ Do teachers seem well prepared and enthusiastic about what they are teaching? Is their presentation lively and en-gaging, or is it dry and straight from the manual?

- How do children seem to relate to each other? Are they allowed to work together, or is each child restricted to sit at his separate desk and be quiet most of the time? Silence is not always golden. Children learn a great deal from one another.
- Do children appear to be cooperative and supportive of each other or more competitive and combative?
- Do children have responsibilities for taking care of the classroom?
- What kinds of learning materials are they using for science?
- Are there manipulative materials (counters, rods, blocks) available for math?
- Does the teacher spend most of the day teaching the whole class, or does she work with small groups and individuals?
- What do students do while the teacher is working with a group they are not in?
- How do kids handle independent work time? Are they engaged with the work they are doing, or is there a lot of fidgeting and acting up that distracts others?
- What is the average class size? In the primary grades, when children may need more individual help, there should be no more than twenty to twenty-five students. In the upper grades twenty-five to thirty is average.
- If you had to describe the general tone in the classroom, what words would you use? *Tense* or *relaxed*? *competitive* or *cooperative*? *friendly* or *hostile*? *lively* or *blah*? *sunny* or *dismal*? *interesting* or *boring*? *orderly* or *sloppy*? *harsh* or *lenient*?
- What is the school's policy on punishment and discipline? Does it fit with home policies?
- Is this a place you'd want to spend your days?
- See pages 34–39 for more specific ways to evaluate kindergarten programs.

No School Is Perfect

Once the choice is made (whether by default or by careful selection) the truth is that no school is going to be perfect. You may have found the most wonderful school and end up with a teacher you consider less than wonderful. Or a school may have all the attributes you were looking for and still end up being not totally right for your child. No school is going to be 100 percent to your liking every step of the way. The trick is to find a school that most closely overlaps with your values and goals. Although you may have the luxury of changing schools, in most instances you will ultimately have to deal with any school's strengths and flaws. In the end, whether you have no choices or many, once the decision is made, your job is just beginning. That's what the rest of this book is about.

KINDERGARTEN

For children, parents, and teacher, the start of the kindergarten year is a momentous occasion, marked with the tug and pull of mixed feelings. Let's consider what each member of the triad might be thinking.

CHILD'S POINT OF VIEW

At last! It's the big day. I'm finally going to the real school with the big kids. I guess that makes me big, too. Except I know that compared with most of the kids at the bus stop I'm not really so big at all. But I'm excited and a little scared, too. Jennifer, my friend, is going to kindergarten, only she has a different teacher. Billy, the kid next door, says my teacher is sometimes nice but sometimes mean. He says she yells. Will she yell at me?

I remember there was a kid I played with on visiting day when I met the teacher. I don't remember his name, though, or even what he looks like. I don't see him. There are so many kids in the class, and the teacher looks different.

When my mom said good-bye, I felt like I was going to cry. Some kids did, but I didn't. What I wanted to do was play with the blocks, only too many kids were building. The teacher said I would have a turn later. If I were home, I could play with my own blocks, and I wouldn't have to wait or share them either.

I needed to go to the bathroom for a long time, but I wasn't sure where it was. I asked one of the kids, his name is Robbie. He didn't know, either, but we found it together.

It was a long time till lunch, and I kept wondering how I'd get home. I hope my mom is there. We had fun on the playground. There's a big slide I like a lot. So does Robbie. We had fun, and he goes on the same bus as I do. I hope he comes to school tomorrow. He says he might not.

PARENT'S POINT OF VIEW

As the big day arrives, so do some bittersweet feelings. Looking at him, it's hard to know how this baby of mine grew up so fast. Where did the time fly? It's painful to be turning him over to a teacher I hardly know and who cannot know this child as I do. But in a corner of my heart I know that the six hours of the school day are going to be a real plus in terms of my own schedule. Still, I'm worried. Will the teacher really understand and appreciate this little boy? Does she know how to be firm without being mean, like some teachers I've known? Will she think I've done a good job, or will she dislike him? Will she appreciate his sense of humor and his curiosity and flair for the dramatic? Or will she consider him a noisy, pesty kid who wants too much attention? Will she think he's smart, even though he usually leaves out fifteen when he counts to twenty? Is he going to make friends? Will he be happy here? Will he behave himself and do what's expected of him? What is he going to learn? Should he know all of the alphabet? He doesn't seem at all interested in learning to read. At least, not like his older sister, who couldn't wait to read and write. Is he really old enough? He just made the deadline for this year. Maybe we should have waited another year.

TEACHER'S POINT OF VIEW

For several days now preparations have been under way. Equipment has been taken out of the storage closet. New art supplies are on the shelves. The room is set up and ready for action. All the name tags are printed, and what remains is to meet the faces that go with the now-familiar names. It's warm and sunny outside and it feels more like summer still than fall. But the busyness has already begun. What will this new group be like? Back on visiting day they seemed like a spunky group. Will there be many like last year's Tammy, who cried bitterly and daily when her mother left for the first week of school? How long will it take to get to know these children—not just their names, but their likes and dislikes, their interests and approach to people and things? How long will it take to establish that wonderful sense of community that flowed in last year's group? Will their parents feel confident about me and what I'm doing with their children? Will I have any like Willa's mom, who thought I wasn't teaching enough reading, or Bobby's mother, who thought I was pushing too much? What is there about the first day of school that makes even an experienced teacher feel both anxious and eager to get going?

While these are just three among many "voices" one might hear, clearly each member of the triad comes to the kindergarten door with a different perspective. Nevertheless, the goal for each is much the same—to have a successful year. How well they achieve that goal will in part depend on the kinds of expectations they bring with them. Unfortunately, there are more misconceptions about kindergarten than about any other grade in elementary school.

During the past several years some kindergarten programs have undergone radical changes. Experts have debated the best entrance age, the right curriculum, and even the length of the school day. As a result, parents (as well as teachers) may have difficulty in knowing what to expect from the school and from their child. In order to get the most from this first year of school, parents need to understand how and why some of the changes have come about.

● ■ ▲

How Kindergarten Has Changed

Thirty years ago entry to kindergarten was usually a child's first experience away from the familiar world of home and family. Indeed, in many places attendance in kindergarten was (and remains) an option, not a required year. Traditional schools went from grades one to six. If there was a kindergarten, it was viewed as an extra, not a prerequisite for first grade. For many children the first significant adult outside the family was their kindergarten teacher. Ideally she was a warm and "motherly" person who knew lots of songs and games to play. Essentially kindergarten was not to be taken seriously. While it was the first year of school, it was primarily considered a time for informal play and social experiences. Formal skills such as reading, writing, and math were on the back burner waiting for the rigors of first grade.

In many schools children attended either a morning or an afternoon session. Often the youngest were enrolled for the morning; afternoon was reserved for the older fives. Although the programs were similar, the afternoon children were sometimes given small academic lessons in letters and number skills. It was assumed that young fives would need an afternoon nap and were less "ready."

Today almost half of the children who enter kindergarten have already attended some kind of preschool. This is not their first experience away from home. They may well have had two or more teachers by now and played with many children. As a result, many have learned to be more independent and assertive of their rights. Indeed, some research shows that they may be more aggressive than those who have been at home.

Not only have children's experiences changed, parental expectations have also shifted. In the last several decades there has been a growing awareness of the importance and long-lasting effect of early education. As a result, more children than ever are attending preschool and kindergarten. Although in most states kindergarten is not compulsory, today 90 percent of all five-year-olds are enrolled. Twenty years ago less than 50 percent attended.

Not only are more children going to kindergarten, but the school day is also longer. Increasingly the half-day program has been expanded to a full day. But educators are by no means in complete agreement that more is better. Some feel that the full-day program reflects the needs of working parents more than it does those of children. As one former teacher put it, "Now they'll have time to do more workbook pages and the kids won't even have half a day to be kids and play." Others feel that much more than time has been gained. An advocate of the full-day reports, "With a half day we'd no sooner get their coats and boots off than it was time to get dressed for the bus. Now we have time to really do many more things without the need to rush them from one thing to the next."

Although full-day programs are relatively new, early studies show that both teachers are correct. In schools with inappropriate programs the full day has been expanded to more of the same. In schools with solid programs the added time lends itself to fuller and richer experiences that enhance the opportunities for learning.

In addition to the other changes noted, over the last few decades entry-age requirements for kindergarten have been creeping upward. You may be surprised to know that if you entered school thirty years ago, it's a safe bet that you were close to a year younger than today's kindergartner. Why is this? Basically these new age requirements reflect dramatic changes in what is expected of today's kindergartners. Increasingly the curriculum now offered to many kindergartners closely resembles the formal programs that were typically taught in first grade a generation ago. In such schools the nature of kindergarten has undergone radical changes.

While kindergartens of the past were pretty much alike, today programs vary tremendously in terms of what is taught, when it's taught, and, most especially, how it's taught. Let's take a look at two radically different classrooms. These two models, kindergartens A and B, represent extremely dissimilar approaches to education. Although many schools, even traditional public schools, have a mix of traits from both models, the profiles presented below are purposely painted for contrast.

Two Kindergartens— A Study in Contrasts

KINDERGARTEN A: It's 8:35 A.M. and the last bus has just pulled into the schoolyard. Most of the kindergartners are already in their room. Looking around the room, one sees a bin full of blocks, puzzles on the sill beside the window, a dollhouse with furnishings, a box with balls, and a tray with boxes of crayons. But this is not the time for blocks, puzzles, or crayons. There is an easel, and the teacher is sitting beside it waiting for the last of the stragglers to sit down in the circle of chairs she has arranged. A few children are talking. Some are sitting on their chairs swinging their legs, looking up at the lights, or watching the teacher.

As the last child joins the circle, the bell rings, and the teacher announces who will hold the flag for the pledge of allegiance. She marks the attendance cards and tells the children what they're going to learn today. "Who remembers what we call this letter?" she asks as she holds up a card with the letter *M*. When one child blurts out the answer, she asks, "What did Timmy forget?" Timmy looks down at his feet as several children answer, "He didn't raise his hand!" Now the reading lesson continues. Using pictures of objects, the class "plays" a game of finding objects that start with the em sound. Children play by coming up to the chart on the easel and pointing to a picture that starts with *M*. This game is followed by a worksheet featuring more practice with the letter *M*.

Everyone in the class is working at the same time. The teacher goes from one table to the next to be sure that each child is following directions. After reading, the children will go to gym, and at ten o'clock they will have milk and crackers followed by a lesson featuring the number 4, with more questions, answers, and worksheets.

As they work on their mathsheets, the teacher reminds them there is "no talking." She corrects each worksheet and awards stickers to those who complete the task perfectly. Others must correct the errors she marks with red pencil.

Lunch is followed by nap time, when everyone is expected to rest quietly on his or her cot. No talking, no toys, and no fooling around. If weather permits, there is a thirty- to forty-minute playtime outdoors. Today it's rainy, and playtime is minimal, with little time to get the blocks out before it's time to put them away.

During the afternoon the class works at the Distar language program (a formal program that limits language to simple parroting of right and wrong answers). The children sit in a circle looking at the book the teacher holds. Pointing to a pictue of a cat, she asks, "Is this a dog?" No one answers until she snaps her fingers to signal, and a chorus of *no*s follow. Then, reading from her scripted manual, she says, "This is not a dog. This is a cat." Again she snaps her fingers and the group repeats what she has said. The language lesson culminates with yet another worksheet that is scored with stickers or red pencil.

For Halloween the teacher provides orange paper and patterns for tracing pumpkins. Precut black triangles are pasted on, and now the room is decorated with a sea of look-alike jack-o'-lanterns. After art the children go to the school library. The school librarian may read them a book or show them a filmstrip. Later in the year they may be allowed to select a book to take home for the week.

If time permits, the teacher will sing some songs before the bus arrives. By late afternoon the children leave the room with a trail of papers.

KINDERGARTEN B: It's 8:35 A.M. and children are still arriving. Three children are already at the painting table. One is making a pumpkin; the other is dabbing bright splotches of blue on his paper. "Raining!" he says, "It's raining!" A third child is painting her name in giant letters. There are an *M* and an *A*, and now she is concentrating on the *R*.

In the block area four children have returned to the farm they began creating the day before. "Take this lion out of here. No lions in a barn!" one boy says. "See the sign?" He points to a card that says BARN.

Seating at a round table two children are rolling bits of clay into balls. "I made three," one child says. "I made five," says the other. "I have more ... see ... one, two, three, four, five." Nearby the teacher is at the water table with three children who are testing various objects to find out which ones float or sink.

A latecomer rushes to the block area with two dinosaur figures from his backpack. "No way!" one of the builders insists. "Can't be dinosaurs in the barn!" After a short pause the child with the dinosaurs says, "So, I'm building a museum."

Near the book corner an aide is reading a storybook to several children. "Not I, said the little duck!" they chime in to the familiar refrain.

At 9:30 the teacher brings the entire group together for a meeting time. Here they talk about what they have been doing and make their plans for the day. A message chart written by the teacher tells about events of importance.

Hello
Today is October 20th

Today is Randy's Birthday
Happy Birthday, Randy!
Today We Go to Library at 11 o'clock.

Randy's birthday sparks a good deal of discussion about birth-days in general. Each sentence on the chart is printed in a different color so that it is easier to scan. The structure of each sentence is purposely simple and repetitious. Before long many children will recognize familiar words by sight.

Taking attendance includes counting the number of boys, the number of girls, and how many children all together. The teacher adds this to the chart along with the names of the children who are absent. During this meeting time, major events or personal news may be shared and added to the chart. Since the children have recently made a visit to a farm, much discussion will center on related topics. With Halloween close at hand, the time is ripe for cutting the pumpkin they brought back from their trip.

At the close of the meeting some children return to projects already under way. Others move on to new tasks. Those who painted may now work on the replica of the farm, while those who were working with blocks may now paint or experiment at the water table or help with scooping out the pumpkin seeds. In some cases the teacher assigns tasks. In most instances the discussion is initiated by the child. During the course of the day the teacher is observing, making suggestions, and encouraging children as they work.

Before lunch the class goes to the school library. Here the librarian helps them with selecting books to take home. She also tells them a story or reads them a picture book. When they return to their classroom, it's time to get ready for lunch. Cleanup time is a cooperative venture, not a hit-and-miss affair. Children have assigned tasks, which include sweeping, cleaning tabletops, stacking chairs, feeding classroom pets, watering plants, and putting blocks, puzzles, and books away.

Lunchtime is followed by a quiet rest period. Few children actually go to sleep. Most relax with quiet games that can be played without disturbing others.

Rest time is followed in the afternoon by an hour-long play period, usually outdoors. But it's raining, so today they'll play in the room and adjacent hallway. Active play includes plenty of physical action coupled with dramatic play. When playtime ends, children participate in "writer's workshops." Some make books entirely with pictures, others write or dictate original stories or record an event of interest. Before dismissal they take turns listening to and "reading" their writing with the class.

Classroom A is an extreme example of a teacher/subject-centered approach, while classroom B represents the child-centered model. In these two classrooms the approach to learning is dramatically different. In classroom A, the teacher defines the lessons to be learned in a neat, sequential fashion. Essentially the children are passive participants. It is the teacher who initiates the lessons. She states the questions—they are to give the answers. Reading, writing, and math are taught as isolated, compartmentalized lessons, and few or no connections are made between the children's ongoing activities and the skills to be learned.

In classroom B the teacher has provided more diverse materials and opportunities for learning. Here the children are active participants in the process through direct experience with materials and people. The teacher poses open-ended questions that spark discussion and thought instead of immediate "correct" answers. Similarly, the materials she provides invite the children to experiment and explore. They are learning not just letters and numbers but the excitement of learning itself. Writing, reading, and math are not taught in isolation but arise from real needs and interests. Signs on blocks, letters to people, lists, storybooks, the morning message chart are all an integral part of the day. Counting, comparing, or guess-timating are all part of the meaningful math lessons of the day.

EVALUATING YOUR CHILD'S KINDERGARTEN

Between the two models presented here there are a multitude of variations. As indicated earlier, many schools are likely to be a blend of both models. No grade in schools today is in a greater state of flux than is the kindergarten. Is one model better than the other? Many experts believe that schools that lean toward model B offer better learning environments for young children.

While at first glance it may seem to parents that model A has the look of a "real" school, most early-childhood educators believe that such programs are inappropriate. In a position statement entitled "Developmentally Appropriate Practice in Programs for Four- and Five-Year-Olds," the National Association for the Education of Young Children says that current trends that place an "overemphasis on achievement of narrowly defined academic skills ... are primarily the result of misconceptions about how young children learn."

Parents often understandably confuse what looks like academic learning with meaningful learning for young children. When we hear children reciting numbers or see them circling numerals on a worksheet, it looks like "math" to most of us. Yet the child who is counting out cups for a party or looking for the right size block is likely to be learning more math than he would from a textbook or a formal lesson.

Young children learn best by doing. Learning isn't something you give to children like an inoculation. Education isn't something you "do" to kids; rather it involves the child as an active participant. In providing an environment that motivates young learners the teacher sets the scene with stimulating and challenging materials. Instead of "telling" children what they are to know, the teacher facilitates learning by observing what children understand and moving from that place to more challenging kinds of thinking. She poses problems and encourages children to ask their own questions and look for multiple ways of finding solutions.

WHAT TO LOOK FOR

To the casual observer most kindergartens may look more like playrooms than like typical school classrooms. There are no individual desks in rows with a teacher's desk in front of the chalkboard. More often than not, the kindergarten room is larger and has more open spaces. You'll find several learning areas and clusters of tables that can be easily rearranged as needs arise. Superficially, both models A and B are likely to look somewhat similar, although the way each uses materials is very different. So, appearances can be deceiving.

Let's take a tour of the work areas and explore how they are used in a model B (child-centered) type kindergarten.

MATH AREA: Counting and sorting materials are available here along with simple balance scales, pattern blocks, and raw materials for measuring, weighing, counting, and comparing. In the fall chil-

dren may be handling acorns found in the park, seeds from pumpkins, plastic cubes, Cuisenaire rods, and math puzzles.

BLOCK AREA: An ample amount of floor space is left open for
cooperative block structures. Low shelves for block storage hold
blocks of the same size and shape, stacked in an orderly fashion.
Props for blocks, such as toy animals, people, and vehicles, are
stored with the blocks. After a trip to a real zoo, museum, farm, or
store the children build their own working model of what they have
seen and learned. Such constructive play develops children's ability to use symbols, to make one thing stand for another. As their
miniworlds become more elaborate and detailed, so does the need
for cooperative problem solving and communication. Unlike worksheets that offer pictures, here children have direct experience with
concepts such as "longer" and "taller," "more" and "less,"
"same" and "different." They discover that two small triangles
make one square and that four unit blocks equal one long block. In
working with blocks the language of basic math concepts and the
language of social studies are both learned in memorable and meaningful ways.

ART AREA: Several easels or a large flat table with space for four
to six children to stand up and paint at is provided. Another,
separate table may be set up with varying materials from day to
day: clay for modeling, collage materials for cutting and pasting
activities, materials for printing, coloring, and other art explora-
tions. Here again, children are creating their own symbols, making
their own representations of a cat or a house, or finding a nonverbal
way of expressing their own feelings. This experience with symbolic expression is related to the later use of letters and numbers;
in fact, playing with their own symbols provides children with the
underpinnings for dealing with the more formal and abstract symbols they will be using in math, reading, and writing. Working
with paint, clay, and other art materials also helps children refine
the small motor skills they will later use with paper-and-pencil
tasks. Instead of coloring inside the lines, here children are making
their own lines and using their own meaningful experiences to
discover how to use materials and ideas.

DRAMATIC PLAY AREA: Here the raw ingredients are found for pretend play. You are apt to see housekeeping equipment, a puppet stage, a storefront with register and food boxes, as well as dress-up accessories. As interests in the room shift, so, too, will the themes and content of dramatic play. A domestic scene or the replay of a TV show may dominate for several days, while a restaurant complete with menus, waiters, trays, and checks may blossom another week. Through dramatic play children try on a variety of roles that are not possible in reality. Such play is not frivolous. It helps children to understand themselves and others, clarify their own feelings, and enlarge their ability to make themselves understood. In acting out stories of their own making or replaying familiar tales, they step outside themselves and into roles that demand both leading and following, listening and telling, thinking, planning, and doing. Indeed, such play often has a variety of rich curriculum embedded in it.

READING AREA AND AUDIOVISUAL CENTER: A bookcase or rack displays a variety of picture and easy-to-read books. Included in the collection may be books made by the children themselves. A teacher or aide may be reading to an individual child or a group of three or four. Some children may be looking at books independently. Nearby there may be an audiovisual listening center with books, tapes, and headsets so that children can listen independently to pretaped stories. In some rooms there may be a computer and/or a TV and VCR.

SCIENCE AREA: A low table is set up with a changing variety of materials to investigate. There may be magnets or magnifying glasses or a tub of water with objects that sink or float. Collections of seeds, shells, or rocks are displayed and examined here. Children can sort objects by size, shape, texture, or other criteria. Opportunities for building science concepts are not necessarily confined to this area. For instance, caring for the classroom pet, watering plants, cooking together, outdoor excursions to study shadows or the changing seasons—are all part of an ongoing science curriculum.

OUTDOOR AREA: A good-sized open area set up for climbing, running, jumping, sliding, and using big muscles is usually found not far from the classroom. Here active physical play often combines with dramatic play and satisfies the kindergartners' need to use their whole bodies as well as their minds—hanging from the monkey bars or playing run-and-chase games. Through active play, children get a basic sense of themselves as able and active doers.

Although these discrete areas sound rather compartmentalized, the kinds of learning going on tend to overlap. Whether children are building, climbing, painting, or listening to a story, they are learning social skills and what it means to be part of a group. Math experiences are not limited to the math areas. Indeed, some of the most important math concepts are learned as children cook, plan a party, build with blocks, take attendance, or share a snack. In all of these experiences the need to use numbers is connected to a meaningful event. Numbers are not learned in isolation; they are learned best in the context of real and active doing.

Similarly reading is not confined to the reading area. Classroom experience charts, signs on block structures, storage containers marked with pictorial symbols, and words are found in all areas. In every area of the room children are developing language skills. Such learning is not reduced to repeating words or sentences or answering the teacher's questions with a yes or no. It includes the language one needs to make oneself understood while playing side by side with a friend or to participate and express opinions in a group discussion. Building with blocks, sorting a collection of fabrics, or playing pretend all call for rich and differing kinds of language. In contrast to little lessons taught from workbooks or ditto sheets, here language flows from real experiences with content that has substance and meaning for the child.

DANGER SIGNALS AND WHAT TO DO ABOUT THEM

What can you do if your child's prospective kindergarten is, in your opinion, far from ideal? What if it most closely resembles model A? Does this mean your child will have a bad start in school? Not necessarily. Keep in mind that children learn in both kinds of settings. In fact, those who attend model A schools are apt to have an earlier edge on counting and letter names and sounds. They may also be better acclimated to routines typical of traditional first- and second-grade classrooms.

However, parents should provide such children with more opportunities for free-flowing physical play and socializing with friends during their out-of-school hours. You can also find useful ways to balance and enrich their learning experience with more of the open-ended activities on pages 74–78.

For some children the demands for academic performance in a model A kindergarten may be particularly problematic. Your helping them at home with playful games may give these children just enough support to carry them over the rough spots. But five-year-olds should not need tutors or prolonged drill sessions at home to push them ahead or to "keep up." Indeed, if your child is struggling with expectations that are inappropriate, you may need to take other actions. Often the attributes described when teachers recommend retaining children in kindergarten (see pages 79–82) are apparent early in the year. You may want to act preemptively here. Your child may be better off with an extra year in a good preschool setting than in a classroom where he is destined to "fail."

Ideally, of course, schools should be tailoring programs to match the abilities of all students. However, when reality falls short of the ideal, children should not be the ones who pay the consequences. Fortunately, more and more schools today are moving toward programs that are child-centered. A school may have both an "academic" program and an alternative "developmental" program. The latter is sometimes called prekindergarten (see pages 60–61). When parents are faced with no alternative programs within the system, the best alternative may be to withdraw from that system for another year. That doesn't mean you simply take the child home and wait for him to mature. You will actively need to find small-group, preschool, or individual experiences that challenge your child to continue growing.

THE THREE RS IN KINDERGARTEN

During the kindergarten year, children begin their early work with the three Rs. If they are fortunate, their introduction to reading, 'riting, and 'rithmetic will meet their individual and developmental needs. Rather than formal lessons with abstract symbol systems the emphasis will still be on firsthand experience with real things and people and on the excitement of learning. Assigned tasks and an emphasis on pencils, paper, and books come later, when children are ready and eager for them.

READING

One of the great debates in education centers on when and how children should learn to read. Experienced teachers and parents know that long before children come to school, the process of learning to read has already begun. In fact, some can already read. Parents of early readers often say, "She taught herself." These "spontaneous" readers are relatively rare. They are usually children who have grown up in homes where books and reading are valued, where parents not only read to children but are seen enjoying reading themselves. Early readers are frequently children who insist upon hearing the same story again and again. They begin memorizing every word of a favorite picture book and then begin recognizing words that are repeated. With persistence and a lot of questions, early readers learn to "crack the code" in an effort to satisfy their own desire to know (though all these factors may be present without a typical child showing the faintest signs of early reading tendencies). Of course, sometimes the motivation has more to do with satisfying an adult rather than the child's own desires, which is a far less desirable phenomenon. In any case, an adult or older child is usually very much a part of the team. Keep in mind, too, that early reading is no indication that your child is a genius or that a nonreader is a dolt!

More typically, most children *do not* know how to read when they enter kindergarten. Many, however, have sight recognition of familiar words, such as their own names or the names of products, fast-food stores, and signs on the road. Many are able to recite the alphabet, point out and name numbers and letters, and even know how to write some of them. Children who have been read to also bring a working knowledge of how books work from front to back. Experience with listening has taught them that a story has a beginning, middle, and end. Even if they cannot read words, many can "read" and interpret the pictures. They have a developing awareness that the dark squiggles on the page are translatable into spoken words and they may even know that as people say the words, they read from left to right. All of these "readiness" skills are basic to the actual business of learning to read. Best of all, they are learned informally in the pleasurable context of sharing storybooks and time with the caring adults in their lives.

How the school takes these beginning skills and pleasurable associations with reading varies from one school district to another. In many schools today the approach to reading in kindergarten is heavily laced with arid textbook exercises. Daily lessons in letter names and sounds, in matching and tracing, are presented formally. For some children such lessons represent little or no challenge at all. For others they are beyond comprehension. At best, they introduce the average child to a mode of teaching that continues to be typical of traditional classrooms.

In a more child-centered school, the approach to reading is quite different. Instead of teaching lessons manufactured to fit the curriculum, the curriculum and lessons grow to fit the children's interests and abilities. Reading is very much part of the day, but the approach is less formal. It flows from the rich experiences that begin with the children's own oral language. Indeed, both reading and writing are ''subjects'' to be learned not in isolation but rather as essential modes by which to communicate.

Although some children do learn to read during the year, it is not expected that all of them will do so. As one school principal put it,

> *We try hard not to have families feel that a child must learn to read in kindergarten. Lots of kids are simply not ready. But there's hardly a child in the room who's not interested in books and who doesn't want to sit down to listen to a story. There's a lot of whole group activity around sounds and letters, especially when they're doing experience charts. That's a reading activity everybody participates in. They make lists of words that start with the same sounds or of words that rhyme. There's no formal basal reader program in our kindergarten program or a reading-lesson time every day, but there is an enormous amount of reading and writing. By the time they go on to the first grade, most have at least some beginning reading skills.*

More than just reading skills, children in such programs are likely to have positive attitudes about the process of learning itself. Here the ablest are not bored, nor are the least mature frustrated. Instead, children with varying skills all have contributions to make. They are able to operate at their own rate rather than at an arbitrary rate set by a series of lessons manufactured as if education for fives can be reduced to a one-size-fits-all formula.

At almost any time of day you'll find

▲ A teacher or student teacher sitting with an individual child and a book they've selected.

• Individual and whole-group experiences in dictating stories and information that the teacher writes down. For example, after a trip to a bakery the children will spend time discussing what they saw. As the teacher records what they say on an "experience chart," they see their spoken words transformed into print. This helps children understand the connection between oral and written languages.

▪ Using the experience chart, the teacher may call attention to words that are alike or to letters and sounds. For example the daily morning meeting might begin with these messages:

Good day!
Today is Tuesday. It is a windy day!
We will go to gym today.
We will go to gym at ——.

▲ Using the chart the teacher encourages children to find words that are the same (*we will*, *gym*). She might ask them what sound or letter *we*, *will*, and *windy* begin with. She might also ask if anyone has a name that begins with the same sound. Wendy and William's names might be added to the chart.

• Objects in the room are labeled by the teacher and in many cases by the children themselves.

▪ A library of books sits on easily accessible shelves. There are comfortable places for children to sit down and browse on their own or with others.

▲ Storybooks are read out loud to the group every day, usually before lunch.

• First, last, and most importantly, opportunities for children's oral language are supported through play, group discussion, and in activities throughout the day.

42

Not only do they have an enormous amount of experience with language and print materials, by the time the year ends, most have some solid beginning reading skills. They usually

- ▲ Know many letter names and sounds
- • Recognize many sight words
- ▪ Know the mechanics of handling a book from front to back
- ▲ Have an understanding of the mechanics of reading from left to right, from one line to the next
- • Enjoy listening to stories
- ▪ Can recall events with some sense of sequence from beginning, to middle, to end
- ▲ Can predict what will happen next in a story
- • Can express opinions and discuss a story from their point of view
- ▪ Can make a connection between a story and their own experiences
- ▲ Can tell stories of their own and enjoy dictating or writing them down in their own phonetic spelling

All of these skills are important pieces in the process of learning to read.

WRITING

When you think of writing, chances are what comes to mind is penmanship. Most of us can recall those endless and sometimes painful experiences of practicing how to shape our letters. In the traditional kindergarten such lessons continue to flourish, despite the fact that many children (especially boys) lack the fine motor skills to succeed at such tasks. Left out entirely is the more basic idea of writing as a way of communicating and its obvious connection to reading. Ideally, the thrust of writing at any age (and at five in particular) centers on writing for meaning rather than for perfecting penmanship.

In many kindergartens around the country teachers are using a new approach to ''writing as process,'' inspired by Donald Graves, of the University of New Hampshire, and others. Rather than being constantly drilled in writing and spelling, children are encouraged to ''write'' words and stories using their own primitive spelling and crude penmanship. While the traditional teacher assumes children know nothing about writing until they are taught, this newer approach recognizes that even young children are more knowledgeable about sound and letter recognition than most of us ever assumed. Indeed, looking at children's early spelling reveals that many five-year-olds have a good basic grasp of phonetics. Granted, the efforts are not refined, but the rudiments that are there are generally quite serviceable. By encouraging children to use what they already know, the teacher is not reteaching lessons that no one needs. Instead, the child's own need to know becomes the motivating force that puts the child at the center of his or her own learning. The connection to reading is apparent. Writing and reading go hand in hand.

"This is a horse jumping a fence and a horse being ridden."
Mathew, age 6.

Schools that have adopted the Graves approach provide time each day for a ''writer's workshop.'' Children may write or dictate a caption or story about a painting they have done or an event of interest. Since the children themselves have written the stories with their own personal spelling, it is not surprising that they have little difficulty in "reading" what they have written. So, part of the writer's workshop is used for sharing stories or captions. It is a positive way of launching writing and reading simultaneously.

As for penmanship, children's motor skills as well as their desire to make themselves understood do eventually develop during the early years of school. Of course, the old adage that practice makes perfect is partially true. Yet many of us who practiced loops and lines have handwriting that is still less than legible. However, practice in the context of meaning inherently gives the practice more purpose. In the long run it may even produce a generation of adults who don't say they abhor writing when what they really mean is that they abhor penmanship.

In addition to their own writing, kindergartners learn a great deal about the process of writing by watching adults translating spoken words into print. Group-made experience charts are printed as children recall events of a trip or experiment. At other times an individual child may dictate a story while the teacher writes what the child says.

In doing so, the child's mechanical limitations as a scribe need not inhibit his growing abilities to express ideas in his own words. As the letters and the words flow onto paper, the child sees how letters and words are formed. Of equal impact is the personal delight in having his own ideas given a form that can be read and reread. Writing in kindergarten should not be a matter of merely learning to print letter symbols, but rather an integral part of language and reading development.

Math

As you might expect, in many traditional kindergartens, math, like reading and writing, is taught as an isolated activity. Despite the fact that most children come to school with some fundamental sense of numbers and counting, most manufactured math programs begin with the assumption that children know nothing and can be "taught" through a series of increasingly complex lessons. All too often the lessons start off simply, but rapidly move along to abstract ideas—for young children—that undermine learning. This is especially true of workbook exercises that skip over the young child's need for repeated experiences with concrete materials. A workbook page with pictures of four apples and a line of 4s to trace is no substitute for handling four real apples or counting four legs on a chair, needing four straws for four children, or finding out that four kids in the class have red sneakers on. The point is, an understanding of 4 is not learned once and for all by doing a worksheet. Children need to learn about 4-ness and 5-ness and other numbers in multiple and meaningful ways.

While it's true that kids pushed along can do adding, subtracting, and even learn to count to one hundred in kindergarten, the effort often leads to negligible long-term gains. As one school principal put it,

> *For kindergartners understanding numbers—what 2 or 4 is —is an important goal. If you're teaching kids to add, before you do so, you want to be sure they understand what is 2 or 4. That kind of understanding doesn't come from learning how to add. It comes from multiple experiences with a variety of objects. So, in preschool, kindergarten, and even good first grades, children have loads of experiences with counting. To parents, some of these experiences may not look like math. In one of our rooms the children counted the seeds of a pumpkin. It took them several days to count seeds and glue them on adding-machine paper, which went around the entire room. For most it was a first experience with a huge number, and they came away with an understanding of the largeness of a very large number.*

Five-year-olds shouldn't plunge into abstract math exercises before they have had repeated real-life experiences. To do so is to skip over fundamental connections between reality and pencil-and-paper tasks. All too often parents and teachers don't realize that children don't see the connection or meaning of 2 + 2. They may learn it, much as children delight in counting by rote. But such learning is usually hard to hold on to and a weak basis for the more complex math processes to be learned in years to come.

Beyond the Three Rs
Social Studies—Connecting School and the Bigger World

At the heart of a solid kindergarten program there should be an ongoing involvement with the community beyond the school walls.

Trips into the neighborhood and beyond provide the grist for understanding the world and how things and people work.

A visit to a farm in the country might be followed by a trip to a farmers' market in the city where children see how food grown at the farm gets distributed to grocers who sell it in neighborhood stores. In following the food chain from the farm to their own tables, children see not only how people work but the specific ways in which we are all dependent on one another. This basic theme of interdependence and one's place in the scheme of things is echoed in the classroom. Building models of farms and markets gives children opportunities to bring the world down to child-size and meaningful proportions. Through dramatic play they try on roles and work cooperatively.

During the course of the school year they will take many trips. They may visit a bakery, a bottling plant, a pizza place or fast-food restaurant in the neighborhood. In each case, they will look at the jobs associated with the place they are visiting and study the ways in which work is organized.

In contrast to pictures of community workers on the bulletin board or a textbook about "Our Community," going out into the real world makes school and learning come alive. Each journey is rich with language experiences that are the raw materials for painting, writing, reading, math, science, and most of all a lively interest in and a budding understanding of the connections between school and the real world, the world of their parents.

KINDERGARTEN—
STILL A SOCIAL EXPERIENCE

It has become fashionable in formal academic-style schools to consider the social aspects of kindergarten old-fashioned. Yet, from the child's point of view, the major experience of coming to school is spending the entire school day in the company of other kids. Indeed, the social impact of being in an environment with lots of kids must be a positive one, or learning suffers.

In my own experience with first- and second-graders, those children who had difficulty in the classroom often had more of a social problem than an academic one. Such children tended to display an inability to control impulsive behavior or tended to be withdrawn and less able to participate in group activities. They grabbed things from others, destroyed other children's work, or annoyed kids by barging in on cooperative or solitary activities. Although children are pretty tolerant of each other, they do reject those who consistently interrupt or interfere with their efforts. Kids who have not learned friendlier approaches to others may either end up withdrawing further or continue to provoke negative static.

These kinds of disruptive behaviors may indicate that a child is "overplaced" in a curriculum that is beyond him. However, it may also be that social development and individual initiative were undervalued at an earlier stage.

During my years of teaching, this kind of social immaturity increased strikingly as our school's kindergarten curriculum changed. As blocks, paint, and dramatic play were replaced with sit-down lessons in language and letters and numbers, the children who arrived in first and second grades seemed less able to deal with one another. Whatever gains they may have made on standardized tests were, in my view, seriously offset by a decided lack of social savvy and intellectual initiative. After a year of rigid training they waited for the teacher to tell them what to do and when to do it and to evaluate how it was done. "Should we start?" was a persistent question. Once assigned tasks were completed, many had trouble finding independent or cooperative activities to go on to. Many had already come to expect the teacher to direct all aspects of their day, including their interactions with their classmates. Lacking inner controls of their own, trouble erupted as soon as children had some freedom of choice. In my final years of teaching, it took almost six months of the school year to give many of my students a sense of how to take some responsibility for, not to speak of delight in, learning and how to develop opinions that could be expressed with words instead of fists.

Valuing social development does not, however, mean doing so at the expense of intellectual growth. This need not be an either/or issue. Children can't learn about living with others simply by memorizing little homilies such as "Do unto others . . ." They need to do and to be done unto. Similarly, they don't learn to think by parroting sentences. They learn how to express themselves and how to take into account other people's points of view by struggling to find words that communicate their opinions and feelings. This kind of learning comes from an environment that gives time and value to interactions between children.

To the school-age child, learning to live with and become an accepted member of the group is as basic as learning the three Rs. Perhaps even more so. More important yet, it is not comfortably separable from learning the three Rs. A child who is uncomfortable with himself and others is operating like a car with wet spark plugs. It can be done, but not without a lot of jerky starts, stops, and backfires. In the long run such kids frequently fall behind academically as well as socially. When kids can't make a comfortable fit in the social world of the classroom and playground, too much of their energy and attention gets diverted from "school" tasks.

Emphasizing social development is neither trivial nor outdated. It is basic to the goals of kindergarten as well as every other grade. Fortunately, good teachers have always found ways to combine the excitement of learning with the pleasures of being an accepted and accepting member of the classroom community. It is part of their job to do so.

In a kindergarten in Vermont a group of fives in celebration of the two hundredth anniversary of the signing of the Constitution created their own set of rules. It is interesting to note that their self-made rules are probably more elaborate than any teacher-made list would be. Their rules also reflect a greater social awareness than perhaps most adults would expect.

B-2's Constitution in Honor of the 200th Written by B-2 on 9/17/87

No hitting.
No going up the slide.
No pushing people.
No going on the swings when there are puddles under.
No saying swears.
No throwing or eating sand.
No pulling hair.
We should do things for the teacher.

If somebody hurts you, don't hurt back.
We should be quiet at circle time.
Don't say dumb things.
Don't pick your nose.
No telling people that they're smelly.
Be nice to the birds.
No throwing blocks.

Don't drop blocks on people's feet.

No eating at the listening center or the computer—crumbs bother things.

No popping bags—it scares the animals.

No lying.

No pulling down other people's pants.

No erasing other people's names on the animal chart so you can be first.

If somebody says "stop it," then stop it.

No telling secrets.

Of course, making rules is a lot easier than living with them. But it is a place to begin. They are more likely to be followed when children play a part in creating them.

Parents, too, can play an active role in providing opportunities for children to be together outside of school. Informal time to play one to one with agemates is important for all children and especially for those who are enrolled in kindergartens that limit social interaction. The degree of social interaction is something to take into account in choosing or evaluating your child's school.

ART—NOT END PRODUCTS

In traditional kindergartens many of the art projects really have more to do with crafts than with art. Generally the classroom teacher provides a model and possibly some of the pieces needed to assemble an end product that is "mass-produced." While such exercises involve children in following directions and provide practice in activities like cutting and pasting, they cannot replace the informal and more exploratory experiences children should have with art materials.

In working with unstructured materials such as clay, paint, collage, and crayons, children are free to create their own symbols and express their own feelings in nonverbal ways. In the process, they are also learning about the nature of the materials themselves and how colors blend, paint runs, clay smooshes, and paste blobs. At every step there are decisions to be made, problems to be solved, and surprises to be discovered.

Rather than depending on the teacher to tell them what to do next and how to do it, there is time for learning about the cause and effect of adding too much water to clay or too much paste between paper. Instead of focusing on a completed end product that looks like everyone else's, here the child can take pleasure in the process. While there may be a less-than-perfect end product, it is uniquely the child's own. Rather than training the child to imitate or depend on others for what to make and how to make it, the child is empowered to trust his or her own representations of the world in meaningful and personal ways.

If your child's school experience is predominantly in a craft-oriented program, you can always provide more open-ended unstructured materials at home. Remember, though, to set up materials so that they can be used with independence.

MUSIC AND MOVEMENT

Whether the kindergarten teacher is also the music teacher or there is a music specialist who works once or twice a week with the children, music is an important and often neglected area of kindergarten programs. Music involves expressiveness, creativity, and discipline, and a good program involves all three. Knowing the nature of music and the nature of five-year-olds, an appropriate music program incorporates movement into music. Children not only sing, but clap, snap their fingers, click their tongues, skip, run, and jump to music. They also make music with simple percussion instruments, such as xylophones, tambourines, triangles, cymbals, bells, and woodblocks.

Movement, as a separate subject, is closely tied to music but has a different emphasis. Children are encouraged to use their bodies to express what they hear in music and to convey various emotions. They may also act out stories in pantomime. An important goal for young children in a movement program is to help them explore the potentialities of their bodies in space and to give them a positive sense of themselves through their bodies.

PHYSICAL EDUCATION?
YES, BUT WHAT KIND?

Physical education is often very important to children and their parents, who often see it solely in terms of competitive sports. While in the upper elementary and older grades physical education is often synonymous with team sports, such concerns at this age level are inappropriate, not only from the point of view of physical development but of social and emotional development as well.

Children of this age do not have the physical coordination to play such games successfully, nor are they ready for following the complex rules of formal games. Rather than pitting kids against each other, this is the stage when children need to strengthen their abilities to work and play cooperatively with each other. Winning and losing are often too painful for the still-tender feelings of young children. As they mature, they are less egocentric and better able to enter the spirit of team sports and competition.

A good physical-education program for young children is varied. At different times children might work on tumbling and gymnastics, throwing and catching a ball, or running and playing cooperative games. As in movement, children learn about what their bodies can do and get many experiences in using their bodies in a variety of ways. A good physical-education teacher also emphasizes the emotional and social issues that arise when children play games together. For kindergartners, learning rules and playing by the rules are very difficult concepts, and the games they play should be suitably simple. As in other "nonacademic" areas already discussed, one wished-for outcome of the physical-education program should be the development of skills and knowledge that lead to lifelong pleasure.

GETTING OFF TO A GOOD START IN KINDERGARTEN

Long before the first day of school arrives, you and your kindergartner-to-be will be getting ready for the main event. Depending on where you live and your school's entry procedures, the process may include registration day, screening day, and visitation days during the spring preceding the fall entrance date.

REGISTRATION

Registration procedures vary tremendously from one community to the next. In some schools it is solely a paperwork occasion for adults. In many schools it is also a day for screening tests that involve your child.

Notices for registration are usually mailed to parents and announced in local newspapers during early spring. If you are a newcomer in your community, or your child was born elsewhere, the school may not have your name on its census roll. If you have any doubts about being on the census roll—or, in fact, about any aspect of the registration and visitation process—you should contact the school district and inquire about the dates of registration, the kinds of testing done, and how long you will be there.

Generally you will need to bring a birth certificate to prove that your child meets the age requirements, as well as health records that show proof of immunization requirements. You may be asked to fill out a short history of your child's health and development. The school nurse will want to know if your child has any allergies or chronic conditions that require special attention. In the event of emergency she will need to know where to reach you and who can be called if they cannot contact you. (Remember, if you go back to work after the school year begins, you will need to update this information.) If you are going to depend on another family member or caregiver to pick the child up on occasion, you should indicate this now. If there are custody problems and a parent is *not* to pick your child up, this is the time to say so clearly.

SCREENING

During registration, or on a separate day, your child may be given a series of "tests." In some districts the procedure may involve more than a visual and auditory test to identify children who may have difficulty seeing or hearing. In many schools there are more elaborate screening tests aimed at evaluating your child's developmental readiness for school.

Essentially these tests are designed to assess your child's strengths and weaknesses. So a poor performance in, say, language or fine motor skills, might indicate to his new teacher a need for extra attention in those areas. Ideally such screening-test results are used not to "fail" kids or keep them out of school but rather to place them in appropriate programs that match their learning styles and needs.

If you are anxious about the tests, your child is apt to pick up on your feelings. To allay your anxiety, you would do well to call the school and ask what kinds of tests will be given and for what purposes the results will be used. While there is no reason to coach your child for this occasion, you can prepare her best by knowing yourself what to expect. Keep in mind that from your child's point of view this is a big day. For many it is the first time they are entering the big school building. They may be eager, and they may also be somewhat anxious. In some screening sessions a child may meet a whole team of grown-ups: the school nurse, a teacher, teachers' aides, a speech therapist, the school psychologist, the principal, and maybe the gym teacher. In addition, she may be rubbing shoulders with a dozen or more other possibly anxious children. If there is an extensive screening program and you have younger children, you may want to leave the baby with a sitter or friend. Make this into a special outing, one that is focused on your almost-ready-for-kindergarten child.

Before the screening day give your child a brief and reassuring sense of what is going to happen. Explain, for instance, that the school nurse is going to test her eyes by asking her to look at some pictures and test her hearing by having her listen to some sounds. With kids who are especially uneasy about doctors and nurses you may want to do a small, playful rehearsal. You can certainly assure your child that there are no shots to worry about.

If the screening reveals that there are any visual or auditory problems, you will be advised to seek further testing by a specialist before school opens. Catching such problems early can be significant factors in his or her school performance. You cannot assume that because you don't need glasses, your child won't either. If your school does not do at least this rudimentary testing, you should have your doctor do so. In fact, before school begins, it is a good idea for your child to visit her pediatrician for a general physical checkup.

DEVELOPMENTAL SCREENING TESTS

Many schools today are also administering developmental screening tests. According to the *National Survey of Kindergarten Program and Practices,* close to 60 percent of schools administer screening tests to evaluate children's readiness for school. Some states are required to test children in order to identify those with handicaps that may need special attention, as well as to identify those who may be "gifted." At their best, such tests can be used to plan for children's special needs; at their worst they may be used to prematurely evaluate and place children in fast, average, or slow tracks that may later prove inaccurate but hard to break out of.

Although a group of kindergartners may all be chronologically five years old, there are apt to be real differences in the children's developmental age within that group. Just as all babies do not learn to walk at the magic age of twelve months, children of five come to school with differing skills and rates of development. Consequently, testing can be used to identify those children who will need special educational experiences or, in rare instances, those who would be better off postponing entry to school for another full year. In districts that have rigorous academic expectations for kindergartners, there is sometimes a prekindergarten class (see pages 60–61).

If testing results indicate that your child's readiness is in doubt, make an appointment to discuss the findings with the school principal and/or those who make the placements. You are entitled to know on what basis any decision has been made and what kind of program is being recommended. From the start you should be part of the team that weighs the options and participates in decision making. If you feel that the day of testing was just an "off" day, you may want further evaluations. There is no reason to feel defensive or that you have failed in your job as a parent. Children are born with differing abilities and varying speeds of development. Keep in mind that a child's developmental age is not the measure of his or her intellectual ability. A very bright five-year-old may be able to count, recite letters, and write her name, but may be otherwise more like a four-year-old in terms of emotional and social behavior.

What's On the Test?

There is no universal screening test for kindergartners. Some districts buy and administer a combination of manufactured tests. Others design their own exams. So there are great variations in the kinds of skills tested. Indeed, when one looks at sample lists from different schools, many of the tests sound like checklists more appropriate for the end of second grade.

Many tests today include some or all of the following:

INFORMAL INTERVIEW	▲ The ability to talk about one's age, family, pets, toys, and opinions
VISUAL DISCRIMINATION	• The ability to match like objects or letters

VISUAL MEMORY	▪ The ability to reproduce a pattern with blocks
COPYING	▲ The ability to reproduce simple shapes with paper and pencil
AUDITORY MEMORY	• The ability to recall and repeat a series of numbers
	▪ The ability to follow a series of directions (for example, clap your hands, pick up the book, and walk to the door)
MOTOR SKILLS AND BODY SENSE	▲ The ability to identify parts of the body and to follow simple commands, such as hop on one foot, walk on the line, jump five times

One of the most popular developmental screening tests currently in use is the Gesell Institute's Developmental Examination. It is interesting to note that a simplified list of the various parts of the test can lead to false conclusions about what is tested and what is expected. I mention this because in looking at summaries of the skills tested one often runs into lists in magazine articles that include such items as: knows his birthdate and address, can write numbers to twenty, writes first and last names and letters, knows left from right. If all of this sounds a bit beyond your child's current abilities, don't worry! According to the "norms" given by the test makers, full and correct responses to the items listed above are not expected of five- or even six-year-olds. For instance, although all kids are delighted to talk about their birthday, and many can tell how old they are, norms for the test indicate that most cannot tell the month and date correctly until they are seven.

Similarly, although 70 percent of girls and 56 percent of boys can write their first names at five, it's not until six that most can manage both first and last names. Nor does the test expect fives to write to twenty! Five-year-olds typically not only omit numbers and mix up their order, few can write beyond six. Again, the ability to do so is more typical of six- and seven-year-olds. As for knowing their addresses, many seven-year-olds don't even know the meaning of "address" or consider their phone number a reasonable response. Nor can most children correctly distinguish their left from their right without help until they are seven. Parents who are interested in knowing more about the Gesell test will find a fuller explanation in *School Readiness* (Harper & Row) by the authors of the test, Frances L. Ilg, Louise Bates Ames, Jacqueline Haines, and Clyde Gillespie of the Gesell Institute. For most parents it will be sufficient to know that there's no need to hire a tutor or push your five-year-old to perform like a seven-year-old in order to "score" high. Keep in mind that experienced testers are not just noticing what the child can or cannot do. They are watching how the child approaches a problem; how he deals with tasks; his body language; the way he handles himself and the materials; the way he relates to the tester; and his willingness to try or reluctance to make a mistake, deal with frustration, remember directions, and follow them.

SHOULD PARENTS PREPARE KIDS FOR TESTING?

Are there things you should do to prepare your child for this test? Not really. In fact, doing so may actually invalidate the test *and* make your child overly concerned about "performing." Unfortunately, some parents get so caught up in the status of having their children accepted into the "right" school or the "right" group that they actually hire tutors to prep children for these tests. All too often this drive for early success has more to do with a parent's needs for status than with the child's best interest. Remember, the object of the tests is to get a realistic appraisal of the way your child functions at this moment in time. This is not an intelligence test, nor should the results be considered a definitive measure of anything. One of the dangers of testing at any age is to put too much stock in the results. On any given day a test may be invalid for a great variety of reasons.

A shy child or one who is hyped up and anxious may not have slept well the night before or may be more concerned about "getting done" than about doing well. To the very young child the newness of being separated from mother in a roomful of testers and others who are being tested may prove to be a major distraction. The ability of the tester to put your child at ease, as well as the nature of the setting, can also be important factors.

Because of these and other variables, some educators feel that testing young children is of limited value, either in predicting success in school or in appropriately placing a child. Many feel that observing a child at play in a small group of three or four children, in addition to an informal interview, can give a far better picture of a child's development than can formal testing. Many educators also feel that kindergarten programs should be flexible enough to fit the developmental needs of a range of children and that children should not have to fit a single, rigidly defined curriculum by passing a test.

Ideally, all five-year-olds should be screened, not for admissions purposes but rather to assess their individual strengths and weaknesses, particularly in the area of language development. These screening tests should examine the child's intellectual, physical, and emotional development. The scores on such tests should be less important than the information they yield in helping to plan an appropriate program for each child. Screening not only can help identify those with poor motor skills or superior language ability, it can indicate the child's learning style, which in turn helps in planning for successful instruction.

HOW OLD IS OLD ENOUGH?

As indicated earlier, both chronological and developmental age requirements have been shifting upward. Today's kindergartner is typically a year older than the entrants of a generation ago. This aging-up is in part a reflection of new and more formal kindergarten programs. However, it also relates to studies that show better long-term success in school for children who are chronologically older. In most states today, public school programs no longer accept children whose fifth birthday comes after September 1st or, at the latest, October 1st.

While this may seem an "unfair" hardship to parents whose children just miss the entry date, keep in mind that being the youngest in a class is generally less desirable than being among the oldest. In fact, over the years older students tend to achieve more success than their younger classmates. So, missing the deadline may be disappointing now, but might be a real gain in the long run. Even children who appear to be "bright" or "advanced" intellectually may be physically or socially less mature. Most experts feel that pushing such children under the wire puts them at more risk than early entrance is worth. Studies show that boys especially profit from later entry since boys typically develop more slowly than girls do. In fact, current wisdom holds that girls should be five, whereas boys should be five and a half before kindergarten entry.

MAKING DECISIONS ABOUT ENTRY

What if your child's birthday is two days after the cutoff date and she seems altogether ready? If a child just misses like this, will schools adjust? Or suppose the developmental test shows your child falls into that gray area known as "questionable"? Before making a decision, it's important to know what kind of program your district offers.

If there is only a one-size-fits-all kindergarten curriculum, with the accent on workbooks and formal lessons, the choice of later entry is probably advisable. If your district automatically promotes all children to first grade after a year of kindergarten, again for some children later entry may be a better option. No studies or book can give you the answer to your child's individual needs. You may be right in feeling that your child either is better or is less ready than his age or developmental tests indicate. Discussing the options with the school principal can help you both make a decision that fits the best interest of your child and his individual needs.

In many private schools today there is "mixed-age grouping." Some five-year-olds are in a group for fours and fives, whereas others are placed in the fives-and-sixes group. Similarly, in many public schools there are fives who enter kindergarten while others begin in a *prekindergarten* or, as it is sometimes called, *developmental kindergarten*. Often the decision to launch children in less-academic programs means that such children may need two years of growing before going on to first grade. But not always. Many times children who appear less ready in September make great developmental leaps during the year and go on with agemates to the first grade. In fact, in many school districts that have instituted what is called a developmental program, the results have been so positive that they are studying the wisdom of using this less academic model for all children.

In a sense, the accelerated demands of overly academic kindergarten have played a part in creating the need for more preentry screening and, ironically, are ultimately leading to a rediscovery of the "developmental" kindergarten. Unfortunately, in some districts there are no alternatives to kindergartens that expect five-year-olds to perform like sixes and sevens. If your child is caught in that kind of bind and testing indicates "questionable" readiness, you may be better advised to postpone entry to school. A successful year in a good preschool program is often a better choice than a year in a kindergarten that is programmed for failure. You will find guidelines for selecting such a program in *The Preschool Handbook,* by Barbara Brenner, the companion book to this volume. According to Ames and Ilg, "the most serious reasons for school failure in the primary grades is overplacement"—in other words, putting children into programs that are beyond them. Children who are "overplaced" at kindergarten and automatically promoted to first grade may play "catch up" or "hold on for dear life" for years to come.

SKIPPING KINDERGARTEN

In recent years it has become fashionable in some communities to look for ways to "skip" kindergarten. "They don't learn anything there," parents complain. "My child already knows the alphabet and can count to one hundred. So, what's the point? My kid's going to be bored!" More often than not these are well-intentioned parents who think that a kindergarten program involves nothing more than learning to count or recite the alphabet. Many also see their children's achievements as a reflection of their own self-worth. Having a "smart" child proves what smart parents they are. These are people who like to boast about their wonderkids' IQ scores and grade placement. Forgotten completely is the fact that kindergarten involves the development of the whole child. Also overlooked is the probability that putting a five-year-old into a typical first-grade situation is like promoting a child to the level of her own incompetence. Indeed, it's like punishing a child for being precocious.

Physically, socially, and intellectually there are real differences between fives and sixes. Verbal smarts are no guarantee of social or physical maturity. Even in the primary grades the smaller and younger child is often at a disadvantage, both in the classroom and on the playground. Pushing kids ahead is rarely ever a gain, especially at this stage, no matter how "bright" we like to think they may be.

READY OR NOT . . .
HOW CAN YOU TELL?

Occasionally there are children who for one or many reasons are simply not ready for kindergarten. They may be chronologically the right age but emotionally unable to take the giant step into the daily demands of kindergarten. How can you tell? According to Ames and Ilg of the Gesell Institute, there are warning signs parents should look for.

In most cases the situation is quite apparent. Although many children cry or tend to be clingy when it's time to leave mother, most overcome their reluctance after the first week or two of school. However, for some children the pain of separation and the scenes of despair continue for weeks on end. If that is the case with your child, he may not be ready yet.

Persistent crying over leaving home or mother may be a warning sign. Often the storm begins early in the morning. The child may need to be fed and dressed and literally forced onto the bus or dragged into school. This, too, is an indication of a lack of readiness.

In some instances the child may go off to school with few protests but "fall apart" when he returns home. Although most kids have a bad day from time to time, the child who regularly comes home in tears or on a rampage may be sending a not-ready signal.

In addition, there are some children who find it impossibly difficult to participate in a group setting. Usually it is the teacher who reports that a child is perpetually in the eye of a storm. He may consistently bother other kids. He may hit them, throw things, or destroy their efforts.

While the decision to withdraw a child from a school situation is painful, it may be a more positive move than holding fast. A shorter school day in a nursery school setting with fewer children may be a better choice for making the transition from home to group life. Forcing children to attend a kindergarten against their will at this stage may color their attitude about school for years to come.

• ■ ▲

APPLYING TO PRIVATE SCHOOLS

If you are considering private school enrollment, the process usually begins a full year or more before entry. In many instances private schools require entry exams and lengthy interviews. Children and parents often get caught up in the stress of "making the grade" or fear of failure as they face a battery of admissions tests. Unfortunately parents often fear that their child's entire academic career hinges on getting into the best kindergarten in town. "Best," in this instance, means the school that leads to the "best" high schools, which, in turn, lead to the "best" colleges, "best" graduate schools, and "best" jobs. Eager as they may be to give their child the best kind of future, such parents may be overlooking the most fundamental issue—what kind of school will meet the "best" interests of their child now?

Keep in mind that evaluations before admissions are a two-way process. Rather than depending on the reputation of a school, take the time to see the school with your own eyes and ears. You'd be surprised how much you can learn about a school's philosophy and practices from your own gut reactions to the tempo and climate of the place. In addition to talking with the people in admissions, ask parents of current students about the school. If your child attends a preschool, his current teacher may have good suggestions. Not only is she likely to know about the various options, she also knows your child and what kind of school might best match his needs and style.

In large cities you may need guidance in discovering the options open to you. Specialists who provide advisory services can help you zoom in on choices that match your needs and philosophy. To find such services, check the yellow pages of the telephone book under "School Information." In smaller cities or towns you may need to do your own research. Again, use your yellow pages to find a listing of the schools in your area and start making appointments to visit.

It is a good idea to make a list of questions beforehand to ask the interviewer. You may need an afterschool program or special transportation arrangements. Some aspects of the program may be more important to you than anything else. Jot down questions, issues, and concerns as reminders in case they are not covered in the parent orientation or don't come up naturally in the interview.

KINDERGARTEN ORIENTATION (OR VISITATION)

Most schools have some kind of kindergarten orientation program for entering students. Usually they are scheduled for the May or June preceding entry. This visiting day is different than registration day. It is an occasion planned to give children a glimpse of things to come, an opportunity to try some of the equipment and to meet their future teacher and even, perhaps, some of the children who will be classmates in September.

Generally this is an informal occasion. In some cases the current kindergartners go to visit a first-grade classroom while the newcomers are in their room, or visitation is held after school hours. Other schools invite five or six future kindergartners at a time to visit while kindergarten is in session. Current kindergartners may then play a part in showing the newcomers the ropes. Usually parents of visitors are expected to remain in or near the room.

Even if your child has been to preschool, this may be a mildly anxious event. Much as children look forward to going to "big school," getting close to the real thing creates its own excitement and tension. Your child may join right in or behave with unaccustomed shyness. Don't make an issue of it if he's clingy. In a new situation many kids need extra time to watch and absorb from a little distance. You don't need to apologize for this or push the child to "act his age." Experienced teachers know that such behavior is quite typical for some kids. They also know how to make the child feel welcome without overwhelming him. You can sit down near the action or as close as your child's comfort allows. Usually this informal session ends with a picture book and a small snack. Most schools have only one visitation day, although some may have a series of visits throughout the spring.

After the event, in talking about the visit steer clear of emphasizing what the child didn't do. From the child's point of view, even if he was only looking, it may have been a perfectly satisfying outing. As a result of the visit, school may now no longer be that big, mysterious building, but rather a place with toys he has handled or seen, children he has met, and a teacher he can picture. Over the course of the summer, as the subject of school arises, this visit can be a reference point for the interesting things he'll be doing when September comes.

If your school does not have a visitation program, you may be able to arrange a small visit anyway. Check with the principal's office or the kindergarten teacher. You may be welcome to bring your child for part of a session, or you may be invited to come in after school hours for a short visit. If you have the time, you may even be able to help get a visitation program launched through the school parents organization. In some communities your child's preschool teacher will take a group of kindergartners-to-be on a visit to the big school. This kind of linkage between schools can be helpful to children who are about to make a big transition. There is comfort in knowing that a trusted and familiar adult knows this world of big school and new teacher. In rare instances, teachers either pay a home visit or send a letter to new students (and their parents) before the year begins. This, too, helps ease anxiety by allowing the child to get acquainted with this new and significant other in the familiar setting of home. It serves as a pleasant opener to what will hopefully be a warm and friendly relationship.

BEFORE THE BIG DAY

Aside from the formalities of registration and visitation, getting ready for school is an ongoing process. In dozens of small but significant ways your child has been getting ready for the big day. He may have watched his older sister or a next-door playmate going off to school for a year or more. Now at last it's his turn, and the excitement builds. So does the anxiety. Before school actually begins, there are things you and the school can do to make the transition less stressful.

DEALING WITH THE ANXIETIES OF SEPARATION

Despite the fact that your child may have been to nursery school or day care, entry into kindergarten is likely to produce a bit of anxiety over separation. Some schools ease the stress by scheduling short class sessions during the opening weeks. They may also have only half the group come in on one day and invite the other half in on the following day. This gives children and teachers a more gradual and less hectic time to get acquainted with each other and new routines. In such schools parents are often expected to stay in or around the vicinity of the school for a few days. While this may strike some parents as a great nuisance, many early childhood educators believe it is time well spent. Indeed, for many children, knowing that Mom or Dad is nearby gives them the security and freedom to enter into a new and sometimes awesome experience with less tension and greater confidence. Once children know that school is a safe and friendly place and that the teacher is someone they can depend on, they are less fearful of this exciting new place they have entered. No matter how much they may have looked forward to kindergarten or how long they have attended preschool, this experience is palpably different. During this transition stage, children must accustom themselves to living in a larger group, with less one-on-one attention from the teacher. The curriculum is apt to be more demanding and the structure of the day less flexible. Faced with a variety of real as well as imagined expectations, it should not be surprising that the early weeks of school can be stressful, and even the spunkiest five-year-old may need the reassurance that a parent's presence can provide.

In the event that your school makes no provision for this transition stage, you may need to make your own arrangements. Rather than sending your child off on the school bus, you may be able to take her to school and pick her up at the end of the day as well. For many children the trip back and forth represents a bigger hurdle than the school day itself. Often children worry about how (and if) they will get home and who will be there. Working parents may not be able to take this time off, but they may be able to arrange for a relative or familiar caregiver to accompany their child. After a few days your child will probably be ready to do at least one way by bus. In fact, before long she may insist on doing so both ways. For most children going on the bus represents a great adventure they anticipate with mixed feelings of eagerness and apprehension.

Once he gets to school, your child may have some second thoughts about crossing the threshold of the classroom. He may become shy, clinging, or even tearful. There is no reason to feel embarrassed or to shame him by saying, "Don't act like a baby." You may need to assure him that you will stay with him (if that is permitted) or that you will be wherever the designated area is and/or that you will return before it's time to go home. The arrangements you make will, of course, depend on the school's policy. Some schools insist that children be left at the door, tears or not. Others are more flexible and recognize that some of their entrants need Mom or Dad nearby for a few minutes, hours, or even days. If you anticipate that your child will need that support, and if it is not general policy, discuss your concerns with the teacher before the first day. As a parent, I had that experience and was able to make an arrangement to stay. By mid-morning my son told me, "You can go home now."

While there are those who believe in letting kids "cry it out," most early-childhood educators feel that wrenching the child from the parent is an unnecessarily harsh and inappropriate way of dealing with separation. They also know that children who need this kind of short-term support system will usually make a better long-term adjustment to school.

"How Do I Get There and Back?"

Since the journey between home and school is often the least supervised part of the day, it can be worrisome to both kids and parents. Whether your child will be walking to school or going by school bus or car pool, it is a good idea to establish the pattern before school begins.

WALKERS: If your child will be walking to school, you'll want to be sure he knows the safest routes there and back. During the first days (or weeks), you or another adult will probably walk with him and meet him at the end of the school day. However, even though he won't be going alone at first, it may be a good idea to "rehearse" the walk several times before school begins. Knowing how to get there and back gives everyone involved a sense of security. These walks need not be pressured or have the feeling of a fire drill. Keep them informal and don't load the conversation with cautionary tales that may lead to anxiety.

During these rehearsal walks, point out landmarks that will help him remember where the safe crossings are and talk about the dangers of taking shortcuts. You may also want to caution the child about not accepting rides or talking to strangers along the way. If your child is not going alone, save the "stranger" information and "safe haven" talk for a later time. Children have enough fears to deal with at this stage without adding extra stress. If your child must walk alone from the beginning, you'll need to handle this discussion with care. It should be possible to deliver the message without making the child fear that every stranger along the way is a potential threat. Remember that in the vast majority of kidnapping cases the abductor is someone who knows the child and is often a parent. In families where a custody problem exists, this is a weekend as well as a school-day problem.

There's no point in overdoing the caution by painting a picture of a big and dangerous world. Rather than emphasizing the dangers, give your child a game plan. In many cities and towns storekeepers have instituted "safe haven" signs that signal places where children can find help. If your neighborhood has such a system, point the signs out to your child. In communities where the need exists but no program is in place, you may be able to institute a plan with the help of your parents organization. Even if there are no official "safe havens," you can point out safe and familiar shopkeepers or neighbors that your child can turn to along the way.

After you have done the walk together, play a game of follow the leader, allowing the child to take the lead and show you the way. This will reassure both you and your child that he does know how to get there and back.

BUS RIDERS: If your child will be going off on the school bus, you can probably arrange for an older and more experienced child in the neighborhood to ride with your beginner, at least for a few days. Show your child where the bus will pick him up and drop him off. You will probably want to see him off and meet the bus during the early days of school. If your job doesn't permit this, arrange for another adult to do so, someone to whom your child is already attached. In some areas kindergartners are picked up at and delivered to their homes. If this is not true for you, you will need to establish the best route to and from the bus stop. The suggestions for walkers will apply here.

Keep in mind that the ride to and from school is often the hardest part of the day. In rural areas it can be long and arduous. Since the driver is usually the only adult on board, there are frequently behavior problems when so many children are essentially on their own. For kindergartners especially this can be hard to take.

If your child comes home with regular complaints, I suggest that you follow up by calling the principal or the bus garage supervisor. When our youngest child started school, she complained about a bully on the bus for several weeks. Initially we felt we should stay out of it, but when she arrived home one afternoon with teeth marks on her arm, sobbing that she was ''never going back!'' I called the principal. It was then that my husband and I discovered that the bully on board had been disturbing several children. His parents were called in and the child was taken off the bus for a while. The family had to deal with the inconvenience of transporting their own child, and the incident helped him to understand the rights of others.

According to many principals, the most persistent behavior problems they deal with happen on the bus. As a result, some schools have hired aides to ride and supervise. In some places, parent volunteers take turns assisting. In some areas bus drivers are now being sent to special training classes to learn techniques for handling disruptive behavior. If your child is having consistent problems on the bus, don't ignore them. Talk with school officials or your parents organization. Your child's school day should not begin and end with a sense of having to travel through a combat zone.

ESTABLISHING AN EARLY-MORNING SCHEDULE

BEDTIME

A week or two before school opens, it is a good idea to try modifying bedtime hours. During summer it is not unusual for kids to go to bed a bit later. When school opens, everyone's internal clock is out of order, and no one is ready to rise and shine. Even a child who has had an adequate night's rest is apt to feel a bit weary after a long day in school. Those who are running on too little rest are likely to be even more exhausted and cranky.

Slowly readjusting bedtime a few weeks before school can help kids gradually become accustomed to the new schedule. If they don't have an alarm clock of their own, this may be the perfect time to buy one. Naturally, you can't depend on the clock to do the whole job, but it is not a bad idea to let an impersonal clock give the first wake-up call. It is another step toward giving the child more independence, even if you do have to follow up.

CLOTHING

By five, kids are quite capable of dressing themselves, *if* they have been encouraged to do so and if their clothes have been chosen to facilitate independence. Tempting as some fussy duds may be, keep independence in mind when you're shopping.

Remember that the teacher may have twenty-five or more children to care for. Choosing easy-on-and-off clothing empowers a child to "do it myself" early in the morning and in school. Steer clear of special clothes that kids need to "be careful" about or "keep clean." Children should be dressed for comfort and active play. They should be able to paint, climb the monkey bars, and sit on the floor without worrying about clothes.

To save time in the morning, it is often helpful to lay clothes out the night before. Let your child have as much of a role in making these choices as you feel comfortable with. That way you won't have the early-morning hassle over "what should I wear?" or "I can't find my blue shirt."

If tying shoelaces is still difficult (and it is for most fives), why not select sneakers with Velcro closings or shoes that slip on or come with buckles. Yes, they need to learn eventually, but it will be easier in a year or two. For now the object is to fuel independence.

BREAKFAST AND LUNCH

A good breakfast is so important that many schools now serve the first meal of the day as children arrive. Don't count on it, though. If big breakfasts are not an established part of your day, you're not likely to put them across now. However, remember that for kids starting the day with no breakfast is like taking a car out on the road that's on empty. Kids don't need a three-course meal, but they do need a nourishing start. If possible, avoid sugared cereals and doughnuts, which give an instant surge of energy but lead to mid-morning slumps. Keep in mind that studies show that kids who have a good breakfast outperform those who don't. In fact, that is a piece of information that will impress even kindergartners, who are typically eager to do well.

If the traditional breakfast fare has no appeal, go with lunchtime favorites, such as peanut butter and jelly on whole wheat bread. Or whip up fruit-and-milk drinks in the blender to go with toast or raisin bran muffins. Time is always an early-morning problem. Having it all ready to assemble the night before means less friction in the morning.

If your child is going to an all-day session, you may have the option of either buying or sending lunch. If you are packing lunch, keep it simple and stick to longtime favorites. Don't worry about your child's preference for the same old thing. Food jags are typical at this stage. Eating with others often helps kids become more adventuresome. For the time being the same old thing may be a comfort in a day that is filled with so many new experiences. Think about it. How many thirty-five-year-olds do you know who still eat peanut butter and jelly every day?

SCHOOL SUPPLIES AND OTHER PARAPHERNALIA

Kindergartners don't usually need much in the way of school supplies. They may want them, but generally the school will supply crayons, pencils, and other necessities. Your child's teacher will probably send a letter before or soon after school begins if special supplies are required.

You may need to send a change of clothes for "emergencies," because accidents do happen. A smock may also be needed to cover up clothes for painting or cooking. Be sure to put your child's name on any clothing you send along, and inside boots and sneakers.

If you are buying supplies for home, look for oversized crayons and fat primary pencils especially designed for small hands. You will find these with most school supplies. They are easier for the young child to grasp and control.

Keep in mind that going shopping for school paraphernalia of any sort represents a new and exciting event. The lunchbox or backpack stands for something special in the child's mind. In a sense, they are the tools of the trade for a new and important venture. They are also tangible evidence of one's having become a schoolchild.

PROBLEMS DURING THE FIRST WEEKS OF KINDERGARTEN

During the first weeks of school it is not at all unusual for kids to come home with wet pants. "Accidents" do happen. In addition, some start sucking their thumbs again or come home cranky or whiny. Kids who have given up naps a year or more ago may come home exhausted. There may be sleeping problems at night as well. Nightmares or refusing to go to sleep are not uncommon. All of these problems are usually of short duration and are symptomatic of normal stress related to beginning school.

Once the children begin to feel more at home in the school setting and know they can trust the teacher as a warm and caring person, these signs of anxiety tend to abate. This is especially true when parents understand how temporary the situation is and refrain from shaming the child. This is a time when children may need to be babied a bit at home, while they are doing the "grown-up" business of starting school.

Although there may be other lapses, particularly after a long absence, most kids bounce back to their normal five-year-old selves a few weeks after school begins. On the other hand, if signs of stress and inappropriate behavior persist for a while, parents may need to look more closely at the situation (see pages 47–50).

How Parents Can Support the Learning Experience

Although the shank of the child's day is spent in school, parents continue to play a significant role in guiding and supporting development. This is important for all children, and especially so for those who happen to be in schools that focus primarily on an A-B-C and 1-2-3 curriculum.

While parents may wish that there were other options than the school available to them, in many communities there are no immediate alternatives. At best, informed parents can work together to bring about change. By joining forces with parent activist groups and talking with administrators and school board members, parents can push for better kindergarten programs. However, change does not happen overnight, and your kindergartner's needs are immediate. So what do you do in the meantime?

▲ Avoid being openly and aggressively critical of the teacher or the school with your child. This only tends to create an unbearable conflict for the child, who has to live in both worlds. If you have complaints, take them to the source.

- Be supportive and enthusiastic about the work or projects your child is doing in school. Remember the tremendous amount of energy your child is expending. He needs to feel you respect and value what he's doing (even if you despise his teacher and are unimpressed with the work assigned).

- Keep the channels of communication open. If you don't see the point of what your child is doing in school, ask. Set up a conference with your child's teacher. (See pages 233–40)

Whether your child is in an ideal kindergarten or not, here are some things you can do to balance and enrich your child's experiences. Remember, making use of all of these activities would be a full-time job and add up to more pressure than pleasure. Be selec-

"Me and Sarah are looking out the window." Mio, age 5.

tive and pursue only those activities you and your child enjoy together.

▲ Despite the fact that your child is spending the day with a group of children, time for sustained social interaction may be limited. Opportunities to play one-to-one with classmates and neighborhood friends may need to be arranged for after-school hours and on weekends. It's not just fun; it's an important dimension of learning.

• Programs that keep children confined to paper-and-pencil tasks and sedentary activities overlook the five-year-old's need for active physical play. Provide opportunities to run, jump, climb, and stretch those big muscles after school and on weekends.

▪ No readiness activities are more important than keeping alive children's delight in books. Take time to share picture books with your child every day. Build pleasurable connections with the world of books. Don't assume that the school is doing this. You should be encouraged by studies that show that children who have been read to at home usually do learn to read earlier and with greater ease. In fact, experts have recently suggested that teachers would do well to replicate the kind of one-to-one read-aloud storytime with young children in school. In a typical classroom the group sits at a distance from the teacher. They can see the cover and pictures of the book the teacher has selected. However, at home the child usually selects the book, sits close to the reader, can see the print as well as the pictures, helps turn the pages, interrupts to ask questions, and is involved in the telling of the story. Many studies indicate that the home-style story time is more effective than the group approach. In fact, children who have difficulty in learning to read have usually had little of such intimate and pleasurable book experiences.

After you've shared a picture book, you can occasionally ask your child to retell the story in her own words or have your child "read" a familiar storybook to you by interpreting the pictures. Try borrowing some wordless picture books from the library and encourage your child to tell her own stories. On other occasions, after reading, you could suggest that your child act out favorite stories with puppets. Obviously, you won't always do a follow-up activity after sharing a book. Use only activities that your child enjoys and wants to do. You don't want to end up with a pressurized "ready for enjoyment" time at home!

▲ For independent "reading" experiences, look for books and tapes that children can enjoy on their own. You can record some of their favorite storybooks so that they can listen when you don't have time to read together.

• Provide plenty of art materials for your child to use and explore without having to produce a finished product. This is especially important for kids whose only experiences in school are in manufacturing teacher-designed projects.

▪ Find opportunities to reinforce counting skills with tasks around the house or on outings. Setting the table, serving crackers, returning bottles, climbing steps, counting red cars or seats in a row or lights in a theater are just some of the found opportunities that are ever present. Children love to count, so keep the fun alive. Avoid drilling or pushing on to higher and more complex math concepts.

▲ Find playful opportunities to reinforce sound and letter recognition. On your way to the supermarket or while you are fixing dinner, you can play games of "I'm thinking of something that rhymes with moon.... It's on the table.... It's a ... (spoon)." Or "How many fruits can you think of that start with the sound 'bee'"? Again, keep the fun in such games.

• Avoid turning afterschool hours into minischool sessions. *Bank Street's Bunny Books* (published by Barrons) feature games and activities that are designed for parent-child interactions. You will also find learning games ideas in *Kids and Play,* by Joanne Oppenheim (Ballantine), *Reading Games* and *Math Games,* by Peggy Kaye (Pantheon), and *The New Kindergarten,* by Jean Marzollo (Harper & Row). You may also find Bank Street's *Choosing Books for Kids,* by Joanne Oppenheim, Barbara Brenner, and Betty Boegehold (Ballantine), a useful guide, since it includes a whole chapter on books for five-year-olds. Also see Jim Trelese's *Read-A-Loud Handbook* (Penguin Books) and *A Parent's Guide to Children's Reading,* by N. Larrick (Bantam).

▪ Let your child see you reading the newspaper, books, and

magazines. Talk about something you're reading and enjoying or finding interesting. If an item in the newspaper is of interest to the whole family, share it. Instead of talking about how important reading is, show them by being a reader.

▲ Provide a variety of writing and art materials. Wide-lined paper and hefty wooden pencils are easier for small hands. But don't overlook the value and attractiveness of watercolor markers, fat crayons, paint, chalk, clay, paste, fabric scraps, big sheets of blank paper, as well as empty egg cartons, toilet paper rolls, used wrapping paper, and other "found" materials. All of these unstructured materials give children open-ended opportunities to explore and experiment. They are also helpful for honing fine eye-hand skills. Indeed, gaining control of small muscles with art materials is less tedious and just as valuable as "practicing" letters again and again.

• If you have not joined the public library, now is a perfect time to do so. Many libraries have story hours, films, and other programs for young children. Most children's rooms will give a child a card when they can write their own name. Your librarian is usually a wonderful resource person you can turn to for help in finding appropriate books.

▪ Visits to museums (science, natural history, children's, and art) are more than wonderful family outings. They provide grist for new and wider interests that lead quite naturally to follow-up reading. Similarly, visits to zoos, aquariums, or historical sites whet the appetite for finding out more, with obvious connections to books and magazines.

▲ Museum and zoo gift shops often have books and related games that can extend the experience. You may not want to buy them here, but you might make notes on selected titles and track them down in your local library.

• Taking children to plays, movies, or renting films for the VCR can also lead to book connections. Children's stories that are dramatized can be enjoyed both before and after the original text is shared. Children are often quick to recognize and compare the differences between the two mediums. In fact, one experience may enhance the other.

▪ Without your realizing it, your own reference library may be full of informational books kids would find fascinating. They may only be able to browse or read captions, or you may need to paraphrase the heavy text. Yet, sharing parts of adult books can be a very satisfying experience to both parent and child. Long before children are ready to use an atlas, field guides, encyclopedias, or other reference books independently, parents can introduce such resources as interests arise. If your own library is limited, this may be a good time to fill in the missing pieces. A trip to a bookstore, library, natural history museum, or zoo for material on African wildlife may be the perfect treat for the whole family, especially if the subject is just being studied in your child's classroom.

▲ A well-chosen concert or ballet can be a thrilling experience at this stage. Seeing and hearing live music is quite different from listening to tapes or watching TV. Programs designed for children are ideal but not the only kind of entertainment they can enjoy. Obviously, they are not likely to sit through Brahms's Requiem, but children are quite receptive to a variety of musical experiences and the splendid visual excitement of a concert hall or ballet theater. Indeed, taking your child along can enhance your own experience in rediscovering small pleasures that you may take for granted.

• Even if no concerts or theaters are nearby, you can share your enthusiasm for music with your child by means of records or tapes.

▪ Don't miss opportunities to exercise matching skills. Let your child help matching socks, putting silverware away, and cleaning up the workbench or desk.

▲ Encourage your child to tell you about a painting or building he has made. You can write down the little stories he dictates. You can also suggest that he ''write'' his own stories. Instead of drilling him on forming perfect letters, provide opportunities to use writing in meaningful ways. Remember it's not an end product you're after. You may not be able to read it, but your child will.

• Involve your child in cooperative activities that call for reading, writing, and doing. Cooking together using measuring equipment and following directions puts reading, math, and doing into action with tasty payoffs. Have your helper assist with making shopping lists, signing thank-you notes, or even writing simple messages.

▪ Provide raw material and assistance for creating birthday cards, original storybooks, signs, puppets, and constructions.

▲ Encourage your child's interest in the natural world. Plants, animals, weather, stones, sand, and water are all fascinating ingredients that children like to investigate.

• Expand his horizons with small trips where he can observe real people doing real jobs. Make several visits, at weekly intervals, to a construction site as a house is going up. Go to the supermarket while they're unloading the produce, or the ice cream store while they're making ice cream. Encourage your child to ask questions and to recall what he saw. Avoid turning discussions into a quiz. Stimulate conversations that invite kids to express their opinions and to make connections through new and old experiences. Let them replay the real jobs they have seen.

HOMEWORK IN KINDERGARTEN?

You may be surprised to learn that some schools today are giving kindergartners homework assignments. Usually the tasks assigned are short. Most often they involve drill and practice in writing letters and numerals. Schools that believe in such assignments feel they are teaching good work habits from the start. They also believe these little lessons can give parents a way of being actively involved in what the child is learning.

Although early-childhood educators believe in the value of parent involvement, most tend to doubt the value of such assignments. Almost any of the suggested activities just listed would provide richer learning experiences than writing one's name five times. Too often the drill-and-practice kind of assignments teach children how mindless and boring homework can and will be. They are also a symptom of a current trend of pushing academic demands on ever younger children.

If your child is in such a kindergarten, you may have no choice (and no problems). Your child may find such tasks entirely doable. Some children even like the status symbol of being big, which they equate with having homework. Others may balk from the start. Keep in mind that the younger the child, the more parental involvement will be needed. Some of the suggestions in the primary-grade chapter (see pages 161–63) can be used with kindergartners.

Although you may feel these assignments are inappropriate,

avoid criticizing the teacher (or task) in front of your child. Avoid belittling the child's efforts or turning it into a contest of wills. Your child may not have the dexterity to complete the task, or you may be expecting too much. If you have questions, take them to the teacher. If your child is having difficulty with completing the work, the teacher should know about it. Find out how long the assignments should take and ask about her expectations. You don't want to get into the position of policing homework or having nightly confrontations with your five-year-old. Remember, it's not just skills that are on the line, it's attitudes.

If you feel strongly about the inappropriateness of homework in kindergarten, talk this through with the teacher. You may be surprised to learn that the idea came from the top down, in other words, as an order from the administration. As an active parent you may be able to get your parent association involved in studying and ultimately changing that policy.

CAN KIDS FAIL KINDERGARTEN?

Until recently the idea that children could "fail" kindergarten was considered absurd. It still should be! This is not to say that all children are ready to go on to first grade after a year in kindergarten. Most are ready. However, occasionally there are children who would clearly benefit from another year of kindergarten. Such children should not be regarded as "failures" or slow learners. Indeed, the decision to hold a child back may have nothing at all to do with his or her intellectual ability. Nor should it depend on passing or failing a standardized test. Although end-of-year testing has become increasingly common in kindergartens around the country, educators continue to debate the validity of such testing. Most early-childhood experts advise that a standardized test is a poor assessment tool for the early years of schooling. In fact, critics say that widespread testing has led teachers to alter their programs. In schools where teachers feel they will be evaluated by test scores, the pressure to prepare kids for test taking often leads to teaching methods that stress pencil-and-paper drills. In effect, the test becomes a curriculum guide. At this time, only a few states require all kindergartners to pass a test before they are promoted to first grade. However, the debate continues, and so does the testing.

As a parent, you should insist that no single test be used to decide your child's placement. This is not to say that all children should be pushed ahead, ready or not, but rather that many different factors need to be considered in determining if the child should go on or not.

One administrator recalls a five-year-old with very strong academic skills who was nevertheless retained. She said,

> *This was a child who could read* The New York Times *and talk about it. But we felt that emotionally she was a five-year-old, and a very young five at that. She was totally involved in her own world. Her emotional and social skills simply were not up with her reading or writing skills. Even her fine motor skills lagged. She was bright and delightful, but we felt she would benefit from another year, which would give her an opportunity to be a leader. And it was wonderful to see the way it worked out. She really did a great deal of growing during the second year.*

Experienced teachers have similar stories to tell. One recalled a bright child who needed constant reassurance that he was doing things "right":

> *He was always looking over his shoulder or at others for approval. He didn't seem to trust his own ideas or abilities. He looked to his teacher or classmates instead of tackling a task with gusto or taking chances. With a second year he was able to take more control. In fact, since he knew the ropes, he was able to show others and develop a fuller sense of himself as a competent person.*

Often the recommendation to retain a child is painful to parents. Some feel that they must have failed in properly preparing their child. Others shift the blame to the child's "laziness" or a teacher's inadequacy. However, in most instances there is no one to blame. Nor should the need for an extra year be seen as a failure.

Children simply don't all develop at the same rate. Your first child may get his first teeth at two months and walk at twelve months, while your second child may be toothless until she's four months and be walking at ten months. Viewed from that perspective, it should be easier for parents to understand that in the long run the child who walks earlier ultimately walks no better than the child who walks a few months later. Nor do children benefit from being pushed to perform intellectually or emotionally in ways for which they are not yet ready.

Unfortunately, in schools with unrealistic academic demands for kindergartners, it is the program that is failing—not the children. In contrast, schools that have mixed-age groupings or greater flexibility of placement allow an individual pace of growth to prevail. Any child may be placed in a group with older and/or younger children without being pushed ahead or "held back." Similarly, in schools that have both academic and developmental programs, there are options. In such schools children are less likely to fall between the cracks and need not either be "held back" or pushed ahead before they're ready. However, if your child is locked into a school with a one-size-fits-each-grade curriculum, the extra year in kindergarten may be a blessing.

The decision to retain a child is rarely made in haste or without thoughtful discussion between teacher, parent, and possibly a school administrator. In most cases the news does not come as a shock in late May or mid-June. By late winter the teacher has probably already raised the possibility in the course of her reporting to parents. In discussing your child's situation you are entitled to know on what basis the decision is being made. The teacher should be able to show you examples of the child's work (paintings, drawings, stories). She may also be able to share anecdotal records that illustrate how your child operates in group situations or with tasks that are assigned. In some instances, performances on an end-of-year exam may contribute to the discussion. Rarely is a test score the sole measure for retention (nor should it be). More often than not the teacher's observations are the chief factor in recommending retention. You are entitled to a full report. It may also be helpful if you can personally observe your child in the kindergarten room while class is in session. For many parents, seeing their child in action (or inaction) comes as a revelation. While it is not generally wise to compare children, often in this situation firsthand observation tells the story clearly.

Although there is no magic checklist, very often the teacher will report that the child

▲ Has difficulty participating in group situations, expressing opinions, making himself understood

- Continues to need special individual attention from the teacher
- Doesn't relate well to other children in small groups or on a one-to-one basis
- Rarely initiates or stays with a task
- Can't control impulsive behavior, strikes out at others, destroys others' work, grabs toys

No child will have all of these attributes. Indeed, almost all children will exhibit some of these traits at one time or another. However, the child who may need another year of kindergarten will fit this profile in more ways than one, and more often than not.

Once the decision is made, parents may be terribly concerned about how the child will respond. At any age children are quite able to read their parents' feelings. If you act as though the child has let you down or has been a "bad boy," then being "held back" will be seen as a punishment or a failure. On the other hand, if you accept the decision as the right course of action, the child is more likely to trust both you and himself.

KINDERGARTEN— A YEAR OF DISCOVERIES

In the best of all possible kindergartens, this first year of school is a thoughtful blend of discoveries. In living with others the child discovers new levels of independence as well as interdependence. He is abler now to function outside the familiar sphere of home and family. In sharing space, equipment, and ideas with classmates, his point of view now includes an awareness that others have opinions, ideas, and desires that may be different from his own. Reality has brought him face-to-face with the need for listening as well as talking, for following as well as for leading, for putting things away as well as for taking them out, for working together as well as alone. He has a new sense of belonging to a larger community, a world with rules of its own that is separate from home and family.

Compared with the wary kindergarten child who arrived in the fall, he is a social being who enjoys the company of others. He is less dependent on the teacher and knows better how to negotiate his way on the school bus, in the lunchroom, on the playground, and in the classroom. Home and family are still the secure base he returns to each day, yet he has a new and lively fascination with those who share his expanding world in school. Although his friendships are less anchored than they will be in years to come, he enjoys the company of agemates. Some friendships made during this time may be the beginning of lasting relationships that carry into the very social years ahead.

All in all, he is more competent physically, socially, and intellectually. He not only has a better command of language with which to make himself understood, he is beginning to understand the symbol systems used to write, read, and count. Most of all, if he's been lucky, he leaves kindergarten with a love of learning, and that's what school is about—this year and for all the years to come.

THE PRIMARY GRADES (1–3)— THE THREE Rs

For parent, child, and teacher, the primary grades represent a new and significant departure point. While the members of the triad all bring great hopes and aspirations to the classroom, each comes with his or her own point of view. Let's consider the multiple agendas that must somehow blend.

CHILD'S POINT OF VIEW

School's pretty good, most of the time. I have some good friends and some not so good. On the playground, there's this kid, he's in fourth or fifth grade and he's always starting fights. The teacher yells at him, but it doesn't do much good. He thinks he's so big.

Second grade is not like kindergarten or even first grade. We have to do much, much more real work. We have mathsheets and spelling and writing and reading. I'm pretty good in math, but reading is harder. A couple of kids are already reading long books with chapters. I wish I could do that, too. Mrs. Lewis, my teacher, says I'll be doing that soon if I just keep working. I didn't think learning how to read would take so long. Spelling isn't easy either. My mom is always asking me, ''Where's your spelling homework, let's work on it.'' She expects me to spell the words out loud, but I get them wrong that way. I need to write them down, but then she says my writing is sloppy. I try to make it neat, but when I write fast, it doesn't look so nice.

Even so, I like school, especially math and science. We're growing molds. They are real gross. And gym is fun, too. We play kickball.

PARENT'S POINT OF VIEW

It seems to me that Chip could be doing better. He seems to like school, but sometimes I wonder if the teacher is really doing enough. His writing is so messy. I think he's doing all right in math, but he still uses his fingers to count. He certainly doesn't know the answers off the top of his head. Maybe I should get some flash cards like we had when I was a kid. His teacher says he's having some problems in reading. He doesn't read nearly as well as his sister did at this age. She gave me some books to use at home, but it's torture! He gets so upset.

Sometimes I think if the teacher was stricter, it would be better. I remember that when I went to first grade, we sat in rows. You didn't talk unless you raised your hand and the teacher called on you. But it's not like that in Chip's class. It looks to me like there's a lot of playing around and talking. His favorite subject seems to be gym. All I hear about is kickball. He does seem quite at home and happy enough with his friends and the teacher. She thinks he has good leadership abilities. During Open School Week I spent an hour in that room. It's a lucky thing I didn't become a teacher. I wouldn't have the patience.

TEACHER'S POINT OF VIEW

I can't believe it's almost November, but things are finally falling into place. It's funny, but even after so many years of teaching I have to admit that during the opening months of a new year I still feel like a novice. Maybe that's not so bad. In effect, every year you really do have to start all over again. Sure, you have a storehouse of experience, but every new class that arrives represents a whole new riddle—or should I say, at least twenty-five riddles or more.

I'm worried about Chip. He's having such a struggle with reading. He keeps calling himself stupid and he's anything but stupid. I don't want him to get discouraged. I have to make more time to work with him alone. Writing is a struggle for him, too. But that's not unusual for boys at this stage. He's a real leader. Others look up to him. I'm also concerned about Mari Ann. She's having such a tough time getting along with other kids. She wants to be liked, but she doesn't like giving in at all. Thank goodness, Peter has had a few good days in a row. But I never know when that temper is going to erupt and he'll start acting out again. He's had such a rough time at home. Now that his dad is out of the hospital, maybe he'll settle down.

For the most part, though, I've got a terrific group of kids. They're really enthusiastic about learning and doing. My big objective is to keep that enthusiasm alive!

While these are just three among many voices we might hear at this stage, obviously each member of the triad brings a different perspective to the door of the schoolhouse. However, their common goal is to make the most of these early years of learning.

How well these goals will be achieved depends in large measure on the kinds of partnerships they forge. Parents who know what to expect, and when to expect it, are in a better position to evaluate what's happening or should be happening.

THE PRIMARY YEARS— NEW EXPECTATIONS

Ask any first-grader what he expects to learn this year and typically his answer is, "Reading! I'm going to learn to read!" He may be interested in any number of other things, but reading is usually first and foremost on his list of expectations. And he is right! Although the process of learning to read normally takes three years, formal instruction in reading, along with writing and arithmetic, generally begins in first grade. Kids expect it, as do their parents and teachers.

Like the foundation of a house, all of the basic skills are fundamental. Throughout the primary years, grades one through three, children are learning to use the three Rs, the symbol systems they will need for all their years in school and beyond. However, these are by no means the sum total of all that children are ready to learn about. Indeed, the primary-school child is as eager as ever to know about how things work, how they are made, where they come from, and how he fits into the scheme of things.

In contrast to kindergarten, the first-grader is very much attuned to doing ''school stuff.'' It is something of a new kind of role with a certain seriousness of purpose attached. There are new routines and demands in the primary grades. The daily schedule includes chunks of time when everyone does reading or math or writing. Whereas fives may have written notes or signs or dictated stories, now writing is more than a free choice. The teacher may give a writing assignment that every child must do. Similarly, pencil-and-paper tasks in math need to be completed.

From my own experiences in teaching, I would say that sixes and sevens are among the most enthusiastic and well-motivated learners one could hope to teach. They are eager to learn and thrive on lots of positive reinforcement in short periods of time. They need someone else to tell them that they are doing well. They are still eager to please their parents and teachers, but they need a new kind of reassurance and praise for their efforts. Their lack of experience can lead them to expect more of themselves than they are yet capable of doing. For example, first-graders frequently come to school expecting to learn how to read instantly. Indeed, their lack of experience can lead to all kinds of misunderstandings. One teacher recalls a six-year-old who completed his mathsheet on Monday and was shocked to discover that there was yet another worksheet to do on Tuesday and another on Wednesday. From the young child's point of view, the world of school can be confusing.

Often initial enthusiasm fades as children discover that success is not instantaneous. Then, too, they may begin to compare their own performance with that of their peers and find themselves wanting. Even if a teacher or parent avoids such comparisons, children themselves are well aware of who the ''best'' artists, readers, athletes, mathematicians are in the classroom. Physically they are still more active than sedentary. Sitting still and being quiet do not come easily, nor is this an appropriate expectation for long periods of time. Nor does understanding come chiefly from books or listening. The primary child still learns best by actively talking and doing.

Some children are perfectionists who consider any goof a catastrophe, whereas others consider getting a task ''done'' more important than how it is done. While they are eager for independence, sixes and sevens need caring adults who can help them define reasonable expectations, who can help them see how far thay have come instead of how far they have yet to go. Years ago a master teacher told me that she believed that children at this age are generally trying to do their best. They are still fresh, innocent, and not turned off. They may fall short of your expectations or their own, but it's not usually because they aren't giving it their best shot!

Viewed from that perspective, a parent and teacher can do a great deal to support both learning and the child's feelings about himself as a learner. Instead of serving as judge and jury, parents and teachers help best when they serve on the child's side as chief counsel, available for opinions and advice. Often what's missing is not effort but productive strategies to carry out those efforts. For parents and teachers the goal is not only to facilitate the child's mastery of skills but to keep alive the child's enthusiasm for learning.

WHAT THEY'RE READY TO LEARN—
MORE THAN THE THREE RS

Every September I asked my first- and second-graders what they would like to learn more about. Invariably their answers went far beyond the three Rs. In fact, their list covered the chalkboard and gave me some insight about their wide-ranging curiosity. It also provided me with solid ideas for individual and group investigation.

Unfortunately, in far too many classrooms children in the primary grades are cut off from the world and from their real interests. For three or more potentially vivid years their school days are filled with little more than a series of step-by-step lessons designed to prepare them only for more advanced lessons. Reading, writing, and math are all too often taught in neat, compartmentalized sessions, as if they were unrelated in any way to each other or to bigger experiences. Rather than meshing lively content with skills, the skills themselves become the total content of school. It is as if children's interests must be put on hold.

It's not that the three Rs are unimportant. However, they are better taught by using social studies, science, music, and art as departure points that naturally lead to a need for reading, writing, and math. Skills should not be taught in a vacuum but rather as useful tools. They are the nuts and bolts that are needed to connect the bigger pieces. The rewards for learning how to read, write, or compute should not be measured merely in gold stars but in the excitement of using those skills as tools for unlocking all kinds of learning.

When children are learning to write, they not only need to know how to shape letters; they need to have reasons to put words on paper. Writing, after all, is not just a mechanical act, it is a way of communicating ideas. Similarly, reading is not merely an exercise in decoding printed words. It is one of life's pleasures, in addition to being one of the ways we find out more about things. In a primary classroom a teacher repeatedly raises the question, ''How can we find out more about ———?'' Despite the fact that the teacher often knows the answer to such questions, in the best teaching situation she looks for ways to lead children to find the answers for themselves; and reading, writing, and math are tools to use in the service of discovering such answers.

INDIVIDUAL DIFFERENCES— ATTITUDES IN THE MAKING

For most children the task of learning to read, write, and do simple computations is entirely doable, but some may have more of a struggle than others for a variety of reasons. In some instances, the approach to skills may not match the child's learning style. For example, if the reading program is solely based on sound-recognition skills, and Jimmy has difficulty connecting sounds with letters, he may do quite well with an approach to reading that emphasizes sight words. But if no alternative program is used, he may lag behind in learning to read. For a child like Jimmy, who is falling behind in reading or math, the solution may be an outside tutor, who can tailor a more individualized reading program to his specific style than the school is willing or able to provide.

For some children, school may be less compelling than other concerns. Children may be distracted from work in the classroom because of personal or social problems. For seven-year-old Bobby, every Friday and Monday were lost days. Bobby, whose parents were fighting over custody, came to school every Friday all wound up in anticipation of the weekend with his father and uncles. On Monday he would arrive exhausted and somewhat overwhelmed by the overly stimulating experiences of the weekend. For a child like Bobby a visit with the school psychologist may be in order. Often, it is not the child but the parents who need support and guidance through a stormy period (see pages 258–60).

Then, too, there are children who simply lack the maturity to cope with the tasks expected of them. Six-year-old Tommy was not physically smaller than his classmates, but he displayed his immaturity in multiple ways. He had difficulty completing any task that needed to be done independently and generally disrupted any group activity. He wasn't being naughty, nor was he lazy. He simply wasn't ready. After several weeks of evaluation it was decided that Tommy should have another year in kindergarten. Ideally, Tommy would have been in a first grade with a more flexible program and children of mixed ages. However, given the circumstances, the extra year in kindergarten was the best choice. Not only was he delighted to go, he thrived and was successful in first grade the following year.

All too often, when the school's agenda doesn't concern itself with individual needs, the child bears the brunt of the burden. Children are expected to fit the curriculum instead of the other way around. But forcing children to fit the mold can rub away their confidence and reinforce doubts about themselves as competent learners. It can also bore them. During the early school years, attitudes about learning are as basic to long-term success as the acquisition of the three Rs.

Rather than letting situations drift, parents need to actively engage the help of those who can best help a child who seems to be floundering. Often that help can be found within the school. Where it is not, parents will need to look to other resource people outside the school.

At every stage the child's own love of learning can only be nurtured when schools and teachers respect children's individual interests, needs, and abilities. Indeed, effective teachers know that kindling and keeping that love of learning alive is just as important as any other skill they teach.

NEW LEVELS OF THINKING

According to Jean Piaget, the Swiss psychologist who studied how children's thinking skills develop, children between five and seven are on the threshold of developing new thinking abilities. He calls this the Concrete Operational stage.

While the young kindergartner usually approaches a problem by means of trial and error, the older child is better able to think before he acts. For example, while a young child is likely simply to jam a square block in a round hole, an older child will be able to consider the shape of the hole, the shape of the block, and the possible fit before acting.

It is also at this stage that children are beginning to be able to think about more than one attribute at a time. Unlike the young kindergartner, the first-grader can deal with two different attributes at the same time. As a result, the school-age child begins to grasp the notion that an object can at the same moment be both like and different from other objects. For example, looking at a collection of dark and light stones, he can classify them according to their hue but also according to smoothness and roughness. Further, he can reverse this thinking; he can go back to his original notion of what makes them alike. This kind of flexibility in thinking is basic for dealing with the complex symbol systems needed in reading and computation.

A child who is in the Concrete Operational stage can also make generalizations such as: if $3 + 5 = 8$, then $5 + 3 = 8$. The child who has not arrived at that level of thinking sees each of these equations as if they were unique and unconnected, so although he may memorize these separate facts, learning for a younger child is more cumbersome and less internalized. It is also more easily forgettable.

In one of the best-known Piagetian experiments, a child is shown two identical containers, each containing the same amount of liquid. After the child agrees that the quantities of liquid are equal, the tester pours the liquid from one of the containers into a tall, thin vessel. Children who are as old as six or seven will still say that the tall vessel has more water. It is not until the child recognizes that the quantity does not change with the difference in appearance that he can be said to "conserve." In other words, he is no longer ruled solely by his visual perceptions. He can begin to solve mental problems in his head. *But he still needs concrete materials to support his thinking.*

Two Different Approaches

Although any curriculum in the primary grades tends to focus on building competence with basic skills, the approach to teaching these skills varies tremendously. Let's look at two very different approaches.

Classroom A

It's 9:30 A.M. and Mrs. Russell's second grade is already at work. During the opening session Mrs. Russell has taken attendance and explained the day's assignments. On the chalkboard there are sentences to be copied. Each sentence has a blank space that must be filled with one of the new spelling words the children are to study this week. Mrs. Russell has also handed out a worksheet that reviews the math the class has been working on in their workbooks. On the board there are also reading-workbook assignments for the three reading groups.

At this moment Mrs. Russell is seated with the eight children who are members of the Thundercats reading group. While she works with this group on the rule for "dropping *e* and adding *-ing*," the rest of the class is expected to sit at their desks and do their work. Desks are lined up in rows and children are expected to stay in their seats. Since each group will meet for thirty to forty-five minutes, children are essentially required to work quietly at their desks for an hour or longer. The teacher's solution is often to assign mountains of dittos to keep students "busy." If this happens to be a morning with gym or art, the reading groups may be taken up again after lunch.

If weather permits, there will be half an hour of playtime on the playground after lunch. Then it's back to the chalkboard and workbooks. Today's math lesson is learning the facts of 10. Mrs. Russell puts nine magnetic apples on the chalkboard and asks, "How many more apples should I add to make 10?" She allows a child to come to the board and add one more. Then she writes $9 + 1 = 10$ and asks everyone to recite that fact. She continues until all of the facts of 10 are recorded on the board. Now the lesson moves on to the workbook page that deals with the same facts. Step-by-step the lesson on one side of the sheet is done with the entire group. Then the second side is assigned as independent work. As each child completes the worksheet, the teacher corrects them. A perfect paper rates a sticker or star.

After math the class may have library or music. On days when there is no special event, the teacher may use the remaining time for science, social studies, a storybook, or a group game.

At the end of the day a little time is taken for cleaning up, making last-minute reminders of assignments, and getting coats zipped and snapped.

CLASSROOM B

It's 9:30 A.M. and the children in Mr. Murray's first grade are talking together about the trip they took yesterday to a local bakery. Mr. Murray has written down what each child recalls as something new that he or she learned from the trip. ''How was this bakery different from the first bakery we visited?'' he asks. ''It's bigger!'' one child says. ''It's newer,'' adds another. ''That's true,'' the teacher agrees. ''They only sell bread there!'' a child adds. ''They don't sell cakes or cookies like the first bakery.''

After further discussion Mr. Murray says that all of this information about the trip will need to be added to the class Trip Book. Sometime during the morning each child will be expected to write a few sentences about what he or she saw and draw a picture of something interesting in the bakery.

During the next hour and a half, skills groups will be meeting. Mr. Murray will be working with a small group, while some of the children work on writing, drawing pictures, or doing mathsheets in their folders. But not everyone remains in the room. Half of the class will go to art. Later in the day those who have art now will have reading while classmates go to art.

During the course of the morning Mr. Murray not only works with small groups on word skills, he also listens to individual students read aloud. Although he doesn't have time to read with each child every day, he will read individually with each child several times during the course of the week.

After lunch the group will come together to talk about what they have been doing and to listen to a chapter of a long book the teacher is reading to them. There will also be an active playtime outdoors with time to run, shout, pretend, and play together.

During the afternoon a solid chunk of time is spent on math. Again, instead of working with the whole group, the teacher will work with small groups, while others are scheduled for music, art, or library. On this particular day five children are seated on the rug with the teacher and a basket of Cuisenaire rods. To begin, Mr. Murray takes out a green rod and says, "I want to find all the 'two car' [two rods] trains that equal green. How many do you think we can have?" Their guesses range from "three" to "five" or "six." Now the teacher says, "Do we agree that there is more than one?" Clearly, they agree. Now the teacher says, "Let's see what two-car trains we can find. But we'll use a system. We'll start with a white rod because..."

In a very real and active fashion the children use a variety of manipulative materials before they move on to abstract calculations. This kind of firsthand experience provides a firmer foundation for long-term understanding of the symbol system of math. Although from experience several children give numerical value to the rods (a rod chart with numerical equivalents is posted), the business of writing number facts is ignored at this point. Even the follow-up worksheet has no numerical symbols. Instead, children are asked to color rod trains that equal the given rod. They can use the rods to do their figuring or they can try to do them "in their heads" and then check their answers with the concrete rods.

In these brief sketches it is apparent that the approach of these two teachers is dramatically different. Simply comparing the physical layout of the room clues one in to the style of instruction. In classroom A the desks are lined up in rows facing the teacher's desk and chalkboard. The teacher decides what the children should learn, when they should do so, and how they are to do it. For the most part, all instruction flows from the teacher, who has all the questions and answers. Indeed, she is the center of the universe. In using manipulative materials, it is essentially the teacher who does the manipulations, while the children watch.

In classroom B there are several large and small meeting places. Instead of desks in rows there are tables (large and small) where children can work together. There is a cozy area with rug and cushioned benches to sit on for whole-group meetings. While the teacher is central, he is not the center of the universe that all must focus on at all times. Some children work with him, others work independently and cooperatively with their peers. In their inter-actions children are encouraged to think about what they already know, in order to make connections to what they are trying to discover. Instead of asking simple questions that produce simple answers, the teacher poses questions that move children to think of a variety of answers and questions of their own.

In classroom A the rules about talking, cleaning up, and other routines are written on charts and enforced by the teacher in firm, no-nonsense tones. No talking is permitted during work periods. Interrupting the teacher while she is teaching a group is also off-limits.

In the more fluid setting of classroom B, opportunities for social and intellectual interactions are very much part of the ongoing business of the day. Children are encouraged not only to share their ideas and feelings but also to share responsibilities for group liv-ing.

During work periods it is relatively quiet in the room, but not silent. Children not only talk to each other, they talk to themselves and can quietly ask the teacher for help without fear of being scolded for interrupting. Indeed, there is a quiet buzz of industry in the room. At the end of the morning, when it's time for cleaning up, the teacher reminds them that they are responsible not just for what they used but also for helping to pick up anything they find.

In classroom A the teacher governs with an autocratic hand, however benevolent it might be. So long as she is in their sight or hearing, students know they must behave or suffer the conse-quences. In classroom B the teacher is in charge, but his approach is more democratic. Where possible, he has created a setting that encourages independence. He involves his students in understand-ing not only what the rules are but why they are needed. Instead of having to live up to adult-made expectations, children are in-volved in formulating expectations that are accepted as necessary for everyone.

While the traditional model of classroom A continues to typify a great many public and private schools today, many others have moved toward variations of model B. Indeed, some traditional schools have incorporated traits from model B. As indicated ear-lier, parents may have decided opinions about which model they prefer. Those who are fortunate are able to choose from a variety of schools. However, many parents are apt to be caught with fewer choices. Model A may be the only show in town. While parent activists can ultimately bring about change, the question remains, what can you do to help your child make the most of the here and now?

In looking at the primary years, we will examine the skills children should be learning, how models A and B differ, and finally what parents can do to support or fill in the missing pieces.

READING

BASAL READING PROGRAMS

In the majority of schools, beginning reading instruction is taught through basal reading programs. A *basal* (which means "basic") reading program generally includes a series of readers, workbooks, activity sheets, and a teacher's manual with lessons planned in sequential order for each grade level from first to sixth grades.

First-graders typically read

▲ Two or three preprimers: very short books with only a handful of words
• A primer: a collection of short stories with a highly repetitive and limited vocabulary
▪ A first reader: a collection of short stories with a slightly larger vocabulary

After first grade such programs generally include two books for each grade level. Some schools use the basal series as a total reading program. Others combine the basal with a variety of supplemental materials.

GROUPING FOR INSTRUCTION

Within any classroom there is bound to be a wide range of abilities. Forty years ago the teacher disregarded those differences in traditional classrooms. Reading lessons were done with the entire class. For those who learned quickly the pace was tedious, and those who lagged behind hung on as best they could. In trying to reach everyone, lessons had to be reduced to the most common denominator, which really suited no one.

Today teachers typically divide the class into three or more groups. The teacher may use the same reading materials but at a different pace with all groups, or she may have entirely different books for each group.

In grouping children together by ability the teacher is better able to focus instruction to meet the particular skills of a given group of children. For example, group A may be working on long vowels, group B on short vowels, while group C is still learning consonant sounds. If truth be told, even within each group there will be a range of abilities, and teachers frequently need to individualize instruction to make it fully successful.

How does the teacher know what group your child belongs in? From several factors. During the first weeks of school she will be observing children individually and in groups. She will be observing how children deal with each other and with assigned tasks. She will be looking at how they deal with frustration; do they stay with a task? Their participation in discussions gives her a good sense of their language development and thinking style. She observes how children use a variety of manipulative materials. Their drawings and the stories they dictate also help her evaluate their thinking and language skills. As experience charts are developed, she begins to know how children approach ideas and visual tasks. She begins to know which children seem to have no trouble in finding the same word in several places on the chart. When she draws their attention to the words with the same initial sound, she soon knows those who will need more practice or less. In addition to all of her own observations, she may have the benefit of an informative report from last year's teacher and, in some cases, she may use a standardized reading-readiness test (see section on testing, pages 228–29) to help in her evaluation.

From the beginning and throughout the year the composition of these groups should remain somewhat flexible. A child in group A may need more time with short vowels and be moved to group B, or a child in group C may be ready for the slightly faster pace of group B. Similarly, children may be moved in or out of group C. As the year progresses, the differences between the groups may widen. Groups A and B typically will complete the first-grade basal readers, whereas group C may only finish the first half of the program. What happens to those who don't finish the first-grade program? Most of them will do so early in second grade.

"Why Isn't Johnny a Bluebird?"

For parents and children, the difference between groups can become a matter of great concern. Although names like Bluebirds, Thunderbirds, and Eagles are used to disguise A, B, and C ability groups, most kids and parents know perfectly well which group is flying in first, second, and last position. Naturally parents are eager for their children to succeed, and being in group A is usually perceived as being better than group B and two times better than group C. However, not being in the "top" reading group should not be a cause for despair. Children don't all learn to talk at the same time, nor do they learn to read at the same rate. The fact that they have reached the magic age of six is no guarantee that they are ready to learn to read. Many bright children who will become solid readers do not begin to read books until mid-year or later. Those who take off early sometimes plateau for a time, whereas others who were slow to start suddenly zoom ahead. Any experienced teacher can tell you about students for whom reading just "clicked" after months of slow and steady plodding.

When parents become overly concerned about what group the child is in or press for speedy progress, the pressure may backfire. Children need to feel successful in whatever group they are in. Kids who learn a little more slowly are not destined to be poor readers or poor students. By third grade, whatever reading group they were in, most children usually have a good grasp of basic reading skills.

A Perfect Reading Program

If anyone tells you they have just found *the* perfect way to teach reading—be suspicious! Over the past several decades "innovative" reading programs have come and gone like other swings in fashion. Every few years publishers introduce new reading programs. Often the so-called new series is a revised edition of an already established program. It may have fresh covers, great art, or even a revised workbook, but essentially it is the same program with a face-lift. Occasionally publishers do launch an entirely new series, heavily promoted as the most up-to-date approach to reading.

In educational circles today the latest "in" idea is called Whole Language. Its basic principles are excellent. There is no packaged program involved but rather an approach that combines many sound teaching practices. Whole Language teachers stress the importance of children's oral and written language and its connections to their everyday experiences. Through class discussions and students' writing, language is used as a tool for communication. Instead of using workbooks, phonic-drill lessons, or basal readers, the Whole Language teacher provides a print-rich environment, which includes a variety of picture books for reading with and to children. Oversized picture books, called Big Books, are used for group instruction. Care is given to select stories with predictable and repetitive refrains for beginning readers.

The underlying philosophy of the Whole Language movement is sound and hardly new or revolutionary. How it will be translated into practice remains a question. Teachers who simply replace their basal readers with Big Books or throw out phonic skills along with old workbooks will not necessarily be improving the quality of reading instruction. All too often school districts insist that teachers change the surface details without planning how they will replace old methods with newer approaches. It's like throwing the baby out with the bathwater. To be effective, the Whole Language approach calls for extensive teacher retraining along with an infusion of well-chosen picture books for classroom libraries. For many traditional teachers it will require rethinking their basic approach to children and reading. While the basic tenets of the Whole Language approach are promising, whether and how schools enact such practices remain to be seen.

Despite an abundance of research and a proliferation of reading materials, the Holy Grail has not yet been found, nor is it likely to be. And the reason is simple. There is no single foolproof program that is appropriate for every child, because children do not all learn in the same way. Not only don't they learn at the same pace, they come with differing learning styles and interests. If there were a "perfect" program, it could only be one that combines many different approaches that match children's varying learning styles.

DIFFERENT LEARNING STYLES

Experienced teachers know that some children learn an amazing number of sight words with relative ease. Such children are dependent on visual cues. They learn to read whole words such as *house* or *mother* by the distinctive shape of the word.

To some kids the business of memorizing sight words is a snap. For others it's a disaster. Such children are more dependent on "auditory" or "phonic" cues. They use letter sounds to figure words out. Still others depend more upon context cues. They rely on pictures or derive a word's meaning from the whole sentence. For instance, a child who may not recognize the word *lightning* on a flash card is likely, in the context of a story about a rainstorm, to read the words *thunder* and *lightning* without difficulty.

Recognizing these differences, publishers have created some basal programs that emphasize phonetically regular words, while others begin by building a large sight vocabulary. It's not a question of one being better than another in some general sense, but rather of offering the best fit for a given student. Although most children ultimately learn to read by using a combination of strategies, the beginning program needs to match the strength of the child's dominant learning style. A classroom with only one kind of program will rarely meet the needs of all children. A perfect reading program means multiple programs that fit individual needs.

THE LIMITATIONS OF BASALS

Any experienced teacher will acknowledge that even within three or four ability groups there are children who don't "fit." As a result, there are kids who get lost in the group or are bored by the pace.

All too often the content of the basal series constitutes the entire reading program. "There isn't time for anything else," teachers have told me. By "anything else" they mean no time for independent reading by students and no time for reading storybooks to children. Yet, at this stage especially, children need to hear stories that are beyond their independent reading skills. Reading aloud to children should be part of their daily experience in school as well as out!

Unfortunately, instead of finding multiple ways for children to connect with books, reading is sometimes treated only as an exercise in basals. In the minds of children, if reading equals basals and basals equal boredom, then reading equals boredom too. In many classrooms, the premade lessons are followed slavishly, whether individual children need them or not or are ready for them or not. It is assumed that the "experts" who wrote the program know what students need to learn at this time better than the teacher on the spot.

Indeed, in some schools teachers are *required* to teach by the book. Their lesson plans are monitored by the principal or reading coordinator, who keep track of what they perceive as progress by comparing what page teachers at the same grade level are on. I taught in such a school. Instead of using the suggested skills lessons as a resource to pick and choose from, such teachers must follow them like recipes. For beginning teachers a premade structure offers a measure of security. In fact, teachers frequently come to rely on them rather than on their own judgment.

For the earliest stages of reading, the controlled vocabulary and early skills lessons make sense. However, when such programs define the content of reading throughout the early school years, they can actually undermine the desire to read. Kids are not only turned off by skills lessons that are doled out like prescribed medicine, they also turn away from reading an endless string of stories that are typically mediocre or worse. Few of the basal readers in use today contain stories that would whet the appetite to read. Instead of finding the best children's writers to create stories with literary merit, most basic reading material is frequently generated to match word lists and skills. Even when good stories by real writers are included, they are adapted to word lists that sap their quality. Publishing a basal series is an expensive proposition, but in budgeting, only a small percentage is spent on the stories themselves. In other words, the quality of the stories tends to be the least valued part of the enterprise.

It is not surprising, then, that a generation of kids who have been taught to read on a diet of dull basals turn out to be less than avid adult readers. How can children become literate if neither their textbooks nor their classroom teachers introduce reading material with real vitality and spirit in it?

WHY A CLASSROOM LIBRARY?

Any primary classroom should have a library of books that children can read independently and books that the teacher can read to the class. There should be factual books as well as fiction and poetry. Even if there is a library program and children are allowed to borrow books once a week, the school library is still relatively far away, and a classroom library is an important resource.

Listening to good stories read aloud is more than a relaxing pastime. In a sense, the teacher's reading has the kind of cadence and expression children can hardly bring to their own reading, so it serves as a model of sorts. Then, too, children of six to eight are capable of comprehending stories that are far beyond their independent reading skills. Of necessity, the limited language of the preprimer and first readers are something of a letdown for children who have grown up listening to well-written storybooks. While there is a sense of pride and accomplishment in being able to read the paltry little stories typically found in primers, the importance of reading *to* children should not be overlooked!

In sharing stories with young children teachers need not stick to books with overly simplified language or one-dimensional characters. The richness of language experiences that good read-aloud stories provide continues to be an important ingredient in producing independent readers. Listening to and discussing books provide solid opportunities to develop language and interpretative skills. These are experiences that prepare the way for more advanced independent reading. The fact that children also happen to enjoy being read to is not insignificant either. When children look forward to hearing stories and ask for "just a little more!" they are well on their way to the next step—the delight of reading stories themselves.

INDIVIDUALIZED INSTRUCTION

While the majority of primary teachers divide their class into three or four reading groups, some use a more individualized approach. In such schools children meet in small groups to work on word skills but read individually with their teachers. Instead of everyone being on the same page of the same book at the same time, children read at their own pace from a variety of materials. By working one-to-one, the teacher is able to zoom in on a child's strengths and weaknesses. Rather than sitting through a long group session listening to everyone else's mistakes and waiting for a turn to read a few sentences, each child reads a good deal more in his allotted ten or fifteen minutes with the teacher. Furthermore, the children themselves play a part in selecting their reading materials. There are several basal series in every classroom, but children also choose from a variety of books in the classroom library that reflect their individual interests and taste. Reading materials geared to ongoing science and social studies are also available. With guidance from the teacher, the child is allowed to select books that are often better written and of greater interest than the usual pap found in most early basals.

When children play a part in choosing what they read, they are likely to be better motivated than children who think of reading as an assigned task. Involving children in the choices helps to establish the idea that reading is an activity they "want to do" rather than something they "have to do."

Visiting a classroom with an individualized reading program, one cannot help but be struck by how absorbed the children are in their reading. During quiet-reading time at one school I visited, children were not bent over books at their desks. Two children were stretched out on the rug, reading side by side. Others sat comfortably in their own separate places, near a window, leaning against a bookcase, at a table with feet propped up on a chair. After listening to one student read, the teacher shared a few words with a child who wanted to talk about a book he was obviously enjoying. "Have you read *Frog and Toad*?" the teacher asked. "It's by the same author. It's about being friends. I think you'd enjoy it." In that short exchange the teacher has listened, touched base, and whetted the child's appetite for more reading.

Of course, individualized instruction calls for different kinds of planning and organization. Instead of preparing for three groups, the teacher must find appropriate reading materials for twenty-five or more children. Rather than running on automatic pilot by assigning every page in the workbook as sequenced, she needs to find skills materials that match or tailor them to a child's individual needs. Scheduling is different, too. Instead of the entire class going to music or art, half of the class may go while the teacher works with small skills groups or individuals. Thus, children are not spending long stretches of time filling in the blanks of workbook pages to keep them quiet. There is an enforced quiet time when children read and work independently, but it does not seem endless.

No one in this particular classroom needed to remind kids to be quiet or to get on with their work. They were relaxed and reading in much the same way that an adult might be who was reading for pleasure at home. For children the benefits are obvious. They are not merely learning how to read, they are acquiring positive attitudes and an appetite for a lifetime of reading for pleasure as well as for information.

Even with an individualized program, small groups do meet. Sometimes children who are reading the same book will be called together to discuss the book or to read portions to each other.

EVALUATING YOUR CHILD'S READING PROGRAM

Perhaps no subject causes more parental anxiety than beginning reading, and understandably so, since reading is a key to so many other areas of learning. Although the job of teaching children to read is essentially done in the classroom, there are a number of ways parents can and should be involved in the process.

Early in the school year make a point of finding out about your child's reading program. Many schools invite parents to visit the classroom during Open School Week. This is a good time to discover for yourself how reading is taught. Ask when your child's reading session is scheduled and arrange to be there at that time. If you have questions about what you see, jot them down so that you can discuss them with the teacher at conference time (see pages 233–39).

Your school will probably also have an Open School Night early in the year. This is a good time to find out more about the reading program. Since this is a group meeting, the teacher will not discuss your individual child's work, but she will usually be able to answer questions about the program generally. You should feel free to ask the following:

▲ What kinds of reading program or programs will you be using?

• Do you use a variety of reading programs and materials to match different learning styles?

■ Will my child have reading homework and, if so, how often?

▲ Are there games or books I should use at home to help?

● ■ ▲

What You Should Expect

In a solid reading program you will observe that

▲ Instruction is given to a small group or individually, so that each child has time to participate.

• All children in the room are not working on the same skills at the same time.

▪ A variety of materials is used to match students' varying needs.

▲ Children are absorbed in the lesson and not fidgeting or being distracted by others.

• The teacher is well prepared not only to teach the lesson at hand but to interact with children and their responses. In other words, there is a give-and-take rather than the teacher slavishly following a manual.

▪ Other books and reading materials in the room are available and in regular use.

▲ Reading is integrated into other parts of the day. It is used informally as well as for the formal daily lesson.

• Books are read to the children as well as by the children.

Outside of the classroom you will also be able to observe, in casual ways, how your child is doing. Beginning readers usually

▲ Are enthusiastic about this new skill they are learning. They are eager to succeed.

• Delight in spotting words they know on signs, menus, newspapers, or packages.

▪ Ask questions about words they don't know.

▲ Take pride in reading out loud from easy-to-read books they bring home from school. In first grade this usually begins somewhere between November and January.

• Still enjoy hearing stories read aloud and now take a greater interest in following along as you read.

Danger Signals and What to Do About Them

▲ If your child seems to be shying away from reading, complaining about school, and generally avoiding anything related to reading activities, you may need to investigate further. It may be that such a child is doing well in school and has other important agendas for his afterschool hours. Just because he is learning to read, you shouldn't expect him to bury his nose in a book at every free moment. Nor should you fear that an occasional complaint is a danger signal. Learning to read is a process that takes several years of real work. It's the child who never voluntarily reads or who says he "hates" to read and seems genuinely pained with reading who may need extra attention.

• From your observations in the classroom or at home you may have serious questions about your child's reading program. Feel free to question the teacher about your concerns. Make an appointment for a conference.

▪ If all the students in your child's class are using the same reading program and working on the same skills, chances are only the average child will be doing well. Able readers are apt to be bored, and the least able will be struggling to keep up. Children caught at either end of the spectrum may need extra help. The able reader may need books for enrichment, the least may need remedial help.

▲ Keep in mind that you may not be able to change the system, but talking with the teacher can help. Avoid being confrontational or antagonistic if possible. The teacher may wish she had other options and recognize the shortcomings of the program. You may be surprised to know that decisions about curriculum are not always made by the teacher but rather by administrators. Your objective is to make the teacher an ally, not an adversary.

• Take time to look at activity/workbook pages your child brings home. If you are not seeing any, check with the teacher at your first conference or call. It may be that your child's teacher doesn't use many worksheets or only uses them at school; or their absence can mean your child is having difficulties he'd rather you didn't know about. Knowing what skills they're working on in school can help you provide appropriate support. As a busy, working parent I did not discover until mid-winter that one of my own children was falling behind in second-grade reading. Her workbook was never sent home, and her grades were "S" for satisfactory. It was not until she was absent and her work was sent home that I discovered she was getting short vowels all mixed up. Her teacher did not seem to recognize the problem, but together we were able to work on it, both at home and in school.

▪ Remember that some mistakes and corrections on papers are expected. The bigger issue is whether the child seems to make the same mistakes again and again. If so, help may be needed.

▲ When children are learning how to break the reading code, parents often ask for extra workbooks. Although sometimes additional practice can be helpful, there are problems in turning afterschool hours into drill and practice sessions. Often informal games can accomplish more than yet another workbook. Indeed, for many children, workbooks themselves are a turnoff. If you feel your child needs extra help, discuss it first with the teacher. She may be able to help you focus on your child's individual needs. That way you won't be trying to teach too many things at a time and possibly making a bad situation worse. One of the best resources for playful learning games is a book called *Games for Reading*, by Peggy Kaye.

If your child is having a great struggle with reading, either you or the teacher may want to request a special conference. There is no reason to feel defensive or apologetic about the problem. The main issue you need to address is what can be done to help the child.

In some instances the teacher may be willing to work with your child individually. She may also have suggestions about how you can help at home. She may give you specific skills to work on and materials to use. If you find that working on reading with your child causes too much friction, you may need an alternative plan, such as hiring a tutor.

▲ Children who are having consistent problems with reading may need more specialized help than either you or the classroom teacher can provide. Ask your child's teacher whether the school has a reading consultant or learning-disabilities specialist who can do an evaluation. Such a specialist can often diagnose a reading problem and suggest appropriate ways to remedy the situation either in school or with a tutor. In a large school system there is likely to be a reading specialist and even a remedial program. In a smaller school you may need to find such a person outside the system. In either case, your child's teacher or the principal should be able to assist you in finding help (see pages 254–57).

• Children sometimes need extra help and individualized attention that a tutor can provide. However, keep in mind that private tutoring can be expensive. Before you get started, it makes sense to check the school's resources first. If tutoring seems advisable, it is still wise to consult with the school so that the efforts of the tutor and child mesh both with the school's program and with your child's individual needs.

OTHER WAYS TO HELP WITH READING

Although the job of teaching children to read is largely done in the classroom, parents can and should provide a rich and varied supply of reading experiences at home.

For the beginning reader there are dozens of easy-to-read trade-books that you can find in the library or your local bookstore. If you are puzzled about the choices, ask the teacher, a librarian, or a knowledgeable bookstore salesperson to help you. Keep in mind that many so called easy-to-read books are beyond the child who is just beginning to read. In fact some would be a challenge to second-graders. You may find *Choosing Books for Kids,* by Joanne Oppenheim, Barbara Brenner, and Betty D. Boegehold (Ballantine), a useful resource to help you zoom in on appropriate reading materials for independent reading, as well as books to share.

Keep in mind that reading for pleasure should be exactly that —pleasurable. In your eagerness to provide extra practice it's tempting to begin pushing for new levels of achievement. Parents frequently asked me for extra readers at the next grade level. What we all sometimes forget is the value of positive reinforcement. Children themselves usually select a book that's relatively easy. It's not because they're lazy. At this stage they really need the repetition and practice of easy reading to consolidate what they are learning. Long after they have gone on to more advanced skills, they take delight in rereading books that they struggled with earlier. Though they may call them baby books, there's a glint in the eye and a sense of pride in being able to breeze through *Green Eggs and Ham* or *Go Dog Go*. It's a way of showing themselves how far they've come. Children who feel successful about their reading will move on to more challenging material with more confidence than those who are always being prodded to struggle with more difficult material.

Parents often assume that once children can read, they are past listening to storybooks. That's not true. Throughout the elementary school years (and beyond) children enjoy and benefit from hearing stories read aloud. Indeed, compared with the books they can manage on their own, there is a wealth of literature and factual material that will engage and delight them. Children have the ability to follow much more complex books orally than their reading skills would allow. By sharing such books, parents and teachers build not only pleasurable connections to books but also the child's motivation to become a reader.

Here are some specific ways parents can provide significant bridges to reading:

▲ By mid-second grade many kids are ready for simple books with chapters. Frequently they are intimidated by a book that is more than thirty-two pages long with paragraphs of prose on every page. However, when parents take the time to read the opening portion of the book, kids sometimes get hooked on a story and go on to finish it independently. This is a technique that can overcome a reading block at almost any age. But it is particularly important as kids reach this transitional stage.

• Reading at home need not be limited to books. A story in the newspaper or a cartoon may be of special interest to your child. Clipping an item from a newspaper or magazine gives kids an early link to other media that need not be foreign to them until they are "old enough."

▪ In restaurants adults frequently neglect to offer children a menu. They may need help with their selection, but where food is concerned, kids like the dignity of studying the menu and making choices.

▲ Another activity related to food is reading and following recipe directions. A cake mix or recipe for brownies calls for comprehension skills with edible rewards. At this age level kids will need assistance and supervision, but the time spent can be more useful than plodding through a book that they don't want to read.

• When children read and stumble on a word, your best bet is to supply the word and keep the story flowing. Avoid telling them to "sound it out" or saying things like, "Come on, you know that word!" Obviously they don't know that word or they wouldn't be stuck. If you see a pattern to their mistakes, you may want to work on it later, but try not to interrupt or distract the child from the story—however important or inspired your lesson may be.

▪ Beginning readers often have difficulty keeping their place on a page they are reading. Many use their fingers to point to each word. As a result their reading is choppy and disconnected. By providing a small bookmark you can help them learn to scan the line rather than reading word by word. Parents often worry that the marker is a crutch children will become dependent upon. No need for concern. Children who no longer need the marker put it aside when they are ready. Removing it too soon is really not a way to help.

▲ When a child makes repeated errors and seems to be drowning in a text that's over his head, go to the rescue. One technique that works is to share the reading. Remember, keeping confidence alive is as important as any skill you hope they'll learn. In extreme cases, when a book has been poorly chosen, it is better to take over most of the reading than to encourage the child to keep at it. Kids who get all wrung out by books that are beyond them are not likely to feel good about themselves or books and reading.

• Your local bookstore, dime store, or even supermarket probably has many workbooks for primary-grade children. Again, parents often try to give kids a head start by buying books for the next level. The truth is, most kids get enough of these in school. However, if you are going to buy any, avoid pushing for the next grade level. Look for those that reinforce what they are currently learning. Remember, harder is not necessarily better. Rather than pushing drill and practice, look for "activity books," in which kids have to read instructions to do puzzles or experiments.

- Plug into your child's interests and wherever possible make a connection to books. For instance, when seven-year-old Rick became fascinated by rock collecting, his dad brought home a field guide to rocks. Rick couldn't read all of it, but he enjoyed the pictures and captions. His dad read selected portions to Rick. In the library there are wonderful nonfiction books written especially for young readers. But don't overlook the excitement children find in looking at and listening to parts of grown-up books. It's a way of showing a child that you take his interests seriously.

▲ Children are great at asking questions. Instead of answering from the top of your head or shrugging and saying, "I don't know," why not lead them to the place where you can find out together. Admitting that you don't know or exactly remember the answer to something can have its benefits when you answer a question with, "Gee, I wonder where we can find out about (stars, animals, space, etc.);" they lead kids to a reason to read.

- Quite apart from books, there are games that provide playful avenues to reading skills. Word-building games such as Spill & Spell, Boggle, and Scrabble Sentence Game for Juniors are appropriate choices. Forget about the timers and create your own rules. Another favorite toy you can buy is a word wheel with multifaceted letter cubes that can be turned to create whole words. This is a toy that can either be used solo or kids can write down all the words they find in a given time period. Also interesting is the new kind of charade game Pictionary Junior. Instead of acting out what the word card says, players draw pictures of their clues for teammates.

- For independent reading there are many book and audio tape combinations that give beginning readers backup support. Following the text as a narrator reads aloud is not quite as passive as it might appear. It can help kids in learning to read phrases and provides a good model for reading with expression. Before you buy, be aware that not all tapes follow the text exactly. Ask around before you make such purchases.

If the tape and book don't match, the young reader will get lost and frustrated. Of course, you can make your own tapes of favorite stories. Use a bell or other signal to tell young listeners to turn the page.

▲ Programs on TV such as *Reading Rainbow* and *Wonderworks*, or select videos of children's storybooks, build enjoyment and pleasurable connections to books. Seeing and hearing a story may enhance reading the real thing.

• Comic books and magazines are frequently new and exciting to kids at this stage. The frame-by-frame stories with picture cues are light but entertaining reading that may be less intimidating to young readers than straight prose.

▪ Probably the most basic thing you can do is to be a reader yourself. Children who have reading parents have the best model of all for becoming readers. Talk about a book, article, or newspaper story you have enjoyed or found interesting.

▲ If you haven't already begun to do so, begin building a library of books your child enjoys. Book clubs offer paperbacks at the appropriate grade level and usually at reasonable prices. There are abundant good choices in your local bookstore, too. Unlike adults, who generally read a book once and put it on a shelf, kids like to read and reread favorites. Here are some book clubs you may want to join:

Caedmon
1995 Broadway
New York, New York 10023

Beginning Readers Program
Grolier Enterprises, Inc.
Sherman Turnpike
Danbury, Connecticut 06816

Junior Book of the Month
Club
485 Lexington Avenue
New York, New York 10017

I Can Read Book Club
Field Publications
245 Long Hill Road
Middletown, Connecticut 06457

Junior Literary Guild
245 Park Avenue
New York, New York 10167

Scholastic Book Services
730 Broadway
New York, New York 10003

WRITING

Before we can discuss writing, it's important to define what skills we are considering. When your child's teacher reports that your child's writing needs improvement, you need to know if she's talking about penmanship or content. Although the two skills are related, they are really quite different from one another. During the primary grades, children need to learn the mechanics of shaping letters and words. That's penmanship. But the heart of any writing program should have more to do with language and ideas than with the motor skills involved in paper-and-pencil tasks.

REASONS FOR WRITING

Traditionally the whole writing program in the primary grades has been concerned with penmanship (or handwriting). However, in today's classrooms teachers are increasingly emphasizing the content of writing. From the start, children of six and seven can learn to use writing as a means of communication. Indeed, it flows directly from their spoken language and can enhance their reading and thinking skills.

As indicated earlier, in many schools writing begins in kindergarten. Not only do children dictate captions about pictures they have made, they may dictate whole stories. Or they may use their own phonetic spelling to write signs, sentences, or stories of their own. For the most part, fives themselves decide what they will write about. However, starting in first grade, the teacher sometimes assigns specific writing tasks. She may have the children write about a subject related to social studies or science. What follows is typical of good early-grade writing programs that can now be found around the country.

In one first grade, after a trip to a local restaurant the sixes and sevens discussed what they had seen and learned. As they talked, their teacher wrote what each child recalled on a large sheet of chart paper. She used a different colored marker for each child's sentence. On the following day the children began trip pictures and trip stories. Children decided which they would do first. For many, drawing a picture is an ideal way of making the transition to printed symbols. The drawing itself is a symbolic representation of what the child has seen. Often such pictures are rich in small details that reflect what the child has noticed. While an older writer may be able to make a picture in his mind's eye and write about it, drawing a real picture provides a valuable step in conceptualizing what the young writer will focus on.

After the pictures and stories are completed, they may be stapled together in a Trip Book, which becomes part of the classroom library.

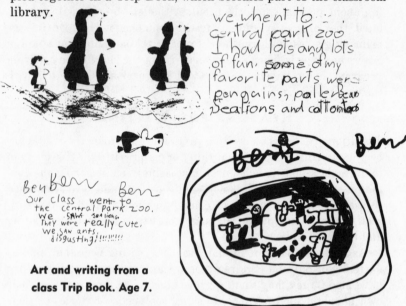

we whent to central park zoo. I had lots and lots of fun. some of my favorite parts were pengains, poller bear, seations and cottontes

Ben Ben Ben
Our class went to the central Park zoo. We saw sea lions. They were really cute. We saw ants, disgusting!!!!!!!!!!

Art and writing from a class Trip Book. Age 7.

Translating what they have seen at first hand into written form is actually a first and important step in learning how to observe, record, and organize ideas. In fact, it is directly related to the next step, which involves translating information from materials they read into ideas they can express in their own words. By writing, the child combines and unifies experiences, making them his own.

After a trip or when a visitor has come to their room, there are thank-you letters to be written. There are recipes from classroom cooking to be copied, notes to parents about meetings or supplies, observations about the class pet, science experiments, or reports on books they have read. All these activities involve writing, and yet none emphasizes the separate issue of penmanship.

Writing is not, of course, limited to factual reporting. Children also write stories, personal narratives, and even "books." One typical seven-year-old in a class I visited was writing a book that chronicled her travail with her little sister. Indeed, writing provides an ideal pathway both for fantasy and for expressing deeply felt emotions about everyday life.

As in kindergarten, a chunk of time is set aside for writing. It is during this quiet time that students are expected to put their ideas on paper. In some instances, what they write will be shared only with the teacher. The content may be very private and privileged information about a problem the child is having in school or at home. In other instances, the writing will be shared with the group.

After children have shared what they have written, their teacher and classmates have an opportunity to question them further. This sharing time gives children a chance to discover for themselves what, if anything, they have left out or not stated as clearly as they imagined. So it is partially from their own peers that they discover how to communicate. From the start the teacher plays a significant part in modeling how questions are to be posed. Since everyone knows that he or she will also be "edited," if not today then another time, students tend to choose their words of criticism sympathetically. It also helps the writer to think of what he's trying to say and how to say it.

After a story has been shared, the young writer may go back and rewrite, using the editorial comments he gleaned from his classmates' comments on his piece.

Instead of recopying the original piece, young writers become quite adept at cutting, inserting, and reworking their second draft. At the start little emphasis is put on neatness or spelling. Each child does have a spiral stenographer's book with alphabetical tabs. When he needs a word spelled, he brings his Word Book to the teacher. Usually the book has already been turned to the correct initial sound, indicating the child has already begun to figure out spelling. If it is a word such as *thing*, the teacher will say, "What do you hear? Listen, *th*." When the child repeats the sound, he may say "*th* . . . oh, it's *t h*—the blend!" Then the teacher says, "Right! *Th*, *ing*." The child smiles and says, *ing*, that's *i–n–g!*" Now the word is written on the *T* page and the child goes back to his writing.

Of course, not all words can be figured out so neatly. A nonphonetically spelled word such as *know* may simply be printed or the teacher may comment on the silent letter. Actually, the individual Word Books become personal spelling books children can refer to.

My Trip to the National museum

By Carrie goto

When the Dutch (frist) *first* came to pigs, cows,
sheep and other kinds of animals (roamed) *roamed* around in people's
backyards. Some people did not like it. ~~that~~
The ~~people~~ put up ~~nces~~ *fences to keep the animals out* and had *special* ~~people~~ *people to watch and* make sure
no animals got in to ~~there~~ *their* backyard or
garden.

° To New Amsterdam.

② and gardens,

③ Having animals in ~~there~~ *their* backyards or gardens,
because ~~they~~ *the animals* (would) *would* mess up the plants or
get everything dirty by smearing dirt
on the houses ~~and~~ *or on* special plants.

First Draft edited
Age 8.

More than that, the books become a tool for reinforcing word analysis skills children are learning in reading as well.

As their reading skills develop, they become more proficient spellers. Indeed, the teacher may develop spelling lists and word analysis lessons from words that children commonly ask for or misspell. However, at this stage neither spelling nor penmanship is the major focus. You may ask, aren't the children learning bad habits? Not really. What should count when children (or adults) are composing is getting their thoughts down on paper. That is the first and most essential priority. If adults put great emphasis on neatness or spelling, the flow of writing is likely to get dammed up. Instead of shaping their ideas, children may actually limit their writing to safe words and super-short stories, especially if they are going to have to rewrite and correct all misspelled words.

Ultimately, in good writing programs some of their writing— usually the pieces they are most satisfied with—gets polished for a final draft. Pieces that are going to be ''published'' in a class book or letters that will be mailed go through a final revision, with corrections made for spelling and rudimentary punctuation. It is at this point that neatness and mechanics are emphasized. Not every piece of writing will get this kind of scrutiny. First and foremost, the objective in the primary grades is to emphasize content.

As children read and write with greater ease and frequency, their spelling and punctuation skills come to be tools they need and use in the meaningful context of writing. Many of the conventions of grammar are learned without repeated drill and practice, but rather through constant experience and use.

There are still schools that continue to limit writing in the primary grades to copying letters, words, and sentences from the board—or from books. Lessons in punctuation are taught in isolation. The weekly spelling list is put on the board with directions to "use each of these words in a sentence." While such exercises may reinforce skills—and may be found in moderation in any writing program—they can hardly be called writing. Indeed, they reinforce the notion that writing is tedious and relatively mindless.

In such schools students are usually given an occasional fling at "creative" writing. But even these assignments tend to be spun from formulas such as "What I did last summer" or "Why I'm thankful this Thanksgiving." Such exercises are generally viewed as "add-ons," something to do if time permits or as a treat. But

> Carrie
> When the Dutch first came to New Amsterdam, pigs, cows, sheep and other kinds of animals roamed around in people's backyards and gardens. some people did not like having animals in their backyards or gardens because the animals would mess up the plants or get everything dirty by smearing dirt on the houses or on special plants. The people put up fences to keep the animals out and some had special people to watch and make sure no animal got in their backyard or garden.

Final Draft.

writing skills don't develop when they are used infrequently. Writing and the reasons for writing need to be an integrated part of the daily program.

It is not that children don't need to learn how to punctuate and spell but rather that these skills and the need for them should not deter creativity or dominate writing in the early grades. If your child's school does not have a writing program, you may be able to get one going through your parents organization. Some parent groups have sponsored visits by guest writers to the school. Such programs can inspire students as well as teachers. Your parents group might also study how other schools are changing their approach to writing.

How Parents Can Help with Writing

Studies show that children who excel in school often come from homes where they have access to books and writing supplies. If your child is in a school that does little in the way of writing, you can fill the void in a number of ways. A note of caution: Avoid turning these activities into pressurized, required assignments! These are suggestions, not prescriptions. Don't try to use them all. Pick and choose to fit your child's interests.

▲ Adapt some of the ideas from this section. For example, after a trip to the museum or a family outing, encourage your child to make a souvenir book. Drawings, postcards, ticket stubs, photographs can be used for making trip books the whole family will enjoy reading.

• Provide lined stationary and reasons for letter writing. Grandparents, uncles, and aunts will be delighted to hear about what's new from your child's point of view. Keep in mind, some children find letter writing downright painful. Preprinted thank-you notes with room for a line or two or original ''art'' may be a better approach.

▪ After watching a show that was especially pleasing (or displeasing), why not write a letter to the star or the station. Your child may even get an answer.

▲ Instead of buying invitations for a birthday party or special event, encourage your child to design her own. The information that has to be included calls for planning ahead and checking for accuracy.

• After sharing a storybook, your child may enjoy writing his own version of a similar story by changing the characters and/or the events, or the ending. How about "Goldilocks Returns" or new lyrics for a favorite song?

▪ Sevens and eights may enjoy keeping a diary or journal. They are not likely to write in it daily, but they like the idea of a private place for personal writing. You could give them one as a gift without then standing over them to see that it is used. Remember, it's private property, so don't pry.

▲ In addition to your standard dictionary, have a children's picture dictionary on hand. Beginning readers like to leaf through the pages and will occasionally use it to look for a word they need to spell.

• When kids need help spelling a word, supply it. You can encourage them to tell you what they hear at the beginning of the word and help them to break it into spellable syllables. But remember, many words can't be sounded out.

▪ Keep a supply of interesting writing tools available. Colored pencils, thin markers, and pens are often an inducement to write.

▲ Kids of this age are delighted with riddles and jokes. Encourage them to make a picture book of their favorite riddles or jokes as a gift for a grandparent's birthday or to keep in their personal library.

• If you have a computer, your child may enjoy writing on it or may find just fiddling around with your word processing program quite pleasurable. You can set up a "file" for her and tape up nearby clear, simple instructions on how to get into the word processing program.

HANDWRITING

Children usually come to first grade with a good deal of experience in writing. Developmentally they begin as toddlers with scribble writing. Typically, by the time they are six, they can write their names and many of the letters and numbers. They may have started in kindergarten, at home, or a combination of both. During the primary years they will continue to refine their writing skills. Many teachers use a book or some formal program giving children step-by-step instruction in how letters are formed.

In contrast to the random kinds of letter writing young children experiment with independently, now they are given some real strategies. For example, the teacher will begin with letters that are related in shape. If she begins with the letter *c*, she will go on to

teach other letters that begin with the shape of *c*, such as *o*, *a*, *g*, *d*, *q*, *e*, *s*. Similarly, she will teach all the letters at one time that begin with a straight downward stroke. The letter *l* would be the starting point for teaching *t* and *i*, or *n* would be taught with *m*, *r*, *h*, and *b*.

Although children frequently arrive in first grade knowing how to print many of the capital letters, often they have learned to do so quite inefficiently. They may, for instance, draw the three horizontal lines for *E* before drawing the downward stroke that would give them a holding line, or, they may write *D* by making a circle and adding a stick to the left. For many children improvement in writing is confounded by having to "unlearn" their earlier approaches to shaping letters.

Learning to shape letters calls for a good deal of practice. In their own way, children of six, seven, and even eight are wonderfully well suited to the task at hand. They have an appetite for tasks that call for repetition and practice. Their fine motor skills are better attuned than they were at four or five, and they are better motivated than they will be at nine or ten, when writing letters is apt to be considered "baby stuff" and boring. So learning to print now is a satisfying if painstaking task, more easily mastered at this age than before or after.

This is not to say that all sixes and sevens find it easy to learn to write. Some children are more adept than others at tasks that involve copying. Others have problems with spatial relationships. They may have difficulty seeing or reproducing letters that go below the line, such as g, j, q, or they may have problems shaping letters that are a full or half space tall, such as l versus i. That's why primary teachers generally prefer special writing paper with dotted guidelines for beginners rather than standard notebook paper.

In addition to demonstrating on the chalkboard how letters are formed and where they begin, good primary teachers also provide special kinesthetic materials that reinforce children's sensory style of learning. Letters on a chalkboard or in a workbook are flat and one-dimensional. To give children a more immediate sense of how they feel, teachers may have children trace letters on cards that are textured with fabric or sandpaper. They may have puzzles with letter cutout shapes that children can handle and fit back into puzzle books. Frequently the teacher will have children practice writing letters with their finger in the air, making big sweeping motions. Or children may practice writing letters in a pan of sand or flour. All of these sensory exercises can go a long way in helping children get a firsthand feel for the shape and direction of forming letters.

Since children are usually learning letter names and sounds at the same time they are learning to write, the teacher will tie the two skills together. She may encourage them to name things that start with the letter, or they may draw a picture of something that starts with a particular letter. For example, my first-graders dictated and illustrated a delightfully silly book full of dinosaurs dancing, dinosaurs driving, dinosaurs diving, dinosaurs digging, dinosaurs drinking, and so on, when we were working on the letter d.

Once all the letters have been introduced, many teachers will assign a daily copying task. It may be a letter home, a recipe, or words and sentences related to their reading work. For many children this is a doable, if boring, task. However, for some, the business of translating from blackboard to paper is arduous if not overwhelming. They may lose their place and reverse words and letters. Children who fall apart on such assignments often have less difficulty copying if they are given the same task to copy from a paper on their desks. If your child is having such a problem, discuss this intermediate approach with his teacher.

Parents often become terribly concerned when children reverse their letters, particularly *d* and *b, p,* and *g.* Or a child may reverse an entire word, writing or reading *saw* as *was* or *top* as *pot.* Although such mistakes can be symptomatic of a learning disorder, in most cases reversals of this kind are simply age-typical errors. Most first- and second-graders do turn letters and numbers around. If your child is still having this problem in third grade, then you will need to check into it. Until then, there's little reason to worry.

By third grade, penmanship programs shift from printing to cursive writing. From the child's point of view this new style of writing has a certain amount of status appeal. It's another visible symbol of being more grown-up. So they are well motivated to labor over loops and lines. Their fine motor skills are also more fully developed, so the task is generally quite manageable.

Of course, there are children for whom the mechanics of writing represent a giant hurdle. Studies show that boys, who generally develop more slowly than girls, also tend to have more penmanship problems at this age. For some, both boys and girls, using a typewriter or word processor ultimately becomes the best alternative. It represents a refreshing form of freedom to concentrate on content without the distraction of having to focus on form. This is not to say that in an electronic age kids no longer need to know how to use pencil and paper. However, for today's students there are more tools available that can do the job.

● ■ ▲

How Parents Can Help
with Penmanship

▲ Provide plenty of writing materials at home. Primary pencils, which are thicker than regular ones, are easier for small hands to use. You will find these in stores with an extensive school supply section.

• Primary writing paper with guide lines is available, and is more helpful especially for first-graders.

■ Unless the teacher suggests the need for extra drill, avoid instituting your own official practice sessions that turn writing into drudgery. Keep in mind that practicing the wrong way is much worse than no practice at all. When kids overpractice mistakes, they end up needing to unlearn and relearn, so the task is compounded. If you're going to help your child, it's important to know how letters are being taught in your school. The teacher should be able to cue you in on the "methods" used.

▲ If you are asked by the teacher to help with writing at home, don't try to work on everything from *A* to *Z* in one sitting. That is bound to be counterproductive. Stick to letters that have related shapes, as described on page 120.

• Don't overlook the value of activities that are related to writing that can help children develop fine motor skills without emphasizing letters. Drawing with crayons, markers, and paint continues to have great appeal and enhance the child's eye-hand skills.

■ Similarly, puzzles and construction toys that demand looking at fine differences provide practice in skills related to writing and reading.

▲ Many of the sensory exercises used in the classroom (see page 121) can be adapted to home.

• Chalkboards are great favorites at this age, both for "playing school" and for practicing letters or numbers. Children love the impermanence and power of quickly erasing a goof and starting over again. Magic slates, those inexpensive pads with an acetate sheet that lifts to erase, are also pleasing writing tools for this age group.

SPELLING

Your child may have a formal spelling book or spelling may be taught in the context of reading and writing. Once children have a firm grasp on the connections between letters and sounds, they are able to make generalizations that simplify learning to spell. Spelling workbooks often have their own agendas that are not necessarily in sync with what the child is being taught at a given moment in reading or writing, especially in first and second grades. So students may be learning the sounds of long *a* followed by silent *e* in reading while the spelling text is working on short *a* words. Although children eventually need to learn both, competing lessons can be counterproductive.

As noted earlier, in many schools today children begin writing with their own invented spelling. By six and seven, they begin keeping a personal alphabetized Word Book that is in fact a spelling book of words they need and use for their writing. Over a period of months these lists and the words that are studied in reading skills become the basis for beginning spelling skills.

By the time children are in the third grade, they are more likely to be ready for the structure of spelling workbooks and weekly tests. Children at this stage are often paired with spelling partners and quiz each other. Generally partners are unevenly matched and have different word lists. There may be as many as three spelling groups that reflect the range of abilities within any class.

HOW PARENTS CAN HELP WITH SPELLING

Some schools send weekly spelling lists home by the middle of first grade, others not until second or even third grade. Check this out with your child's teacher so that you will know what to expect, when to expect it, and whether or not she expects you to help your child on this.

Parents can do a great deal to support children's spelling skills. Keep in mind, however, that your own attitudes about spelling are going to show. If you had difficulty or always hated spelling, don't pass it on. Rather than saying, ''I was never good in spelling, either,'' look for an approach that works for your child. For many beginners the big problem is a lack of strategies for studying word lists. Some children learn best by writing their words on paper. Others find it better to say each word and spell it out loud. If spelling homework poses a problem for your child, here's one approach that might help.

Step 1: Have the child study the word list or print each word on an index card. Then do a preliminary test by having the child spell words you say. Go through the entire list to discover which words need further study. Most spelling lists contain words that can be crossed off as known (or put in the known pile).

Step 2: Now look at the words that need to be studied. Are there similarities between the words? If so, help your child discover the elements that are the same. For example, ask your child to find the words where the *e* at the end is silent.

Step 3: Encourage your child to study the words
▲ by saying them
• by copying them
■ by looking at them, then covering them up and writing them (or spelling them out loud).

Step 4: When he feels he is ready, repeat step 1 and discover how many more words can be put in the known pile.

Aside from helping with assigned word lists, parents can also help spelling skills along with a variety of games and toys. Word-building games such as Boggle, Spill & Spell, Scrabble for Juniors, or Hangman are good choices. You may need to adapt the rules or forget the timer to make them into family games. Also useful at this stage are some of the electronic toys that can be played at the beginner's level, such as Texas Instruments' Speak and Spell. If you own a computer, you may prefer some of the software programs designed specifically for the early-school-years speller.

MATH

Like reading, the approach to teaching math has been subject to much trendiness. Many of today's parents arrived in elementary school in the age of "new math." In the late fifties when the Russians launched Sputnik, there was tremendous pressure for updated science and math programs in our schools. Before Sputnik, elementary schools concentrated on basic computation skills needed to add, subtract, multiply, and divide. With the "new math," emphasis shifted to teaching the language and concepts of mathematics. For example, children were expected to memorize definitions of sets and subsets, the differences between a number and a numeral, or the meaning of *equal* versus *equivalent*. Ultimately, many of the new programs failed because children were unable to put these abstract ideas and definitions to meaningful or practical use. Like reading teachers who throw out phonics, some math teachers also discarded programs that stressed computation skills and any kind of drill or practice. Although the radical new approach "failed," it did change the nature and scope of math instruction. Math programs today combine elements of both the "new" and the traditional approaches to math.

For the child in the primary grades the language of math is best learned when it is integrated into their other studies and informal experiences. Almost any group discussion or project lends itself to a math component. When my second-graders were studying dinosaurs, although they couldn't go to the museum, they were able to get a firsthand sense of how tall or long these fascinating creatures grew by measuring a reel of kite string stretched the length of a school hallway. In doing so, the forty-foot length of a Diplodocus became much more than a fact found in a book.

Similarly, in planning a second-grade party for Halloween we needed to figure out how many packs of plates we would need if there were eight in a package and we had twenty-four children. We also had to find out how many people we could serve with one can of juice in order to discover how many cans we'd need. Then, too, we had to consider how much juice would cost. As children brought in money for the party, there was change to count. In working together, these second-graders were doing a great deal more than simple counting. Not only were they working as a team, they were discovering multiple ways of thinking about solutions to a real-life math problem. And they were testing their thinking with real materials.

In any classroom setting a multitude of everyday events and materials provides the grist for mathematical thinking. The clock, the calendar, a thermometer, money, scales, and rulers, are all used for different ways of measuring. How many days until the party? How many weeks until the class play? How much higher or lower is the temperature than it was yesterday? What time is gym? How will the clock look when art is done? How many people ordered chocolate milk? How many plain milk? How much change should you get?

Adults often assume that because children can count, they are ready to learn to count higher, or that when they can add, the next step is simple to get them to add faster. Math is often seen as a series of tricks to be memorized rather than understood. Often, though, when children are rushed into juggling abstract symbols, they skip the fundamental pieces that are essential to solid learning. It is not enough to know how to add, subtract, multiply, and divide. Children also need to know what it means to do those operations and when to do them.

Indeed, problem solving is the really important thing about math. Though any good program should have enormous amounts of problem solving, all too often the emphasis in schools is on computation. As one teacher put it, "A lot of what's taught as math comes under the heading of stuff you learn to get through school. It's a kind of self-perpetuating thing."

Programs that focus on drill and rote learning of facts before second or third grade can actually undermine children's long-term understanding of math. When we present kids with thick workbooks full of page after page of computations, we are also fostering an "answer-getting" mentality. Kids can (and often do) zip right through the pages without ever discussing the concepts involved or even connecting one lesson to the next. They begin to do them mechanically, at the very time when conceptual learning is so important. Indeed, the underlying message of the workbook itself conveys the very narrow notion that this is what math is all about.

This doesn't mean that formal lessons or practice sheets in math have no place in the primary grades. Of course they do. However, a rich math program is more than a series of lessons developed by a publisher and portioned out day by day in the classroom by the teacher. It begins with multiple real experiences that lead children to an understanding of basic math concepts before they move on to the abstract symbols and operations typically found in workbooks.

THE NEED FOR CONCRETE MATERIALS

While sixes, sevens, and eights are dealing with the abstract symbols of math, their understanding is still dependent on manipulating concrete materials. A picture of a set of six objects on a page is not the same as handling six cubes or six raisins. Crossing one out on a page is not the same as covering one cube or eating one raisin and having five left. By their very design, math workbooks with number symbols and pictures are once removed from reality. Pictures help, but they are a poor substitute for repeated sensory experience with three-dimensional objects that can be arranged and rearranged at first hand.

Of course, the most available manipulatives kids typically use at this stage are their own fingers. For most, this dependence is gradually outgrown. In the classroom the teacher may provide cubes, sticks, chips, beads, or other manipulative materials. She will also show children how they can calculate addition and subtraction facts on a number line. The number line, which resembles a ruler, is more abstract than beads or blocks and provides a bridge to understanding in an active and yet more conceptual way. To solve the equation $6 + 3$, the child learns to find 6 on the number line and then move his finger three more spaces. Or if he is subtracting 4 from 6, he puts his finger on 6 and moves his finger four spaces back. While parents sometimes are concerned that children will become overly dependent on such "crutches," children ultimately give up such supports when they no longer need them. As they become better able to manipulate numbers in their head, they will have less need for fingers, objects, or number lines. However, for sixes, sevens, and many eights these supports provide security and the underpinnings of understanding.

WHAT AN INTEGRATED APPROACH TO MATH LOOKS LIKE

In an integrated program math is taught both formally and informally. In a third-grade room I visited, where the children had embarked on a study of the sun and earth, this problem was posted on the board:

> Everyone do this: Sunrise 6:19 A.M.
> Sunset 5:00 P.M.
> Hours of daylight _____

This was no isolated question, although it was timely. Over the previous weekend, clocks had been turned back, but the study had begun several weeks earlier. On a bulletin board, a large graph was being used to keep a record of the changing patterns of sunrise and sunset. One could look at the graph and quickly see the hours of darkness growing longer. Here is a pictorial way of representing a rather abstract idea. Instead of simply calculating the time between 6:19 A.M. and 5:00 P.M., the numbers are translated into a visual experience that makes the symbols meaningful.

Yet this was not the main thrust of the day's math work. During a scheduled math period students were divided into three skills groups. Several children were working on multiplying by 10, others were doing subtraction with regrouping (what we once called borrowing and carrying), still others were doing addition with regrouping. In every instance the assigned tasks were supported with manipulative materials. For example,

To figure out a subtraction problem

$$\begin{array}{r} 207 \\ -139 \\ \hline \end{array}$$

students were told they could do their computation by using Dienes blocks and record their answers, or they could work out the problems first and check their answers with the blocks. Children easily placed the blocks that represent 207 on their math folders:

THOUSANDS	HUNDREDS	TENS	ONES
	▤ ▤		□ □ □ □ □ □ □

So, here was the dilemma! How could they subtract 9 from 7? Could they take it from the tens place? "Only if we break up one of the hundreds," one child suggests. "Try it," the teacher says.

● ■ ▲

THOUSANDS	HUNDREDS	TENS	ONES

"But it still won't work," another child says. "We have to ex-change one of the tens for ones." So they do.

THOUSANDS	HUNDREDS	TENS	ONES

"Now we can do it," a student says, as he takes nine ones and three tens and one hundred off his folder. "Sixty-eight!" he says. "There are sixty-eight left!"

THOUSANDS	HUNDREDS	TENS	ONES

Instead of beginning with blackboard tricks showing children how to borrow from the hundreds column and carry it to the tens and ones, these children were physically doing what they will ulti-mately be able to do symbolically. Indeed, the teacher works through several of these problems with a small group. It is not until he senses that they understand what they are doing that he assigns a worksheet to provide further practice.

Similarly, in the second-grade room, where children are also learning about place values, the teacher introduces a game called

"Take a Chance." Two players stand before charts that look like this:

100	10	1

100	10	1

The teacher rolls the dice and calls the number 8. Players have to "take a chance" and decide in which column they'll put the 8. The teacher rolls the dice again and calls a 6.

Player A

100	10	1
8		6

Player B

100	10	1
	6	8

It is not until the third number is called that we know who has written the highest number and wins the round.

However, in the next round two players play "take a chance" in this way:

100	10	1
7	9	

100	10	1
9	7	

As soon as the second number is called, the group knows that player B has won the point.

The foregoing game is just a small part of the day's math lesson about place value. Small groups will also work with color-coded chips (green = 100, blue = 10, yellow = 1) in learning to add those digit numbers with regrouping.

By third grade the range of math skills within any class is

diverse. Rather than ignoring that diversity and imposing a single lesson plan for all students, the teacher addresses those differences with appropriate materials at varying levels. By working with small groups the teacher is better able to recognize those students who may need extra time with a concept. She can also provide more challenging work for those who are ready.

Rather than a giant workbook, each student has a math folder with worksheets they are required to do three or four times a week. However, as students begin dealing with written symbols or paper-and-pencil tasks, basic concepts continue to be explored in multiple ways with concrete materials such as Dienes blocks, Unifix cubes, Cuisenaire rods, and chip boards. In doing so, students can learn from the start that the symbols of math represent a reality they can understand.

As is true with other subjects such as science, social studies, music, and art, opportunities for *applying* skills lend math a purposefulness that brings it to life for young children. As a warm-up exercise in the morning the teacher may say, "Today's the twenty-first of October. Who's got another way of saying twenty-one?"

One child says, "Twenty plus one."

Another child calls, "Four times four plus five."

Yet another child says, "Five times five minus four."

Although there are different levels of math thinking in the group, everyone can participate. In fact, there is often a wonderful openness about what comes out.

Through cooking, record keeping, graphing, using money, measuring, and multiple direct experiences children learn the functions and connections that are the underpinnings of math thinking.

EVALUATING YOUR CHILD'S MATH PROGRAM

Many schools invite parents to visit the classroom during Open School Week. This is a good time to see for yourself how math is taught. If you have questions, be sure to jot them down so that you can discuss them with the teacher at conference time.

Your school will probably have an Open School Night early in the year. This is also a good time to ask about the materials your child will be using.

What You Should Expect in a Strong Math Program

▲ Instruction is given mainly to small groups rather than the whole class at once.

• All children are not working on the same skills at the same time. A variety of classroom materials match students' varying needs.

▪ Manipulative materials such as blocks, counters, and rods are used by the children, not just the teacher, for demonstrations.

▲ The teacher encourages children to find multiple ways of solving a problem rather than looking for a single right answer.

• Children are actively involved rather than simply listening or fidgeting.

▪ The math lesson involves more than filling in answers on a workbook page.

▲ Math is integrated into other parts of the day.

• Children use a variety of measuring tools, such as scales, thermometers, rulers, graphs.

Danger Signals and What to Do About Them

▲ If everyone is working on the same page in the same workbook, chances are the math program fits only the average student. In such classrooms the ablest students are likely to be bored and the least able will be struggling to keep up. If your child is at either end of the spectrum, he may need extra help. You may not be able to change the system, but talking about it with the teacher may help. Avoid being critical or antagonistic about the program. Simply discuss your concern openly. The teacher may be willing to provide more enrichment for your math whiz or extra help for the child who needs it. If she cannot, she may have suggestions about how you can support your child's special needs.

• Look at worksheets your child brings home. If none are coming, or if they are consistently full of mistakes, you will need to speak with the teacher. Don't assume the worst. Some teachers in the primary grades do not use a great many work-sheets, or they may not send them home regularly. However, the absence of papers may also indicate that your child doesn't want you to see that he is having difficulty. Early in the year it's a good idea to find out what papers you should expect and how often to expect them. Don't assume that no news is good news. If the first report card or conference is not due until late October or November, your child may lose a lot of valuable time and needed help.

▪ Keep in mind that some mistakes and corrections on papers are to be expected. Nobody's perfect. The bigger issue is whether the child seems to be making repeated mistakes with the same or similar materials. If so, you may need to discuss this with the teacher. Extra help may be needed.

▲ If your child complains about hating math and balks at doing assignments, have him tell you what it is that he hates. Sometimes repetitious drill and practice sheets are what kids hate—not math. This won't necessarily make the drill and practice more palatable, but it may offer you some clues on how to preserve positive attitudes about math in other ways. Let's face it, copying problems from a textbook or doing pages of calculations can be tedious. But parents can help kids understand that practice is how some things are learned. During your conference with the teacher you may want to ask how long assignments should take and discuss your child's balkiness.

• If your child is having difficulty with assignments and needs your assistance every step of the way, again you will need to alert the teacher. Homework, if assigned at all, should not require a great deal of help. For the most part, it is intended to reinforce what has been taught in the classroom. If your child does not understand this work on a consistent basis, the teacher needs to know about it.

In the event that your child is having difficulty in math, either you or the teacher should consider requesting a special conference. There is no need to feel apologetic or to excuse the issue with stories about your own struggle with math. This is the time to focus on your child's immediate problems and how they can be remedied. In some cases the teacher may have suggestions for how you can work with your child at home. The teacher may suspect that a learning disability is at the root of your child's problem. She may suggest or you can request an evaluation (see pages 258–59 on learning disabilities). She may provide extra materials and show you how to use them. If you have negative feelings about your own math competence, you may be the last person on earth who can help your child. If so, it is wise to discuss this with the teacher. She may be willing to do extra work with your child; the school may have a remedial program; or you may need to hire a tutor. Keep in mind that if tutoring seems advisable, it is best to consult with the school so that the efforts of tutor and child may be coordinated with what's going on in school. Although some teachers may feel that the need for a tutor is a failure on their part, children often benefit from the one-to-one attention a tutor can offer. Indeed, the tutor can focus on the individual child's strengths and weaknesses and tailor instruction that hones in on your child's needs.

OTHER WAYS TO HELP WITH MATH

The possibilities for math learning are built into everyday experiences that you can share with your child. Whether you are helping with assigned schoolwork or playing a game, here are some things to keep in mind:

▲ Avoid pushing your child and turning afterschool hours into pressurized teaching sessions.

• Remember that your child needs to develop positive attitudes about math and herself as a math learner. Those feelings are crucial and can influence her achievement. Avoid pushing kids to the next level of skills. Don't try to teach them next year's skills this year. Give them time to consolidate what they know with success.

▪ Parents need to be aware of their own attitudes about math. If you feel anxious or "always hated math," don't pass it on. Math is an area that is subject to sex-role stereotyping. Girls as well as boys need to become competent in math.

▲ Support the way they are being taught. Don't confuse them with your way. Some research shows that helping kids with math can be more destructive than instructive, especially when parents ignore or contradict the school's approach and teach it "their" way.

• When you're helping with math, give your child strategies for solving problems. Help him to make connections to what he already knows. For example, 8 + 2 seems to be easy to recall, but 8 + 3 is not, until kids see that it is just one more. Again, the use of concrete materials such as toothpicks, nuts, or raisins can help clarify abstract symbols and make concepts easier to grasp.

▪ When you play games, encourage your child to be the score-keeper. Children don't have to do heavy addition. They can score points with a single line. Teach them to bundle points in fives like this: ⫴

▲ Keep manipulatives on hand to help with homework that involves computation. Poker chips, raisins, peanuts in shells, or pennies will do the job. For learning place value and re-grouping (borrowing and carrying) a box of a hundred drinking straws is great. Have your child make "bundles" of ten straws with rubber bands; leave loose straws for the ones. These can be used to calculate addition and subtraction problems with two digits.

• Many commercially made games involve problem solving, counting, and adding. Among the best are:

Battleship	Parcheesi
Checkers	Tanagrams
Made for Trade	Yahtzee
Chess	Tri-Ominos
Parquetry Blocks	Any deck of cards
Chinese Checkers	Uno

▪ Many electronic math machines provide drill and practice kids like and can use independently. These are usually of interest to sevens and eights.

▲ Just a simple set of dice can be used for a variety of invented games. Or look at Peggy Kaye's *Math Games* (Pantheon), a book full of game math projects you can make together and play.

• Cooking calls for measuring ingredients and following recipes. Try doubling, tripling, or halving recipes.

▪ If encouraged, young collectors often like to keep written records of their coin, trading card, action figure, or book collections. A card file or the family computer can give the enterprise a seriousness of purpose. Deciding how to organize a collection involves sorting and classifying skills that relate directly to math.

▲ Household chores such as arranging the bookshelf, neatening up art supplies, or unpacking the groceries also call for sorting and classifying by size, use, or other attributes.

• Involve kids in measuring tasks of all kinds. Use conventional measures, such as rulers and scales. But encourage them to use nonconventional means as well (such as hands, feet, a length of yarn). If you are relining shelves or drawers, get your child involved. At the grocery store let your child help weigh the fruit and compare prices. How many more plums do you think could make a pound? Which can of soup costs more? Does it save money to take the biggest or the smallest box of oatmeal?

▪ Find opportunities for children to count change from piggybanks to pockets. Do we have enough for a kite that costs two dollars? How much would two kites cost? How much should we get back?

▲ This is the age when lemonade stands and other entrepreneurial fevers rise high. Help your child figure how much his ''product'' costs and how much he needs to charge to make a profit.

• Kids also love to play store, restaurant, movies, and other pretend games of commerce. Realistic props lend themselves to math thinking such as:

Toy cash register	Tickets
Toy money	Balance scale
Price stickers	Waiters' checks

▲ Many of the above items can be made from scrap paper, but realistic props are especially favored. A set of rubber printing stamps with letters and numbers and an ink pad are great for making signs, menus, and banners. You'll find these in select toystores, stationary stores, or school supply catalogs.

• Find opportunities to get your child to check on the time. Discuss the times when a special event or broadcast will begin.

Concentrate on hour and half-hour divisions to start. Don't try to teach the concept of minutes until the more basic ideas are familiar. Learning to tell time takes time and experience with both analog and digital clocks. A wristwatch is often a prized possession at this age.

▪ If you own a computer, here are some math software programs that may be of interest:

Gertrude's Secrets *(The Learning Company)*
Math Blaster *(Davidson)*
New Teasers *by Tobbs (Sunburst)*

THE PRIMARY GRADES— MORE THAN THE THREE Rs

Social Studies

As you might expect, the approach to social studies and the content of the curriculum vary tremendously from one school to another. Although a school may have a suggested curriculum, how it is implemented is often left to the teacher's discretion. What is taught can vary from one classroom to another within the same school. In the early grades, social studies is often treated as an extra that's tacked on as time permits. Holidays such as Thanksgiving and the birthdays of Washington, Lincoln, and Martin Luther King are usually the chief historical events touched on in the primary years. Typically, during Fire Prevention Week the class may go to the firehouse or a firefighter may visit the classroom, but such visits are often treated as isolated events. No larger concepts about communities, people, and how they interrelate are developed. Similarly, current events and geography are touched on with a student newspaper, such as *My Weekly Reader,* or map skills worksheets that may have little connection to anything else the children are learning.

By the time children have gone through kindergarten and first and second grades, these disconnected bits and pieces become as predictable and lifeless as the annual essay assignment, ''What I Did Last Summer.'' While holidays and pictures of the Thanksgiving Day parade may be part of the American tradition, they by no means constitute a meaningful social studies program.

By second and third grades social studies is often presented as another form of reading, with formal textbooks that are used once every week or two. Rarely do these little premade ''units'' lead to discussions of any depth or spark any further thoughts or investigation. A few children take turns reading aloud, while the rest of the class follow along in their texts. At the end of each chapter there are premade questions that test literal comprehension but little else. In my own experience, the greatest excitement over such programs usually centers on who hands the books out and who puts them away. If they teach anything, it may only be early negative attitudes about history, geography, and the social sciences.

AN ALTERNATIVE APPROACH TO SOCIAL STUDIES

In less traditional public and private schools, social studies—that is, vital studies about people and how they live—is at the heart of the curriculum. It is the core from which a variety of significant learning experiences grow. Indeed, the way in which any content area is studied should be considered as important as the body of facts children may learn.

In the primary grades the focus of the social studies curriculum should be the notion of people working together. While the particular culture and people that children study will vary from grade to grade, the approach to their investigations has certain common threads.

For the children, every study involves

▲ Working as a member of the group
• Formulating what they already know on a subject and what they want to find out

- Using, if possible, some nearby part of the community as a resource for finding out by observing, inquiring, and recording
▲ Using discussions, writing, and reading as a way of understanding/synthesizing
• Reenacting what has been seen through art, constructions, and dramatization
- Connecting and comparing what one knows with what one is finding out
▲ Learning how to ask questions as well as answer them
• Gradually learning how one goes about finding out about the world from multiple inquiries and sources

LEARNING HOW GROUPS FUNCTION

First and foremost, at every grade level, every study itself is a group experience. Whether a class is studying how food gets to the city, how the library works, or what it was like to live in New York when it was New Amsterdam, the process itself involves working together as a group. In doing so children are learning

▲ How a group investigation takes place
• How a group organizes itself to go out and get information
- How to handle information and understand it together
▲ How to communicate ideas and opinions
• How to deal with differences of opinion

Quite apart from the topic being investigated, the role of group experience provides a significant lesson in the business of functioning democratically as a community.

WHAT THEY STUDY

For first-graders, the world of here and now continues to provide the most meaningful social studies content. However, their interests are much broader than those of kindergartners, whose studies move from ''Me and My Family'' to ''My School and My Community.'' When the five-to-sixes go to an orchard, they return to the classroom and make long lists of what they have seen. For the kindergartner it is enough to have gone, seen, and compiled their observations.

In contrast, when first-graders go to an orchard, they are ready to understand how the people who are involved at the orchard fit together. For example

▲ They want to know how the orchard owner knows when to call the beekeeper so that the flowers will be fertilized to make the apples.

• They know apples come to the city, but they want to know whose job it is to crate the apples.

▪ They want to know whether the storekeeper drives to the farm to get the apples or the farmer brings them to the city.

Less egocentric, sixes and sevens are able to think beyond what they see. They want to know how things and people operate, so they may study how the library works, come back to the classroom, and create their own library, or they may study the city by actively visiting and discovering what places, people, and jobs are absolutely necessary to meet people's needs.

For the early school years, the world beyond the classroom doors provides a hands-on laboratory for learning. The group begins its investigations by going out into the community and observing how things and people work. However, before they leave the classroom they are encouraged to focus on what they know, what they think they know, and what they hope to find out.

In a first-grade class I visited, after taking a trip to a neighborhood restaurant the children talked together about what they had discovered. Not only did they discuss what answers they had found to their own questions, they talked and wrote and drew pictures about what was most interesting to them. In addition to noticing the different jobs done by the chef, salad person, waiter, busboy, and manager, they were fascinated by the tools people used and the kinds of storage places needed for food, dishes, and supplies.

This local café was just the first of many restaurants these children would visit over a period of two or three months. In planning the program, their teacher had arranged to take them to several very different restaurants, where contrasts would be vivid. A vegetarian restaurant, a seafood establishment, a Chinese restaurant, and a fast-food place offer built-in learning opportunities for discovering how these places are alike and in what ways they are different and why and, more generally, how the world the children inhabit actually works.

Ultimately the study will culminate in running a restaurant of their own—in this case, a fast-food yogurt stand offering a variety of toppings that they'll sell to other classrooms for a week. In contrast to pure dramatic play, this "business venture" involves serious planning, comparative price shopping, computing costs, setting a fair price, collecting money, and keeping a tally on flavor preferences to predict what to stock the next day. As a group they need to decide who does the buying, advertising, selling, counting profits, cleaning up, and restocking. In effect, the culminating activity combines much of what they have learned outside the classroom with their basic three-Rs curriculum. The result: an active, powerful learning experience enacted on a small but meaningful child-size scale. As in any study at this age, what begins with things that are part of the child's familiar world leads in the end to a fuller understanding of how things happen and what people do to make things work.

To extend that knowledge, children have opportunities to talk with each other and to ask questions directly of those who do the real work they are studying. In the classroom a library of related books may be used by the entire group or by interested individuals. No textbook could teach a similar lesson.

As children move into the second grade, they are ready to learn more about people and places of long ago. Yet history is approached in a way not vastly different from the earlier studies of farm or restaurant. Indeed, the focus should not be on dates and events in time. Whether they study the Massachusetts Bay Colony or Native Americans, the focus should be on looking at people and describing how they lived. In doing so, children are able to understand that people in any age have certain basic human needs, which don't change very much. In any given study they begin by trying to discover how these particular people met those needs—for food, clothing, housing, entertainment, tools, stories, music, art, and spiritual life. Since they understand the world best from their own perspective, they are encouraged to discover how the people they are studying were different from and like people today.

By the time children are nine or ten and have studied several groups of people and some historical figures, they can begin to know how to go about finding out about other people and times. What they have learned in terms of a body of facts is not more important than what they have learned about the process of finding out. By relating what they know to what they are finding out, meaningful connections are developing. In firsthand visits to seaports and museums children are encouraged to speculate on how the geography of a people affected the kinds of houses they lived in, the foods they ate, the clothes they wore, and the tools they used. By re-creating some of those artifacts, children enter into a more compelling kind of study than that which is contained only on the pages of a history book. It is not that books should never be used. Indeed, children at this stage use books for beginning research, for doing reports, and as a source for experiencing the art, folktales, and music of another time.

What they discover in books is then translated and reenacted through art and dramatizations.

Reenacting becomes a way of knowing about one's self and others. In fact, really great readers actually read like that. They enter into a story and re-create it in their own minds. There is a depth of experience that captures what learning is really about. That kind of learning is quite different from the traditional approach to a body of facts that are all-too-soon forgotten. It is also in the context of such experiences that children use their emerging school skills as writers, readers, and mathematicians.

How Parents Can Help with Social Studies

While changing the social studies program in your child's school may be impossible right now, there is much you can do to enrich your child's experiences outside of school.

First, it's important to understand that children at this stage are eager to know how things work, so instead of focusing on facts, dates, and names, turn your attention to what's going on that kids can see at first hand. For instance, on a trip to the supermarket or the dry cleaner take time to help your child focus on the conveyer belt that carries the clothes on hangers, or on the truck outside the market with its conveyer belt and products being unloaded. Take time when you are walking past restaurants to notice the trapdoor in front of such places that usually leads to a storage room. Ask, "Why do you think that's here?" "Where do you think that truck came from?" Stop and take time to watch at a construction site or take a weekend afternoon to go to an apple orchard. Wherever you go, there are things you can point out and talk about. Not only is it a way of sharing time and information, use the opportunity to build connections between what your child knows and wants to know more about. Trips to museums, restoration villages, and historical landmarks whet the appetite for knowing more about history. So, too, can films and storybooks with historical settings. Such experiences can whet the appetite and build connections to content they will be studying in school. A child who has been to Plymouth Plantation, for example, brings that experience and another dimension to a textbook account of the pilgrims. He has smelled the soup cooking on the hearth, felt the chill of the crude cabin, and seen how dim candlelight must have been. In storybooks such as Robert Lawson's *Ben and Me* (Dell) he gets a childlike but humorous encounter with Benjamin Franklin (as told by his mouse Amos) or experiences the excitement and discomforts of the covered wagon with William Hooks's *Pioneer Cat* (Random House).

Often it is easy with school-age kids to get caught up in talking chiefly about family routines and what you expect and want. Getting beyond such nitty-gritty affairs can bring another dimension to your relationship, but try to steer clear of telling your child only what you consider important. Instead, encourage a dialogue about what your child thinks, feels, or finds interesting. Indeed, headlines in the news or on TV may provoke worries and questions that need clarifying and discussion—about a book, a place you've visited, or a show on TV.

Children of this age are also becoming involved in their own family histories. Photo albums, family artifacts, and visits with older relatives give them a firsthand sense of their own history and their specific links with the past.

While you cannot replicate the group experience of the classroom, you can, in a way, do so within the family. After all, your family can be seen as a model for a group of people who have diverse and sometimes conflicting ideas, and that alone presents opportunities for discussion. At the dinner table it should be possible for all ideas to be heard. If someone is misinformed, the emphasis should be not on belittling that person but on how to become informed. In effect, the family is a group that helps children learn

▲ How people listen to each other
• How people deal with disagreements
■ How people come up with a collective decision
▲ How group problem solving goes on

Of course, in reality the family is not exactly a democratic situation. Obviously, parents have roles to play that don't always lend themselves to majority rule. So does a teacher. Both parents and teachers are authority figures, and some decisions are made from the top. However, both in school and at home there are opportunities to treat the feelings and opinions of all members with respect, and frequently there are issues that can be dealt with in a democratic way.

For example, the family may discuss what to do during the weekend. One job may be to find out what the options are at the movies. As a family, then, there are questions over which movie various family members would enjoy and what time and where the various movies are playing. Even in such small events we are teaching children about the process of group experiences and how choices are made.

Perhaps most important, parents play a vital role in helping children to begin to deal with social questions for which we ourselves may have no perfect answers. Rather than avoid such issues of poverty, bigotry, and the inequities children begin to ask about, parents can offer children a sounding board for their concerns. We can help children see how contributing their "baby books" to a book drive for hospitalized or homeless children is a way of doing something to help. Children can learn that while we cannot always "fix" things and make the world safe and perfect, it's still meaningful and valid for them to bring up their concerns and discuss what's on their minds. Indeed, such discussions allow a lot of misinformation to surface and be clarified.

SCIENCE

Any science program in the early grades should be approached in active ways with real materials rather than through textbooks. During these years children need opportunities to observe and record what they are studying. They can learn to keep logs, and to make drawings, charts, and graphs about their experiments. They learn to classify objects by comparing such attributes as color, texture, and size. Tools and numbers are used for measuring, comparing, and looking at detail. They can be encouraged to set up a hypothesis and then test it. In a rudimentary way they are learning the process of thinking like scientists. This kind of approach with young students makes more sense than, say, a study of a distant rain forest or desert that is outside their experience.

The classroom pet is a resource for learning observation skills as well as for developing a sense of responsibility. What is learned about classroom pets gives children some generalizations about other animals' needs. Indeed, when one knows a great deal about one animal, it is easier to study another by comparing ways in which they are alike and different. Similarly, living things such as plants, birds, fish, and insects are a source of fascination, useful comparison, and firsthand study.

A second grade, for example, might begin a study of their local park early in the fall. They would not only investigate the people who run the park and how people use it, they would compare and study the flora and fauna of the park. They might bring back water from the pond along with plants and living creatures for further investigation, observation, and record keeping.

By third grade the ability to deal with more abstract subject material is developing. In one class I visited, children were learning about the solar system. These were some of the questions they had formulated on a chart:

OUR QUESTIONS ABOUT THE SUN AND EARTH

- ▲ What is an eclipse and when does it occur?
- • How close to the sun can you get before you burn up?
- ■ How can the sun stand by itself without falling?
- ▲ Why isn't every planet like planet Earth?
- • Is the core of the sun hot or cold?
- ■ What are clouds made from?
- ▲ What is continental drift?
- • How fast does the sun move?
- ■ Why does the sun have flames?
- ▲ How did the sun get its name?
- • Why does the earth turn?
- ■ How did we find out how far away the sun is?
- ▲ Can humans live without the sun?
- • If there's a face on the moon, why isn't there a face on the earth?

- Is the moon turning when it goes around the earth?
- ▲ What is the autumnal equinox?

While none of these questions can be answered by firsthand experiences, these eights and nines were exploring other experiential strategies for finding answers. On a separate chart the road map to more abstract research is apparent.

How Will We Find the Answers to Our Questions?

- ▲ Do experiments
- Take trips to planetariums and museums
- Read magazines like *National Geographic*
- ▲ Write to the people at the NASA space centers
- Read books and encyclopedias
- Watch TV—science shows like *Nova*
- ▲ Watch movies
- Listen to the radio
- Talk to each other
- ▲ Interview some astronauts
- Look at a map of the stars
- Look in newspapers

On the bookshelves of the room a library of related books and magazines is prominently displayed. There are books at varying levels of difficulty that reflect the wide ranges of student ability and interests. A poster of the solar system is on the wall, along with student-made artwork and written reports that reflect children's interests and varying levels of sophistication.

Throughout these early years of school the emphasis in science must relate more closely to children's developmental need for concrete experiences. Even the eights-to-nines need to translate abstract ideas into real experiences they can touch, smell, taste, hear, or know through their immediate senses. While they are eager to know more about increasingly distant and unseeable facts, their real understanding comes in making a connection to what they have experienced.

As with social studies, much of their science learning begins with observations that incorporate their emerging skills in math, reading, and writing.

How Parents Can Help with Science

The temptation in science is to tell your child more than anyone ever wanted to know. For the sake of learning, parents would be well advised to do more looking and listening with their child than telling. Helping children feel at home in science begins with feeling comfortable yourself.

▲ Stop to notice the details of collected leaves, rocks, plants, and other natural materials. Encourage your child to talk about and compare what she has found with what she already knows.

• If you can handle a pet, do so now. Kids before seven or eight are not terribly good at remembering where their responsibilities begin and end. So the pet will require some involvement from you. Yet the long-term rewards can be significant. Even if you cannot have a dog or cat, a tank of fish or a bird puts children in touch with another creature's needs and habits.

▪ Use the outdoors as a lab for learning. A bird feeder provides a changing parade of different appearances and eating habits. Kids at this age enjoy bird (or other animal) field books and may even start keeping records of species they have seen.

▲ Similarly, a trip to the beach or the park can yield interesting collections of shells, stones, seeds, leaves, and pinecones to sort and compare. Keeping records and collections on display often interests kids for short periods of time.

• Toy stores sell bug kits and planting kits. What you really do is buy the habitat and send away for the species. Much less costly is to provide your own habitat, catch your own species, and then let them go when interest wanes. Library books can give you tips on how to house earthworms, ants, and other easy-to-capture creatures. Also interesting at this stage is a terrarium, which can be made with relative ease in summer and fall. Instructions for early science experiences can be found in such books as *Science Fare,* by Wendy Saul and Alan Newman (Harper), or *The Science Book,* by Sara Stein (Workman).

▪ Simple tools for taking a closer look at details are ideal for these years. A real microscope is better for the next age group. However, magnifiers, small microscopes that can go outdoors, flashlights, magnets, tweezers, empty containers, and your enthusiasm can provide the support for a vast range of investigations.

▲ Growing things in the backyard, on the windowsill, or under a lamp is interesting, especially if children have a hand in the planting. Try a variety of planting materials for multiple experiences:

Avocado seeds	Sweet potato
Cuttings with roots	Orange seeds
Carrot tops	Vegetable plants
Lima beans	Paper white narcissus
Cactus	

• Cooking offers opportunities to make things from scratch and see how they change. Talk about these changes, like whipping cream, melting butter from solid to liquid, or baking cake from liquid to solid, and how children think they happen.

▪ Use the public library for finding easy-to-read magazines as well as books to share on subjects related to science. There are many fine magazines designed for this age group too. Your library may have them or you may wish to subscribe to:

Ranger Rick's Nature Magazine
National Wildlife Federation
1412 16th Street, N.W.
Washington, D.C. 20036

3-2-1 Contact
P.O. Box 2933
Boulder, Colorado 80322

National Geographic World
Department 00880
17th and M Street, N.W.
Washington, D.C. 20036

▲ If at all possible, you'll find it's worth a special trip to hands-on museums, such as the Boston Children's Museum, Philadelphia's Franklin Institute, Chicago's Field Museum, New York's Museum of Natural History, San Francisco's Exploratorium, San Diego's Wild Animal Park, Baltimore's Aquarium, and so on.

• Watch for TV specials, especially on PBS, that will open children's view of the natural world and sciences. Share these programs when possible by talking together and connecting them when possible to firsthand visits to zoos, aquariums, and museums.

ART AND CRAFTS

Instruction in art is often left to the classroom teacher during the early school years. In schools that can afford the staff, there may be a special art teacher who visits the classroom once or twice a week. Such sessions usually last twenty-five to thirty minutes at most. Unfortunately, when budget cuts must be made, art is often the first to get the ax.

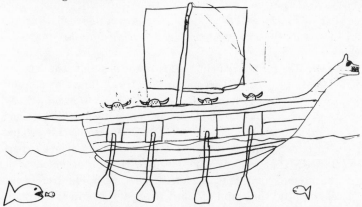

Viking drawing from homework assignment. Nasees, age 9.

In the primary grades art experiences should be happening daily within the classroom as well as with specialists, not as an isolated skill but as another way of expressing one's feelings and re-creating one's view of the world. Art experiences should be integrated into most other parts of the curriculum. Indeed, for many children art is the path into writing and social studies.

Rich possibilities can arise from a more integrated approach to an art curriculum. In my own teaching experience, when our social studies centered on a Chinese New Year's celebration, the art teacher brought in special brushes and black paint, introducing an art experience that related to Chinese scroll paintings. Students also produced colorful red and gold New Year's cards and a papier-mâché dragon head for a dance done to music brought in by a Chinese-American student.

Often art teachers tend to be trained generally, rather than specifically, with the needs of the early-school-years child in mind. As a result, formal lessons tend to creep down into grades where the exploration of materials and experimentation with expression would be more appropriate activities.

During these years, sixes and sevens should have opportunities to try a variety of open-ended materials for drawing, painting, building, sculpting, and printmaking. Few children at this age are terribly self-conscious about their end products, unless too much is demanded of them. This is not the time for vigorous lessons in perspective or how to produce realistic still-life drawings. More central at this stage is the freedom to explore a nonverbal form of expression and the excitement of discovering how art materials work.

Typically, far too many primary art programs center on teacher-directed craft projects. Everyone in the class follows the step-by-step process of reproducing what the teacher has designed. All thirty "creations" may be displayed as "our artwork." While such tasks may teach children about following instructions and producing end products, they are the most limited kinds of art experiences. Indeed, they may lead children to rely on others to show them what to make and how to make it. The fact is, children at this stage seldom need that kind of motivation, nor should the focus be on producing an end product. Doing a painting, working with clay, or building a collage are processes that children find engaging and satisfying in and of themselves.

In schools that value art and creative expression, both classroom teachers and art specialists provide space, time, and materials for children's work in art. The walls of classrooms and the walls of the school itself are alive with the shapes and colors of children's paintings, collages, and other works. Such displays, which change frequently and which include all children's work at different times, let children know that their artwork is valued and, in turn, create in them a sense of pride in their ways of expressing themselves.

HOW PARENTS CAN HELP WITH ART

Since some kids have no art to speak of in school, parents can provide some of the missing pieces at home. Even those who have programs in school would benefit from being able to work on a task for a prolonged and uninterrupted time. All too often in school there's paint today and clay tomorrow, with no opportunity to really work at length in any medium.

At home, parents can provide materials and a work surface where an ongoing project can be kept for several days. Among the favorite materials at this stage are the following:

Tempera paints	Chalk	Fabric
Watercolors	Clay	Plasticine
Crayons	Paste	Papier-mâché

Using unstructured materials is not merely fun; perhaps equally important is the fact that children use these materials to create their own nonverbal symbols of the world. The fact that such symbols are not photographic likenesses of the world is not important. For the child they are the underpinnings for being able to think in the language of symbols—symbols of their own making. Drawings at this age tend to become far more detailed. Indeed, looking at what the child zooms in on can give you some insight into his or her interests and point of view.

This is also a stage when children are delighted to explore small-scale craft projects: knitting, weaving, needlepoint (big size), woodworking, sewing. Since kids from this stage on grow increasingly interested in end products, simple kits that produce results often provide satisfaction. Children also enjoy construction kits, punch-out books, and snap-together models. They may need some assistance, but these are another path for exploration.

Working on such projects at home helps children to extend their staying power and their ability to "stick to it." Such efforts also help them hone the kinds of skills that are used in penmanship, draftsmanship, and problem solving.

MUSIC

Music, like art, is often left to the classroom teacher. In schools that can afford specialists, children may have a weekly session with a music teacher. In either case, some of the music program is bound to include singing together. Children at this age enjoy learning familiar folk songs that are part of their musical heritage.

Years ago teachers in the early grades had to know how to play the piano or some accompanying instrument. This is no longer true. In fact, many teachers feel uncomfortable singing or doing any musical activities other than playing recordings. For children this is a real loss. Like art, music can be a wonderful pathway for exploring rhythm, movement, and creative expression.

As with art, music teachers are often trained broadly instead of for the early grades. Consequently, many bring to their music programs formal studies in musical notation. For most first- and second-graders, such formal lessons are premature. What *is* appropriate for this age group is pointing out what they can readily observe: that notes go up or down when their voices do; that ''fast'' notes look fast (or short) and slow notes look ''slow'' (or long), for example. This gradual approach to the symbolism of musical notation readies them for later, more precise study.

The overriding goal of any music program for the primary years is for children to enjoy music. It should invite children to explore and expand their experiences with singing or improvising on basic instruments (xylophones, other percussives, and recorders), as well as introducing them to musical notation and various types of music.

How Parents Can Help with Music

Some children are eager to learn to play an instrument at this stage. However, most six-, seven-, and even eight-year-olds are usually busy enough learning to master the symbols in their math and reading books without the challenge of yet another abstract symbol system. Indeed, children who begin musical instruments a year or two later often catch up quickly.

Whether they are taking lessons or not, all children continue to benefit from a variety of informal musical experiences parents can provide.

▲ Singing together continues to be satisfying. Folk songs with multiple verses and repetitive refrains are great favorites.

• In addition to pop music, tapes and records can open their ears to new listening. Marches, show tunes, ethnic music, or scores from the ballet, opera, orchestral, or chamber music should all be part of their experience. Select music that features particular instruments or story lines that inspire listening and interpretive skills.

▪ Children enjoy conducting, dancing, or drawing to music that lends itself to expressive interpretations with movement or art materials.

▲ Provide materials for making simple percussive instruments or ready-made instruments such as drums, recorders, xylophones, or autoharps for exploration.

• Look for opportunities to hear live music, whether it's the local high school band or a real concert, show, or ballet.

PHYSICAL EDUCATION

Most schools have some sort of physical education program. In many schools the responsibility for physical education falls to the classroom teacher, or your child's school may have a gym teacher who supervises gym classes once or twice a week. Few schools make provision for active physical play on a daily basis. Yet this is exactly what primary children need.

For young children the importance of active play is often overlooked or comes under the heading of an extra (''if time permits''). However, experienced teachers know that, for children, hours spent in the classroom are likely to be more productive when sit-down time is punctuated with some vigorous activity. Such activity provides not only an outlet for releasing tension and energy but a way for children to use their whole bodies, enhancing their basic sense of their own physical competence. All too often, however, gym programs do not support such attitudes. The competitive games and expectations that would be appropriate for older children are pushed down to the primary years. During these early grades vigorous games with exacting rules that pit children against each other are a poor choice.

Children in the primary grades should have gym classes with a physical education teacher several times a week and time for active play daily. Their gym program should include a range of physical activities, from creative movement, gymnastics, and tumbling to precursors of team sports like kickball. Both boys and girls should be included in all of these activities. Girls today are frequently as interested in sports like softball as boys, and the program should reflect that. The goal is to include a variety of activities so that the program will meet the different needs and interests of all children. In addition, children at this age level should have at least a half hour of supervised recess every day. Weather permitting, teachers should take them to the park or school playground as often as possible, usually several times a week. If you feel that your school is not making adequate or appropriate provisions for physical development, your parents organization may be able to bring about change. The focus needn't be on expensive equipment but on the need for daily time for active play.

How Parents Can Help with Physical Education

Perhaps the first and most fundamental role parents play is in modeling an active life-style. Children learn more from what we do than from what we say. If you do not engage in any physical activities, chances are increased that your children won't either. If you are looking for a change, this might be a good time to find a physical outlet you can share with your child.

Parents can also provide children with encouragement and the sorts of simple equipment that invites them to use their bodies. In addition to bikes, jump ropes, balls, and skates, consider the possibilities for homebound but active kids: an inexpensive chinning bar installed in a doorway, or an exercise mat for tumbling stored under a bed. If you have the room, this is the age when junior, scaled-down sporting equipment comes into its own. Lightweight basketball hoops with foam rubber balls can be used indoors or out. Similarly there are Ping-Pong tabletop sets and volleyball or badminton sets for the driveway.

This is also the age when kids are eager and ready to learn how to swim. If you cannot teach them, look for a trained instructor who can. In regions where snow abounds, this may be the time for skiing and skating lessons.

What's important at this stage is making physical activity a given in their lives. Often parents get hung up on what sports they believe girls "should" do as opposed to boys. That kind of sexist thinking can shape the kinds of equipment they supply. More importantly, it can limit children's view of themselves as active doers. Although team sports will begin to take on importance among the upper ranges of this age group, keep in mind that this is not the only path to fitness. For many children at this stage (and later) solo sports have more appeal than the rough and tumble of competitive team games.

SOCIAL DEVELOPMENT

Along with academics, children in the primary grades are continuing to develop social skills. Parents sometimes assume that once you leave kindergarten, it's a whole new ballgame with no room for socialization. This is a mistaken idea. Kids of six, seven, and eight are very much involved in learning a host of important social skills. Indeed, one of the major developmental tasks of the school-age child is the very social business of finding one's place in the group life of the classroom, lunchroom, backyards, and perennial "clubhouse."

Few things are more central to the young schoolchild than learning how to be friends with somebody. Yet, making friends is easier than keeping them. Indeed, friendship and acceptance among one's agemates are necessary ingredients for gaining a new and more independent identity. While home and family were once the center of the child's universe, now the world revolves around school and friends.

By six and seven, kids have learned from their earlier experiences that being friends requires giving and taking, following and leading, listening and telling. But knowing this is not the same thing as living it. They may be less egocentric than a four- or five-year-old, but accepting the other person's point of view can still be quite difficult. As a result, friendships are relatively unstable. Jennifer may be Emily's best friend today and her worst enemy tomorrow. They still need help from the teacher or other caring adults in learning how to negotiate. However, the social chafing that goes on at this stage is a positive irritant. Because having friends is so dear to the child's heart, she is impelled to give up some of her egocentric ways of thinking and behaving. Though friendships at this stage are less deep than they will become, children are beginning to operate on the principle of "you rub my back and I'll rub yours." But this newfound mutuality is not always easy to maintain. Sixes and sevens can still be impulsive in their ways. Among nines and tens it would be unusual for someone to grab a ball out of someone's hand or to strike out at another child. However, among sixes and sevens it is not that unusual. The primary-grade child can tell you the rules of how to behave, but following those rules is still a tentative matter.

By second and third grades self-made "clubs" become epidemic. From the child's point of view these little clubs satisfy the strong need to have a sense of belonging and acceptance. They also give children the heady power of excluding others. Indeed, one of the chief functions of such clubs is to determine who can and who cannot belong. These mutual-admiration societies are usually short-lived. Often they fall apart when it becomes apparent that only one person can be president.

Typical, too, is an increasing division of the sexes. While preschoolers usually play with children of either sex, at this stage they tend to gravitate to those of the same sex, as if in being "one of the boys" or "one of the girls" children confirm their own sexual identity. It's another kind of belonging.

In primary classrooms where teachers understand and value social as well as intellectual development, children are not tethered to desks with busywork to keep them quiet and out of trouble. There is no expectation for silence. In fact, there is a kind of industrious hum in the room as children go about the business of active learning. Tasks that demand talk and cooperation are part of the plan. In the give-and-take of painting a mural, making a map, researching a project, there is both intellectual and social learning going on. It is in the company of others that kids discover there is often more than one way to approach a task. Cooperative work calls for planning and being responsible for your part in a project. It also calls for being open to other people's ideas as well as asserting one's own.

In group discussions among first- and second-graders one begins to hear a real difference in how children relate to one another. Fives and young sixes can hardly wait to show and tell what they have done. Once they have spoken, there is usually limited response or discussion. Instead of relating to what someone has said, kids are usually more interested in "Can I be next?" Yet, with guidance and experience, children do begin to listen and respond to what others are saying. In a good primary classroom, the teacher encourages kids to participate and express their opinions. Through such exchanges children discover that there are people who have different opinions than theirs or who share their likes and dislikes. Within the group children find not only friendship but a sense of commonality that links them to their agemates. It is a comfort to find others who have trouble with their big sisters and little brothers or who aren't brave about going to the dentist. From group experiences children also discover real differences in people's lifestyles. It is somewhat amazing for some to discover that not everyone in the world has a Christmas tree, lives with their mother and father, or goes to bed at 7:30. In a real sense the social dialogues of schoolchildren are full of information that confirms (and contradicts) their earlier and much more egocentric view of the world.

In living with others the need for rules and shared responsibility becomes apparent. In such primary classrooms the teacher encourages children to formulate the rules that they will live by. When children themselves discover the need for rules, they focus not only on their own needs but on those of others. Of course, making rules is usually easier than living by them, but helping to make them oneself is a better starting point than simply experiencing rules as something formulated and imposed from on high.

PARENTS' ROLE IN SOCIAL DEVELOPMENT

As children move into the wider social world of school, home and family remain the secure base they return to for support and assurance. Although they are eager for friendship and a sense of belonging, the idea of being friends is easier than the reality. Spending all day in the company of those who are also socially inexperienced can be trying. Yet given a choice, most kids this age would rather be with agemates than be at home. Increasingly, as the years pass, a new kind of dependence begins to unfold. As they gain a greater sense of independence from home and the family, they are also growing increasingly dependent on the company and approval of peers. As parents it is not always easy to accept this shift from being the first-class expert to periodic second-class citizenship. Yet it is from their peers that schoolchildren learn a great deal about themselves and others. While there may be frequent reports about how so-and-so has done them wrong, cheated, hurt, called them names, or otherwise acted badly, such sad tales seldom keep kids from going back for more.

For parents it is sometimes difficult to know when intervention is called for or when simply listening helps best. In most instances the latter approach seems to fit the schoolchild's need for a sympathetic ear coupled with a sense of trust that the child can handle the situation independently. This is not to say that parents never need to intervene or get to the cause of persistent complaints about a bully or a troublesome relationship. What parents do need to understand, however, is that as children step into this new and more independent role, the aches and pains of rejection are a natural part of the learning process. In measuring themselves against others, children may fall short of their own expectations. They may not read as well as their buddies or run as fast as others. They may think that when the teacher scolds, she is scolding only them. In any of these situations the child may or may not be correct. What is important is having someone who not only listens but helps them to clarify their thoughts and feelings, someone who treats these small but significant events as if they matter. Because to every child they do matter tremendously.

On some occasions parents may need to look further into a situation that the child seems unable to handle independently. For example, when seven-year-old Cindy woke up tearful every day and became sick before leaving for school, her mother was unable to get to the cause of Cindy's sickness from Cindy herself. An appointment with the teacher revealed that for several weeks Cindy had been rejected by one of the little ''clubs'' in the classroom. Although the teacher was doing her best to break up this tight-knit clique, she had been unable to do so thus far, or to help Cindy find a way in. In time, Cindy formed a group of her own, and her morning upset subsided. Indeed, in time, Cindy herself rejected an ousted member of the original ''in'' crowd.

All through these early school years, children do unto others and they are frequently ''done unto.'' Neither parents nor teachers can totally shelter or protect them from the inevitable rough-and-tumble of growing up among their peers. What we can do best is recognize how important making and keeping friends is to children and how difficult that can be. Parents can also welcome friends and visitors into their home. Playing with one child at a time in one's home base helps children connect in ways that cannot happen in the group situation of the classroom. At this stage learning to be a host and learning how to act as a visitor are both important sides of the social coin.

Encouraging some more official group membership is also useful at this age. Joining Scouts, Sunday school, or afterschool programs provides a ready-made group with adult supervision to smooth out the bumps.

Even as children become increasingly immersed in their group social world, parents need to remember the importance of time for the family group as a social unit. Doing a task together, playing a game, going on an outing, simply enjoying a meal and talk together helps cement the first and continuing importance of the family as a social unit that the child depends on for support.

HOMEWORK IN THE PRIMARY GRADES

Initially many children are genuinely excited by the idea of having homework. It's another sign of being grown-up or at least becoming one of the big kids. However, even those who were longing to have homework often become horrified when it keeps happening beyond day three. Then, too, there are those who bring great fears to the very notion of homework. A child may feel anxious about what is expected of him. And parents, too, may bring their own anxieties from their schooldays to the homework table. Few issues cause more stress and conflict between parents and children than homework.

Although homework is your child's job, not yours, the fact is, young students tend to need more parental involvement than older children. They may lack strategies for studying their spelling words or need to review the directions on a worksheet. A new math concept may have been crystal clear while the teacher was explaining it, but three hours later the lesson is lost, and so is the child. The beginning "researcher" may think he needs to copy every word in the encyclopedia about his subject and feels overwhelmed by the enormity of the task. A book report assigned a week ago is often postponed until the last moment. And no matter how interesting or tedious the assignment may be, most homework is much less appealing than playing with the dog or watching TV.

With young students parents can help to establish good work habits in a number of ways:

▲ Establish a routine time when homework will be done. Some children need a break after a full day at school. Others like to get their work done as soon as they come home. Initially, rather than insisting on a set hour, allow time and flexibility to establish which is best for your child.

• Establish a workspace where your child will be relatively undisturbed and undistracted by TV or siblings. Some children prefer total isolation. Others work better knowing they are not alone or at least with a supportive parent in near proximity.

▪ Your child may need some help in getting started. Take a few moments to sit down and have her talk about what needs to be done. This can help clarify what the assignment is and what must be done.

▲ If there is more than one task, children may need help in organizing what they will do first, next, and so on. Otherwise, they are likely to start jumping from one task to another and become overwhelmed. You can't impose order, but you can give suggested strategies and relate how you use such strategies in doing your own work.

• Organizing their workspace can also help them become more independent and orderly. Desktop holders for pencils, scissors, tape dispensers, and so forth make nice back-to-school or holiday gifts. Such items give children a framework of order and have the appeal of grown-up tools.

▪ Without becoming a policeman, be available as questions arise. Check in from time to time to see how things are going.

▲ Be aware of how long average assignments should take and how often they should be expected. You can get this information from the teacher at your first conference or on Open School Night.

• Assignments at this stage should not take an hour or more to complete. They should be relatively "doable" without much assistance.

▪ Knowing when and how to help calls for great patience and tact. If your child is racing through his homework in order to go outside and play or watch TV, you have a management problem. It may be that the original schedule needs reassessing. Many kids need free time after school and come to their work refreshed a few hours later. Others may need firmer limits on TV viewing during the school week. Selecting a limited schedule for favorite shows and sticking to it may work better than negotiating on a daily basis or outlawing all TV.

▲ Further suggestions about dealing with homework can be found in chapter 7 (see pages 213–18).

WHY HOMEWORK?

Some educators believe that children who get homework from the early grades on do better in school. They also feel that if homework is not introduced before the junior high school years, students are then overwhelmed and ill prepared. According to some educators, an appropriate formula for determining the amount of time homework should take can be arrived at by multiplying the child's grade level times ten. So a child who is in grade two would have twenty minutes of homework, and a sixth-grader would have one hour of work per day.

Homework policies vary tremendously from one school to another. They can even vary from one class to another within the same school. At its best, homework can be used to reinforce skills that are being learned in the classroom. It gives children extra practice in writing, reading, or math without the direct supervision of the teacher. Thus, it can help the child develop independent study and organization skills. Homework also helps the teacher evaluate what children need further help with in the classroom. At its worst, it can be assigned as punishment, or in such large doses that it feels like punishment.

Homework can help you as a parent keep in touch with what your child is (or is not) learning. By helping, you can also show your child that you value what he is doing and are willing to

163

support those efforts. But "helping" does not mean "doing." Homework is the child's responsibility. If you take over that responsibility by doing it or by reteaching every lesson, you will be undermining long-term work habits. For one thing, teachers often use homework to assess what a child has (and perhaps more important, *has not*) grasped in school—as a way to spot problem areas to be worked on in the classroom. If you go through your child's homework correcting and amending everything, you are depriving the teacher of one useful guide in helping your child. Problem areas may be artificially papered over to the child's long-term detriment. You may also be setting yourself up for continuing problems with your child. This is especially true in subjects like math or reading. The teacher's approach may be very different from the way you were taught. Even if you are an expert, you should not need to teach or reteach the day's lessons. This is the teacher's job. If your child is having difficulty with such assignments, contact the teacher and talk about her expectations. You don't want to get embroiled in confrontations with your second-grader. You may find it pays to back off and see what suggestions the teacher has for you. She may prefer to handle the matter in class. This may relieve the pressure for both you and your child. Indeed, if many children are having problems, she may reconsider the length and content of those assignments (see pages 233–40 on teacher conferences).

WHAT IF YOUR CHILD HAS NO HOMEWORK?

Not all schools give regular homework assignments before second or third grade. Many educators continue to delay formal assignments until children are at least eight or nine years old. Children may have an occasional assignment to bring something back to school, to observe something and report on it, or to do a short worksheet. Does the lack of homework mean your child will be behind? No. By the time children are eight or nine, they are better able to take the greater responsibility for their own work. In my experience with sixes and sevens, I found few who actually followed through on occasional assignments or who remembered to bring worksheets or materials back to the classroom.

Many early-childhood educators believe that afterschool hours should offer a real change of pace, a time for more self-directed and informal learning and play. Unfortunately, many children's afterschool hours are overly booked with activities designed to teach. Coupled with homework, such busy schedules can be an overload that produces more stress than pleasure or valuable learning.

We sometimes forget that for most young children school has already meant a long and taxing day. Parents should also keep in mind that many important kinds of social, physical, intellectual, and creative skills are learned through play. Indeed, play gives children a way of reflecting and of trying out new ideas and making them their own.

Children still need time to ride bikes, draw pictures, and even spin daydreams of their own making. They need time to "play" school as well as attend school. It's not just TV that robs them of such moments. All too often it is their busy afterschool schedules, which may have more to do with adult needs than with children's best interests.

Whether your child is assigned homework or not, there are things you can do to reinforce and support what she is learning in school. Despite the fact that I sent home no formal assignments, I did urge parents to work with their children informally on a regular basis. Many of those subject-specific ideas are in the sections of this book labeled "How You Can Help Your Child in Math (Reading, etc.)" In addition to those suggestions, parents can also

▲ Take the time to look at papers that children bring home
• Praise work well done or signs of improvement
▪ Go over errors to see if the child now understands what was wrong
▲ Encourage reading by reading aloud to your child daily
• Establish a quiet workspace where children can work free of distraction

THINGS TO AVOID— HOMEWORK OR NOT

Parents sometimes make the mistake of turning afterschool time into another minischool day. Some have children rewrite their papers or drill them on more difficult math "so they'll be ahead of the class." All too often, children end up practicing how to write their letters incorrectly or go on to new math skills before they have fully mastered or understood basic math concepts. Rushing children to learn how to multiply or count by rote to one hundred before they have mastered simple addition or feel confident about counting from one to twenty can actually confuse and undermine math skills. Similarly, pushing children to painfully ''sound out'' words and read books that are beyond them can turn reading into something they'd rather not do. What parents need to remember at this stage is the importance of building children's positive attitudes and sense of competence. Foster their success with books and games that reinforce what they are learning rather than trying to hurry them along to new levels.

If your child is asking you to reteach or help with every part of his homework, you need to talk with the teacher to find out why or what you should do to help. Students' homework assignments for the day should not take more than twenty to thirty minutes. That's about the size of what children can handle. Occasionally teachers may assign a project that is to be done over a period of a week or more. Long-term assignments at this stage are generally doomed to fail. Young children who are given an assignment on Monday that is to be turned in on Friday simply lack the sense of timing required to fulfill such tasks. Rather than getting into a weekly hassle over this or other conflicts over homework, again, you may need to talk this through with the teacher. She may have suggestions for handling such problems or be willing to readjust her assignments. However, if you think your child is getting too much homework, you may need to discuss this with the teacher, principal, or parents of other children in the class. If this appears to be a classwide problem, you may find it best to approach the teacher or principal as a group.

Remember, even if you consider a homework assignment ''stupid'' or of limited value, avoid voicing your criticism to your child. Take your concerns to the school. Vis-à-vis your child, it's important to be supportive. You may not be able to change the school policy on homework. Undermining the teacher or the assignment can only make matters worse.

In the long run your big objective is to let your child take the responsibility for his homework. Establishing that idea from the early grades onward calls for a delicate support system. It's something like teaching them to ride a two-wheeler. You hold on to the seat until they are steady, but you're prepared either to let go or steady the seat again if they need it.

THE INTERMEDIATE GRADES (4–6)— MASTERING THE BASIC SKILLS

W hen I think back to fourth grade, I remember the staircase in our school that separated the lower grades from the upper grades. In a sense, that "stepping up" marked a new way of thinking about ourselves. We left the little kids behind. Now we had joined the big kids. While the intermediate years are not dramatically different from the primary years, there are real changes in everyone's expectations.

CHILD'S POINT OF VIEW

School's okay and so is my teacher, except sometimes it really makes me mad when she punishes the whole class for something one or two kids do. It's not fair.

We have a computer in our classroom. But you only get to use it for a half hour two times a week, and I don't like that. I'm luckier than some kids because we have a computer at home. So, sometimes in school I help other kids and I think that's good, because a lot of times kids will listen better to a kid than the teacher.

I like gym, too. We do a lot of team sports like capture the flag, war, and team dodgeball. There are kids who get picked first because people pick their friends or the guys that play better. I have friends and enemies. You get enemies because you dislike people who do something better than you and vice versa or because you did something to him, like you teased him. There are kids who are friends and then they are enemies and then they're friends again —they keep going back and forth. My best friend, Matt, has been my friend since second grade. He isn't like some kids, who act like they're better than everyone else because they are in the top math group. Matt is better in math, but I'm better in reading. So, we help each other.

PARENT'S POINT OF VIEW

Danny seems to enjoy school so much more than he did before. Of course, there are still problems on the bus, and a few times I've heard about how unfair the teacher was in punishing the whole class on account of one person, but for the most part, there are no serious complaints. He takes more responsibility for his own routine. He doesn't need someone to pull him out of bed or watch the clock before the bus. Of course, I do have to check to see if homework is done, and sometimes he needs help, especially if it's a written assignment. I can remember feeling the same way. That blank piece of paper and the panic of what to put on it. Basically, life seems to be on a much more even keel as long as he's busy with school or friends or doing something. Of course, I get annoyed when he gets so engrossed he doesn't seem to hear what anyone's saying. And lately, I've been getting a lot of that "but-so-and-so can, why won't you let me?" I guess that's just typical. I did it, too. I felt that he should be in the more advanced math group, but after talking it through with the teacher, I have to admit he's probably better off doing well in a less pressured situation than struggling to keep up. She says Danny has good ideas but he doesn't usually volunteer or talk up. She's working on that. Overall, though, I've got few enough complaints about him or his schoolwork. Maybe it's just the lull before the storm. Sometimes I wish we could freeze time and not have to go on to what comes next. I'm just going to enjoy this while it lasts.

TEACHER'S POINT OF VIEW

Working with ten-year-olds is nothing like my early experience. I used to teach second grade and it was constantly "Mrs. Paley, so-and-so hasn't got his sneakers!" or "Billy took my pencil," and "Sandy hit me!" But with fifth-graders there's none of that. It's almost like an unwritten code of honor. A kid that tells on another kid is going to have trouble with everyone.

On the whole, they're a lively group. Full of questions and hungry for information. They get some of it from their reading, but a great deal of learning comes from discussions and tossing ideas back and forth. Sometimes the depth of their questions surprises me as well as their ability to work together on a joint project. Among themselves they seem to know who can do what best. Of course, there are some who haven't learned how to assert themselves or would rather not take chances. Danny doesn't volunteer, although he's got solid ideas and a lot to offer. And Beth worries me. She has such a fresh way of looking at things, but her words come slowly and the others aren't always patient.

I'm a little troubled, too, by the teasing that's going on since we split up the math groups. I don't call them the top group or bottom group, but the kids do. They're very much aware of who's who and who's doing what. I guess it can't be helped, but I don't like the smug attitudes some of them convey to their classmates. It's gotten some of the parents upset, too. Especially the ones who think their child should be in the next group up. It's this way every year. I'm afraid I'll never get used to it, nor have I found a better solution either.

While these are just three of the many viewpoints we might have heard at this stage, each member of the triad clearly brings a different point of view to the picture. Working together they can forge a support system that strengthens their mutual goals.

INTELLECTUAL DEVELOPMENT

Using the storehouse of information and skills they have accumulated until now, children in the middle years are better able to deal with increasingly complex ideas and symbol systems. By fourth grade most children have mastered the basic skills of reading. For those who have not yet refined the mechanics of reading, extra help will be needed. But most are ready to move on to a new level, becoming readers in a fuller sense. Books are now truly an avenue for finding out information as well as a source of entertainment and pleasure.

By now children are better able to communicate their thoughts and opinions. To take a typical example, in a discussion about the rights of English colonists versus those of Native Americans, I heard one ten-year-old make an analogy to his own property rights vis-à-vis his parents and siblings—a relatively abstract notion, even if still linked to his own real experiences. The ability to grapple with purely abstract concepts such as one might find in advanced math or science will blossom later. Yet, ten-to-twelve-year-olds are able to deal with increasingly complex ideas when they are supported with concrete materials. For example, in building a replica of the Jamestown colony, children can use quite complicated math skills to reproduce a model that is designed to scale. Similarly, to illustrate the enormity of a million or the size relationship between the earth and the sun, children are perfectly capable of constructing models using squares of graph paper and math equations.

While the child in the primary grades was eager to know how things work, the intermediate-age child wants to know why they work, who makes them work, and how we know what we know. For example, if ten- or eleven-year-olds were to embark on a study of Egypt, someone in the class would inevitably ask, "How did the archaeologists or explorers who discovered them know where to look for the tombs? How did they do it?" Although first-graders might ask the same kind of question, they are usually content with a one-sentence answer. For ten- and eleven-year-olds, this kind of question is a departure point for research and discussion.

Since traditional and nontraditional settings often use similar subject matter, the gap between the two appears to close somewhat. Yet their approaches to learning continue to be quite different. Some traditional schools continue to tie their curriculum to textbooks and programmed learning. Other schools use a more active approach that is part of the continuum of what has come before.

READING

In a great many subject-centered schools reading continues to be taught as an isolated skill. Basal readers much like the ones used earlier (see pages 96–97, 100–1) continue to dominate the reading program. Of course, the selections are longer and more complex. Frequently the selections are adaptations from longer books, with length and vocabulary adjusted for "readability." In addition to stories, an anthology is likely to include more nonfiction than earlier reading series. To accompany the text, teachers use workbooks and worksheets that reinforce vocabulary and comprehension skills. The series may also include end-of-book tests that evaluate a student's progress. Often these tests are designed to mirror achievement tests that are given at the end of the school year.

Since children arrive with varying abilities, the teacher usually divides students into three or more ability groups. To reinforce skills students may also be assigned practice lessons with "programmed" lessons that are prepacked in "reading labs." Such lessons often resemble the typical reading-test format you may remember from your school days. There is a short "story" that is heavily embedded with information, followed by a series of questions that test a student's recall of details, general comprehension, and word skills. Designed to be self-correcting, these programs are often used (and misused) for "free time" assignments when the teacher is busy with small-group instruction. Students may like the novelty and independence at the start, but the flat and repetitious format usually loses its interest and turns such assignments into busywork. From the teacher's point of view the value of such work may be in keeping children busy while she is busy with others. Unfortunately, children themselves often begin to do such work without much thought. Indeed, they do such work with a formatted response, and thinking is reduced to the most limited level. There are more productive ways to engage children and still leave the teacher free to work with others.

In addition to a formal reading series, social studies and science are usually viewed as extensions of the reading program. Students may also have some free choice in selecting books from a classroom library and/or the school library. Motivation to read independently is often spurred by contests and charts that show who has read the most books. Teachers may also require written or oral book reports based on independent reading.

Children who are fortunate have teachers who read aloud to their classes on a regular basis. Even more than in the primary grades, this kind of story time is frequently regarded as an extra that's done only when time permits. Adults often mistakenly assume that children who can read no longer need to be read to or that doing so is merely entertaining. What they overlook are the many ways children benefit from listening and discussing a shared story. Experienced teachers know that once they begin reading, students frequently get immersed in the story and go on to read (or reread) the book on their own. In a way, the teacher's reading can break new ground and ease a child's path into books he might never have tackled on his own.

AN INTEGRATED APPROACH TO READING

In contrast to the textbook approach to reading, an increasing number of schools today use a more integrated approach. In such schools formal reading instruction changes radically in the intermediate grades. Students no longer use a basal series, with its textbook and accompanying workbook. By the end of third grade most children have really become comfortable readers, and the focus shifts from word analysis skills to working on a broader range of literary and comprehension skills. There may be one or two children in a fourth grade who still need individualized work in word skills, but for the most part, students are by now competent readers. Because they have the basics down, they can use those reading skills to open new paths of learning and can explore a wide variety of reading materials.

Instead of reading with each child individually, now the teacher can assign a few chapters of a book and students can do that reading independently. Within the classroom there can be several "literature groups" with seven or eight children. After they have read their assignment at home or in class, the teacher will call them together to discuss what they have read. This coming together is often very exciting to students. It gives them another way of connecting, sharing, and comparing ideas from a common experience. Further, they are getting a sense that a book itself has something to give them.

In addition to literature groups, students do a great deal of self-selected reading. The classroom library is rich with many genres from which to choose. Nonfiction that relates to science and social studies is prominently displayed. There are folktales, myths, biographies, poetry, and works of fiction. Resource reference books such as dictionaries, atlases, and field guides are also used frequently.

Students report on their individual reading in a variety of ways. They may keep reading journals or reading cards that summarize a book they have completed. Their write-ups may be presented to a literature group, or they may create a class resource of reviews that others can use in making reading selections. Since students rate books as recommended or not, their book reports also move them toward critiques, or evaluating what they have read.

On the daily schedule of events the teacher reads aloud to the group. It may be a long chapter book that takes several weeks to complete, or the teacher may read myths or folktales that relate to the culture the class is studying in social studies. Children not only listen, there is time given for discussing the reading. Recognizing that children are able to comprehend more complex stories than they can yet read independently, the story time enlarges the child's connections to books and whets the appetite for greater independence.

Compared with the books chosen for the primary grades, the stories teachers now present have richer plots and subplots. The simple all-good and all-bad characterizations in younger books are replaced with characters drawn with greater depth and dimensions. In sharing such literature with students, the teacher is preparing the way for a new level of sophistication that children will ultimately bring to their independent reading.

Perhaps the most significant change is reflected in the way reading becomes a tool for much broader learning, as we shall see in looking at science and social studies.

How Parents Can Support Reading

Despite the fact that children can read, the issue parents often face at this stage is getting them to read. As we have seen, all too frequently reading has been turned into an unending series of required lessons and nitty-gritty practice skills. Instead of having pleasurable associations, children can come to consider reading as work, and work is by definition the opposite of fun.

This is especially true for children who have had to struggle to acquire the mechanics of reading. Few of us choose to spend our free time with activities we are not good at, doing things because they're "good for us." Added to this is the simple fact that there are many other afterschool distractions to which middle-years kids are drawn. Their interest in afterschool activities and friends takes on new importance. Then, too, there is the inevitable allure of TV, with its instantaneous and seductive attraction.

At this stage parents are also concerned about the kind of reading children select on their own. Their appetite for comics and series books such as the *Hardy Boys* or *Nancy Drew* mysteries is often reaching a fever pitch at this point. What makes such junk reading so attractive? Actually there are several reasons that adults often overlook. In the first place, this kind of reading is pure entertainment and totally unlike school stuff. Second, the fact that one book is much like another is a plus from the child's point of view. Since they know the central characters and the format, reading is easy and predictable. Finally, these are the years when children become avid collectors, and comics or books that come in series are highly collectible. In fact, children take some pride in displaying the great stack or long line of books they have read and own.

At this stage parents need not fret about junk reading. For now, whatever brings kids to books can be viewed as a plus. Happily, as children become more experienced readers, most tire of the formula books and are ready to move on. Parents can do a great many things to support reading and help children make the transition from being able to read to becoming enthusiastic readers. Again, no child will want to do all the activities suggested below. Pick and choose those that are pleasurable for you and your child.

▲ Parents should not expect children to be avid readers if they do not read themselves. This is fundamental but often overlooked.

• Continue to read aloud to your child as long as your child seems to enjoy the experience. As noted earlier, children sometimes need someone to break a path, and then they will go on independently.

▪ Often something in a book you are reading can lead to interesting discussions between you and your child. Without turning the experience into a quiz you can certainly ask what she thinks about how a character felt or what she thinks is coming up in the next chapter. Often children will initiate such discussions themselves.

▲ If you are not sure of what books to select, talk with a librarian, teacher, or bookstore clerk. You will find age-appropriate guidance in books such as *Choosing Books for Kids*, by Joanne Oppenheim, Barbara Brenner, and Betty D. Boegehold (Ballantine), or Jim Trelese's *Read Aloud Handbook* (Penguin).

• Not all reading is in books. Magazines, newspapers, rules of games, directions for model and craft kits, and recipes all demand reading for comprehension. This kind of reading in the context of an activity is appealing and supports skills needed throughout life.

▪ Clip out newspaper or magazine articles that you think might be of interest to your child. Stories about sports, particular subjects you've been talking about, or subjects that mesh with a hobby or school project are kinds of reading they might otherwise miss. Even clipping a comic strip you think they'll enjoy makes a nice way of saying, "I thought of you when I read this."

▲ Let them see you reading, both for information and entertainment. Talk about a book or story you're reading. Parents who are themselves readers are giving children an important model.

• In selecting books for their independent reading, involve the child. By this age children welcome suggestions but want a say. They have preferences that should be respected.

▪ If you feel your child is in a reading rut and you want to inspire some new direction, introduce a book you especially love during your read-aloud time.

▲ Whether you're in a mall, a museum, on the road, or discussing a news event, encourage your child to use floor plan directories and maps. Give him simple strategies for using the mall directory or museum floor plan. Point out the arrow that shows where he is now. Trace the route to where he wants to go. If you don't own an atlas, a relatively inexpensive paper-covered atlas becomes an important resource. Also useful at this stage is a globe.

• Children at this age are also keen on facts and important events. They enjoy browsing through almanacs, Guinness record books, and some adult nonfiction books. Even if they can't or don't read from cover to cover, they enjoy reading captions and parts of books that mesh with their current interests.

▪ Nine-year-olds and up are often avid collectors of stamps, baseball cards, political buttons, and comics. They really enjoy collectors' catalogs and become quite adept at comparative "price" reading.

▲ Magazines and field guides that support hobbies and ongoing interests are also valuable paths to reading. Although there are adult magazines children will enjoy browsing through, don't overlook those designed for this age group. Not only is the text easier to read, kids love getting mail. Among the favorite magazines for this age group are the following:

Boys Life
Boy Scouts of America
Box 61030
Dallas–Fort Worth
Airport, Texas 75261

Cricket Magazine
Box 100
LaSalle, Illinois 61301

Cobblestone: The History
Magazine for Young
People
Cobblestone Publishing
20 Main Street
Peterborough, New
Hampshire 03458-9976

Ebony Jr!
820 South Michigan
Avenue.
Chicago, Illinois 60605

Owl: The Outdoor and
Wildlife Discovery
Magazine for Children
Scholastic
P.O. Box 1925
Marian, Ohio 43302

National Geographic World
Department 00880
17th and M Streets, N.W.
Washington, D.C. 20036

Sports Illustrated for Kids
P.O. Box 830609
Birmingham, Alabama
35283-0609

3-2-1 Contact
P.O. Box 2933
Boulder, Colorado 80322

• Follow through on family trips to museums, aquariums, and restoration villages with books or pamphlets related to the event. The gift shop usually has selected titles that could become both sparks to further reading and worthwhile souvenirs. A follow-up trip to the library can extend the experience.

▪ By all means limit television viewing, but don't overlook the positive values it can provide. Programs such as *Reading Rainbow* and *Wonderworks* are designed especially to inspire reading. Often TV productions and videocassettes of children's novels are excellent springboards into reading. Children often enjoy rereading a story they have seen and comparing the dramatization to the original.

▲ TV news and documentaries can also lead kids to want to know more about a particular subject. Science, world events, sports, dance, music, and art programs can be good starting points for independent research. This is especially true if parents say, ''We have a book about ———,'' or ''That reminds me of a story in ———,'' or ''That was interesting. Where do you think we could find out more about ———?''

• If you are not already members at your local library, join now. Many libraries sponsor special events with films, storytellers, visiting writers and artists, exhibitions, and programs, especially during the summer months.

▪ Children do like to have books of their own. You can cut the costs by joining book clubs (see page 112), selecting paperbacks, and getting your library or school to sponsor book swaps, where kids trade books they own with each other.

▲ As children's interests broaden, so does their taste for books in many genres. This is the stage when they particularly like mysteries, biographies, myths, and folktales in addition to realistic fiction set in the here and now or in an historic framework.

• Avoid pushing long and complex books. Keep in mind that kids still get satisfaction from finishing a book and from light, easy reading. Building pleasurable connections with reading as entertainment has lasting value. Reading the "Great Books" at this stage is less important than thinking books and reading are great!

Once children have passed the picturebook stage, parents are often puzzled about what books to read aloud. Here are short but choice lists of books frequently enjoyed by these age groups.

READ-ALOUD BOOKS FOR SEVEN/EIGHTS

The Garden of Abdul Gasazi by Chris Van Allsburg
The Stories Julian Tells by Ann Cameron
Miss Nelson books by Harry Allard
The Shrinking of Treehorn by Florence Parry Heide
Sarah, Plain and Tall by Patricia MacLachlan
Dominic by William Steig
The Real Thief by William Steig
James and the Giant Peach by Roald Dahl
Ramona books by Beverly Cleary
Charlotte's Web by E. B. White
Bunnicula by Deborah and James Howe
The Cricket in Times Square by George Selden

READ-ALOUD BOOKS FOR EIGHTS/NINES

Island of the Blue Dolphins by Scott O'Dell
Bat Poet and Animal Family by Randall Jarrell
Abel's Island by William Steig
Great Gilly Hopkins by Katherine Paterson
Wolves of Willoughby Chase by Joan Aiken
The Cay by Theodore Taylor
Mrs. Frisby and the Rats of NIMH by Robert O'Brien
From the Mixed Up Filer by E. L. Konigsburg
Phillip Hall Likes Me I Reckon Maybe by Bette Greene

The Sign of the Beaver by Elizabeth Speare
Tuck Everlasting by Natalie Babbitt

READ-ALOUD BOOKS FOR NINES/TENS

Constance by Patricia Clapp
Witch of Blackbird Pond by Elizabeth G. Speare
Ben and Me by Robert Lawson
The Egypt Game by Phyllis Z. Snyder
Tom's Midnight Garden by Phillipa Pearce
Time at the Top by Edward Ormondroyd
The Children of Green Knowe by Lucy Boston
The Lion, the Witch, and the Wardrobe by C. S. Lewis
A Wrinkle in Time by Madeleine L'Engle
Bridge to Terabithia by Katherine Paterson
The Indian in the Cupboard by Lynne R. Banks

WRITING

During the intermediate years writing should become a tool that students can use for both fact and fiction.

In many traditional classrooms students are given ''creative'' writing assignments that begin with the same opening sentence. These ''springboards''' sometimes serve as story starters to get the juices flowing. While they are useful, they are by no means the only way to get middle-years youngsters involved with writing. Indeed, for some these creative assignments only create a roadblock. As one child put it, ''A lot of times I have an idea I really want to put down, but I have to do the dumb story instead.''

This is also the time when students are first assigned book reports and research from their reading. Frequently, written work is handed in and corrected for grammar, punctuation, and spelling. Students are then expected to make corrections and rewrite their papers. For many of us the business of painstaking copying is what we remember most about written assignments. Indeed, it may explain why so many adults today say they ''can't write'' or hate to do so.

● ■ ▲

AN ALTERNATIVE APPROACH TO WRITING

A more desirable approach to writing puts the emphasis first and foremost on content. In such programs papers are rewritten only if they are to be "published" in class books. Such papers are the exception rather than the rule. This is not to say that teachers ignore details, but neither do they zoom in on every error on every paper. As a result, students do more writing and less rewriting.

During the intermediate years students write reports and do research that grows out of their work in social studies, science, and literature. Such assignments may take several weeks to complete. Students may not work totally on their own. They may work with a research partner and talk through what has been found out, thereby discovering what pieces are still missing. Indeed, in sharing research and initial writing, students are forced to clarify their thinking in ways that enhance their ability to convey what they intend to communicate. It is in the process of writing that students synthesize information and make it their own.

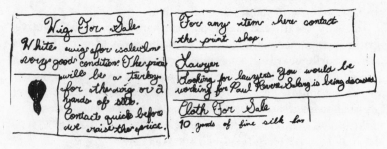

A colonial newspaper published by 11- and 12-year-olds.

In a fifth grade, for example, where they are studying the Middle Ages as a group, the subjects for reports are chosen by individual students, so one child may do a report on Charlemagne while another does research on the clothing of the age. Since individual reports are ultimately shared with the group, the entire class benefits from the work of its individual members and their particular interests.

Not all writing assignments are as long and complex as a social studies report. Students also record their observations of science experiments. They write brief reports about their reading as well as original stories of their own.

It is at this stage that the work begun in earlier grades really blossoms. Children not only do a great deal of self-selected writing; this is the age when they learn how to cut, paste, and edit their original writing. Now that the mechanics of handwriting flow with ease, there is a shift in focus. By now a child is able to look at a draft and say, "I'm not satisfied with this," or "I left something out that belongs here." In other words, they're learning how to think of a piece of writing as something that can be tinkered with and improved.

Children at this age also enjoy writing personal narratives. They write about things that have happened to them. They are not madly introspective, but they do focus on what most concerns them. Children also write in a variety of genres that reflect their readings. Some are heavily involved with science fiction, whereas others are busy with fiction that's derived directly from TV cartoons, sitcoms, or soap operas. Many use lots of sound effects or write sagas about kidnapping, alcoholism, or other problems that may have nothing whatever to do with their real-life experiences outside of the realm of TV. Such "realistic" fantasy is particularly popular with girls. Others use the "talking animal" route to fantasy.

Teachers often set aside some time for students to read their stories to the group. The class is invited to reflect to the writer what they have heard. By listening, the writer often discovers something he has left out or failed to convey. The writer may then turn to the class with particular questions. He may say, "Would it be clearer if I said ... ?" Classmates may also say, "I didn't understand ... Did you mean ... ?" While the tone of these sessions should be generally positive and supportive, comments should also go well beyond simply saying, "That's a good story." A student writer may or may not then use the group's comments in editing and rewriting a new version of the piece.

Over a period of time, each student will work on one or more pieces for publication. It's at this stage that a piece must be fine-tuned in every respect. The final draft will not only be edited by the teacher for content, it must be neatly written, properly punctuated, and corrected for spelling and grammatical errors. The final draft may be handwritten or done on the word processor.

WORD PROCESSING

By the time they are ten or eleven, students are ready to learn to use the computer for word processing. For many students the pleasure of composing is greatly enhanced by working on a keyboard. Not only do they love the "finished" look of their printout, students enjoy the ease with which they can add ideas, juggle paragraphs, and correct spelling errors. They're not ready for complex word processing programs like *WordStar,* but there are many software programs geared specifically for younger students, including *Bank Street Writer* (Broderbund).

Obviously, at this level word processing does not replace the need for legible handwriting. However, it is a skill we believe children in the intermediate grades should be learning. Indeed, for many it represents a new kind of freedom that releases them to concentrate on the content of their writing. (For more on computers see pages 249–52.)

HOW PARENTS CAN HELP WITH WRITING

When children have writing assignments, they frequently get bogged down. Is there anyone who has not at some point been face-to-face with a blank sheet of paper with no idea of how to begin? Parents can play a useful role here in helping the child loosen up and get started. Forget about the wadded-up paper and crossed-out sentences. Encourage your child to talk about what he wants to say. Very often in talking it through, children discover they have a great deal to say and need no further help. If after talking the child again says, "But I don't know where to begin," parents can help by recapping the big ideas that have come from your discussion. Encourage your child to put the discussion down as notes or in simple outline form.

When a paper is finished, ask your child if he wants to read the paper out loud to you. This gives children a chance to discover missing ideas and missing word endings for themselves. Encouraging them to do as much editing as they can fosters their own critical abilities and independence. How far you go with correcting spelling, punctuation, and grammar will depend on various factors. Some teachers may not want parents correcting their children's papers. Some children resist such help anyway, feeling that if you make corrections, you're picking on them. You'll have to use tact and good judgment on this issue. Keep in mind that making mistakes is one way of learning. If this is a first draft, then the teacher will probably not expect a letter-perfect paper. On the other hand, if this is going to be graded and your child is not going to be devastated by "criticism," you may want to point out obvious errors that need attention. This is a good time to take a snack break and give some positive reinforcement about the work done so far. This pause for refreshment is usually enough to send the writer back to do a rewrite. On some occasions, when the deed has been laborious, the rewrite may need to wait for morning, when the child is refreshed.

Quite apart from written assignments children can be encouraged to do independent writing at home. Avoid pressuring them to perform. The following are merely suggestions that your child may enjoy :

▲ This is the age when children love to keep secret journals or diaries. A gift of a blank book and writing tools is often a favorite. Be sure to honor the privacy of such writing.

• Some children at this age also enjoy writing to cousins, summer friends, relatives, and pen pals. Personalized stationery and a supply of stamps are often all that is needed.

▪ Encourage children to design and write their own party invitations and holiday cards. A box of notepaper and art supplies also make writing thank-you notes more attractive.

▲ Writing to athletes, writers, entertainers, or political figures often brings rewarding return mail that children treasure.

• A news story on TV, on the radio, or in a newspaper or a magazine can often spark questions. Encourage children to address some of their questions to those in the news.

▪ Some families write an annual newsletter at holiday time to report on everyone's latest interests and doings. Kids can be encouraged to write their own portion of the news.

▲ Similarly, neighborhood "clubs" and individual kids sometimes enjoy publishing a newspaper with jokes, news, and original stories. The opportunity to use a hand-operated printing press or the family computer often are part of the motivation.

• Family trips or special events are fun to capture in photos.

You can then supply a scrapbook for combining the photos with captions and individual narratives about memorable occasions.

■ Learning to take written messages from telephone calls is a lot easier if you borrow the format used in offices. Kids should be able to take name, number, and a short message. Keep a supply of message pads and pencil at hand near the phone.

▲ Post a chalkboard or memo pad for intrafamily notes. Sometimes a memo about a chore that needs doing is received with less friction than reminders that may have a nagging quality. Encourage kids to use the memo board for sending messages as well as receiving them.

● Similarly, an appointment calendar can record events such as dental appointments, meetings, and games. Encourage kids to check the calendar and note down events themselves.

■ If you have a computer, there are a number of software programs for young writers. As mentioned earlier, look for a word processing program such as *Bank Street Writer* (Broderbund) designed specifically for young students. For more playful writing look for software that combines writing and graphics and others that can be used to print posters, banners, and cartoons. These are some of the best: *Print Shop* (Broderbund), *Comic Strip Maker* (Walt Disney Software), *The Newsroom* (Scholastic), *Bank Street StoryBook* (Mindscape).

▲ Children who are especially fond of writing original stories may also enjoy seeing their stories in print. Here are some magazines that publish selected pieces by children:

Cricket Magazine
P.O. Box 300
Peru, Illinois 61353
> *Runs contests monthly for writing, poetry, and art on varying themes by children six to fourteen.*

Dynamite
730 Broadway
New York, New York 10003
> *Accepts jokes, tricks, and funny ideas from children ten and up.*

Stone Soup
P.O. Box 83
Santa Cruz, California 95063
  Prints original stories. Children can also apply to become book reviewers.

Highlights for Children
803 Church Street
Honesdale, Pennsylvania 18431
  Publishes original stories, art, and poetry by children three to twelve.

You will find more newspapers, magazines, and organizations that run contests and publish children's work in *All the Best Contests* by Joan and Craig Bergstron (Ten Speed Press, 1988).

SPELLING

In the intermediate grades most students continue to have spelling workbooks with a weekly list of related words that are to be mastered. In addition, word lists from social studies and science should ideally be integrated into the weekly lists.

To facilitate their learning of these words, students are often paired with a spelling partner. Teachers generally team a strong and a weak speller to quiz each other. Students are responsible for working together on a regular basis all week. Once a week the teacher gives a written test in order to evaluate students' progress. As in math, students are grouped for spelling by ability, so not everyone is working on the same words.

HOW PARENTS CAN HELP WITH SPELLING

All of the suggestions in the primary chapter (pages 124–25) are still applicable.

▲ Also useful at this stage are a variety of games for the whole family that combine learning and play. Although some of these may have been bought earlier, they will now be played with more sophistication.

Spill & Spell   Upwords
Scrabble   Boggle

• An electronic spelling machine from Texas Instruments called Speak and Spell offers varying levels of spelling difficulty. Kids like the independence of being able to practice on their own.

▪ Also useful if you have a personal computer are a variety of software programs designed for spelling at different grade levels. One of the best is *Spell It* (Davidson). Check with your child's teacher for suggestions.

▲ Many kids at this age enjoy crossword puzzles and like books of word puzzles designed especially for young people.

PENMANSHIP

Most schools make the transition from printing to cursive writing in third or fourth grade. Mastering the fluid lines of script takes time and practice. Instruction in cursive writing is usually done with the whole class. The teacher models letters that are related, and students work at their desks. Often a handwriting book is used so that students can trace letters to get the feel and direction from models on their pages.

Most children make the transition to script over a period of months. However, for some students handwriting remains a hassle. As indicated earlier, for them word processing offers a legible alternative.

HOW PARENTS CAN HELP WITH PENMANSHIP

Students who have difficulty with the fine motor skills involved in handwriting are not likely to sit down voluntarily and practice. Yet there are related activities they may enjoy that can help them hone their fine motor skills and eye-hand coordination:

▲ Art materials such as paint, chalk, colored pencils, and crayons all lend themselves to more open-ended drawing and writing experiences.

• Chalkboards and Magic Slates with lift-up sheets provide less-permanent records of "goofs."

▪ Other art materials, such as beads, looms, clay, scissors, and glue, also provide satisfying practice with fine motor skills and completing a task.

▲ Similarly, craft kits and model building help children build their tolerance for sticking to a task that demands both patience and that eyes and hands work in concert.

• Some children also need the sensory stimulation provided by tracing cards that are flocked with sand or fuzzy material.

While most children learn to write quite adequately, there are some who will come to depend more on typing and word processing skills for clarity. Keep in mind that making too much of an issue over beautiful handwriting may short-circuit the more central business of writing for meaning and content.

MATH

By the time children have reached nine or ten the range of abilities in a class is so broad that departmentalized ability grouping is a necessity. In order to meet children's varying levels of achievement, diagnostic work should be done at the beginning of the year. In this way programs can be chosen that match students' needs. Groups are fairly stable, but there should be room for movement from one group to another when a student's progress (or lack of it) warrants a change.

Since this is the first time in their school years that some children are grouped by ability in math, there can be repercussions. Children themselves are extremely aware of differences in the classroom. They know which the high, middle, and low groups are. This is a new piece of reality that some students and parents have difficulty in dealing with calmly. Typically, for the first few weeks there are parental complaints that need to be addressed by the school. Most common is, "My child is bored," or "My child should be in a higher group." While there needs to be respect for such parental evaluations, often a demand for higher placement reflects a parent's desire rather than the best interests of the child.

During these three years children are expected to learn all the basic operations of addition, subtraction, multiplication, and division. They will also learn fractions and decimals and all the basic operations connected with fractions and decimals. By the end of sixth grade most children will be ready to start algebra. However, there are some students who will continue working toward mastery of the basics.

Some drill and practice is to be expected. Teachers use such exercises to reinforce what children are learning. However, the important word here is *some*. The entire math program should not be one drill lesson after the next.

As students work at more advanced levels, they continue to use manipulative materials. Although they are increasingly able to think in their heads, materials such as Dienes blocks, Cuisenaire rods, Chips, and Unifix cubes continue to demystify what they are doing in concrete terms (for illustrations of these manipulatives see pages 128–32). Instead of learning easily forgotten "tricks" in computation, children's basic concepts should be strengthened by using manipulatives that bridge the gap between reality and symbols. Once concepts are understood, there is less dependence on manipulatives.

As in the earlier grades, a solid chunk of time is scheduled daily for math instruction. However, the uses of math are not limited to math period. In social studies, science, woodworking, art, music, and gym, math is very much a part of the problem-solving business at hand. In contrast to typical textbook word problems (which they also do) their mapmaking or wood-building projects demand the use of measuring tools, computation, and problem-solving skills. When students dye yarn, math is involved in preparing charts and records of the process. From firsthand experience they understand the importance of presenting clear information. The same is true of cooking projects, when precise measurements make the difference between success and failure. Similarly math is used for scorekeeping, statistics, planning schedules, and layout work on a student newspaper. As in the earlier grades, children should be learning how math fits into their everyday experiences and needs.

CALCULATORS

Although parents often worry that having calculators available will turn students into math illiterates, in truth, being able to use a calculator is an important skill. Obviously, children still need to know their number facts. Learning basic operations has not become obsolete. However, knowing how to use a calculator as a tool should not detract from such learning. In fact, teachers often have students check their math with a calculator. Most schools today use calculators as part of their math curriculum.

When they are learning how to use the calculator, the emphasis should be on how to set up the problem. In a sense, this is related to paper-and-pencil calculations, where the student must decide what the question is and how to arrive at the answer. If students don't know whether to multiply or divide in a given situation, it doesn't matter if they know their multiplication tables or have a calculator. In either case, problem solving, not the answer, is at the heart of the matter. Seen from that perspective, a calculator scores as a tool. Its usefulness is only as good as the thinking that is required to use it well.

How Parents Can Help with Math

Helping children with math can be (forgive the pun) problematic. For some parents the world of decimals and fractions seems like a bad memory they'd rather not (or can't) recall. Negative attitudes about math are easy to transmit. For others, the step-by-step procedure in the math-learning process now seems a ridiculous waste of time. "Let me show you a shortcut," they say. With the best of intentions the parent who is able in math may nevertheless confuse the child with tricks that contradict or are totally different from the teacher's approach. As adults we often focus on answers while children still need to grasp the underlying process.

▲ If you feel uncomfortable with math, don't pass it on! Avoid giving your child a sense that being weak in math is something he or she inherited from you. For the parent who feels unable to help, it's important to alert the teacher that your child is having a problem and you don't know how to help. The teacher may even be able to give you a textbook that lays out the steps and clarifies your own problems.

• However, keep in mind that you should not be getting deeply entangled in teaching your child how to do math. Helping is one thing—taking over its teaching is inappropriate. If your child needs that kind of help, you may need to arrange a conference with the teacher to sort out what steps, if any, need to be taken.

▪ Avoid showing your child shortcuts or a "better" way of doing it. Keep in mind that that kind of help generally leads to confusion and creates for any child a conflict between home and school.

▲ In helping with math homework give as much positive re-inforcement as possible : For example, if there are just a few errors in your child's calculations, you can focus on the fact that "you did a great job with most of them. Let's see what happened with these." On examples that are incorrect, have your child talk through the step-by-step process she followed in doing them. Often in doing so, the child discovers the mistake herself or at least you will hear where the confusion lies.

• When most of the examples are wrong or your child says, "I'm stuck!" use the same technique. Encourage your child to talk it through. This will usually give you a clue to the problem.

▪ If the child does not seem to understand a math concept, you should encourage him to ask the teacher for help. Doing it for him under those circumstances will not help anyone. Assure him that one of the reasons the teacher gives home-work is to find out if students understand what she's teaching or if they need more help. Should it seem necessary, send a note along indicating that you believe your child needs to go over some specific issue and you did not want to confuse the school's approach and your own. Keep the note friendly, not critical.

▲ If the problem continues, you will need to make an appoint-ment and discuss the problems your child is having. The teacher may have suggestions that will help you to help your child. She may give him some extra time or suggest you find a tutor. Whatever is recommended, follow through. Math problems have a way of growing since one skill builds upon another.

• Encourage your child to use math skills as they relate to everyday events. For example :

   ▲ Have him add up the check at a restaurant. Older kids can help figure the tip.

▲ Have her estimate how much a purchase will cost. "We only have x dollars. How many can we buy?"

▲ On trips turn the "how much farther?" question around. Let them figure it out.

▲ Have your child half, double, or triple recipes you need more or less of.

▲ If you're about to purchase items like rugs, curtains, or fabric, involve the child in measuring and estimating what you need.

▲ If you're planning for a birthday party, get your child involved in getting the prices and setting a budget for must-haves and would-like-to-haves.

▪ There are many hand-held math drill machines in the toy store. Some of these are useful. Once kids have a concept, they can pick up speed through drill and practice. Toys such as Texas Instruments' Speak and Math are like old-fashioned flash cards. However, the electronic mode often makes them more attractive to kids since they can be used with more independence.

▲ Similarly, there is drill and practice software for the home computer. *Math Blaster* (Davidson) and *Math Man* (Scholastic) are good examples. This is not to say that your child "needs" a computer. However, if you have one, don't overlook other math-related software that is appropriate for this age group. Intermediate-grade students will find new challenges in using *Logo* (Terripin and Apple), *Factory* (Sunburst), *Puzzle Tanks* (Sunburst), *The King's Rule* (Sunburst), and *Building Perspective* (Sunburst).

▪ Many of the games popular for this age group have math skills built into the play. Games that demand strategy and logic, such as checkers, chess, Pente, and Othello, are appropriate and challenging. Also useful at this stage are:

Monopoly	Cribbage
Uno	Yahtzee
Parcheesi	Tri-Ominos

▪ Be sure your child knows how to use a calculator and encourage him to check his answers with it.

USING SKILLS IN NEW WAYS

SOCIAL STUDIES

What do you remember about social studies in elementary school? Is it the rolled-up maps the teacher pulled down on special occasions ... a map you could never quite get to look at without interruption? Or does social studies bring to mind a big book with pages of dull reading followed by questions assigned for homework? Although its content may vary from one school to another, social studies in the intermediate grades is often taught as an extension of reading. As in science, the content is often taught without making any meaningful connections between children's experiences and what they are studying, or between what they are learning today and how it relates to what they studied earlier. The emphasis is often on accumulating a body of facts that, not surprisingly, are less than memorable or meaningful. How many dates, names, treaties, or trade routes can you recall? Can you define the terms *longitude* and *latitude* beyond saying that they are horizontal and vertical lines on a map?

For many of us social studies got bogged down in memorizing forgettable facts. It was a lost opportunity for considering big ideas that would help us better understand our present and future. Currently a great deal of attention is being focused on what our high school graduates don't know about geography and history. In response, it's safe to predict that publishers and schools will react by pushing more texts and tests at an earlier age. While the need for a more engaging approach to social studies is apparent, it is unlikely that new textbooks alone will solve the problem.

An Alternative Approach to Social Studies

In contrast to the textbook approach, many schools, both public and private, treat social studies as the heart of their curriculum. While the subject matter in these classrooms may appear to be similar to that in more traditional schools, their approach to social studies is more active and less tied to dates, names, and memorized facts.

By the time children arrive at the intermediate grades, developmentally they have a new and better sense of time, in many ways closer to an adult's way of thinking about the past. However, although students learn specific dates and events, the emphasis should remain on social history rather than on chronological history. It is people—getting students to feel their way into another culture and how that culture has dealt with all the basic problems of human existence—that is the true focus of this sort of social studies program. In the broadest sense the social studies program of the intermediate years is a continuation of the approach used in the earlier grades. Although the cultures they may study cannot be examined in the same firsthand way as a local community, children can make the leap into the past by reenacting some experiences in active ways. For example, instead of simply reading about tools and how things were made, they actually dye yarn, weave cloth, dry fruit, and build replicas of communities. By looking at the art, listening to the music, and reading the literature and folklore of a culture they can begin to imagine what it was like to live in another

Cartoon from colonial magazine.

time and place. While the content differs at each grade level, the way in which students learn to approach such a study is consistent and has long-term value. Instead of emphasizing linear time, the study of any people unfolds around themes such as what kind of technology they had, their economy, and what their beliefs, folk-tales, and customs were. In looking at the way various cultures have met such needs, children are able to learn in a fuller sense what makes a people distinctly who they are or were.

In beginning a study of colonial times in a classroom I visited, the teacher asked his fifth-grade students what they knew (or thought they knew) about the New England colonists. Though they knew only a few things, a series of early discussions and readings led to a rather far-reaching list of things they wanted to know more about:

OUR QUESTIONS ABOUT THE NEW ENGLAND COLONIES

1. What kind of people settled in the New England colonies?

2. What kind of land was there in the area?

3. How did they make a living?

4. Why did the colonists come to New England?

5. Did the colonists use slaves?

6. How many people came?

7. How did religion affect the new settlers?

8. What was their relationship with Native Americans?

9. What were the roles of women in the colonies?

10. What kinds of houses did they build?

11. What role did children play?

12. What kinds of education did they have?

13. What was the climate like?

14. What important leaders came from these colonies?

15. How did the colonies affect the New World?

Of course, reading is basic. It is part of what makes history come alive. Students in classes like these read extensively on their subject area, nonfiction as well as fiction. They do written reports from this reading and independent research on chosen related topics. Such assignments are part of both their schoolwork and their homework. Arts, crafts, mapmaking, and music are all integrated into such a social studies program.

Instead of covering several cultures quickly, students take the time to study one culture in some depth. The study of the colonies will last five or six months. Rather than a single textbook, a library of related books is available for research. The teacher has provided a good mix of books about the people, their tools, and their customs. From such a library children develop a sense of books as resources they can use to find out a great deal. Students' research goes far beyond the usual encyclopedia approach. Teachers provide and read aloud a good deal of folk literature from the culture studied. At this age students are particularly captivated by Native American myths and legends. Such stories help them feel their way into a culture.

On a bulletin board there are displays of students' geometric paper quilt designs, reflecting an awareness of colonial needlework. On a classroom shelf there are colonial "artifacts," such as baskets, lanterns, and pottery. Some of the reproductions were brought in by the teacher, others were made by the children. Two modest-frame looms with work in progress are on a countertop, and above them are yarns that have been dyed with Concord grapes, pokeberries, and sumac.

When older students study Egypt or the Incas, they look at their ancient math system and how they kept records. They listen to the music of a culture and improvise with related instruments. The culminating activity for a study might well be a full-blown play with music, costumes, sets, and story created through a cooperative group effort. For example, such plays begin as improvisation and skits and develop into a sequenced story. The plays are never written down, but are learned through repetition. Since children are not memorizing a script, the plays often maintain a fresh, improvisatory quality, even in the performance, and lines change somewhat right up to the end.

Naturally, children have a lot of reactions that are ethnocentric. One of the teacher's jobs is to pick up on those reactions and help children compare cross-cultural views. As their knowledge of the studied culture deepens, so does their identification with that culture. Initially, in studying the Eskimos, for example, children might be repelled by certain aspects of the Eskimo's food. The idea of cooking with blubber or eating bear meat at first strikes some as abhorrent. As they learn about the Eskimo way of life, its relation to the environment, and the issues of survival involved, they begin to see "repulsive" customs through Eskimo eyes. Such identification with and appreciation for other cultures is an important goal of social studies. It helps children see beyond their own cultural experiences and biases. Learning to respect other ways of eating, dressing, and believing opens their eyes and minds to the amazing diversity of life as it has existed in the past, present, and hopefully in the future.

Although there is no national curriculum, the upper grades frequently focus on the Middle Ages, the Aztecs, or other ancient civilizations. In doing so, students become interested in the methods and tools of the historian, the archaeologist, the anthropologist. Hearing about how humankind has discovered its own past becomes part of social studies, as well as using graphic displays, such as time lines, that show events of the past in different parts of the world.

Yet, in studying the past the focus is still on everyday events such as "How did they get their food?" and "What kinds of clothes did they wear?" Students may be interested enough to study about a leader such as Charlemagne, but serious study of wars and political history will wait for another year or two. For now it is enough to enter into a culture and get a sense of how it was to live in another time.

How Parents Can Help with Social Studies

Although parents cannot reproduce the kind of lively program they might wish existed in their child's classroom, school readings in social studies can be enlivened by discussions at home. Parents can also lead their children to other resources that relate to subjects children are currently studying.

▲ Keep in mind that this is the age when children are often interested in reading biographies for the first time. Your librarian may be able to suggest appropriate choices that relate to current studies.

• Parents can also borrow books from the library to introduce children to myths and legends of cultures they are studying.

▪ Trips to nearby historical restorations or museums with historical artifacts are often good family outings at this stage.

▲ Try some recipes together or restaurants with food from other cultures or times.

• Many commercially made games can be both enjoyable and educational for family play. Some of the best are made by Aristoplay.

> *Made for Trade (early American life-craftsmen)*
> *Hail to the Chief (presidential and constitutional history)*
> *Where in the World? (world geography)*
> *By Jove (mythology)*

▪ Make use of your own resource books. In a discussion about the nightly news or a school-related topic, make use of the atlas or globe. If you're a *National Geographic* collector, make them accessible.

197

▲ Kids also enjoy working with map puzzles, making maps of their own, and learning how to read and use maps in malls or on family trips.

• Computer users would enjoy *Where in the USA is Carmen Sandiego?* and *Where in the World is Carmen Sandiego?* (Broderbund).

Within the family parents and grandparents can also give children a sense of their own history. Kids enjoy hearing or recording anecdotes from older relatives about how it was when they were growing up. Family photo albums, artifacts, and traditions are a source of interest and pride and are worth sharing.

As indicated earlier, the family itself remains the first and most continuing force in teaching children about living with others. While not all decisions in a family can be made in a democratic way, when possible, children should be active participants in decisions and in expressing their opinions. It is within the framework of the family that children learn a great deal about respecting other people's rights and opinions and how we resolve differences without getting into shouting matches, slamming out of rooms, or socking it to someone. Such lessons are taught by the example parents set in their own behavior.

It is also within the family that we can address some of our mutual concerns for the injustices children see and worry about. Although parents cannot always right all the wrongs or solve the problems of poverty, drugs, homelessness, bigotry, and war, we can help our children understand that these are issues that concern us, too. Parents can show children how they take responsibility by working with organizations in large or small ways to bring about change or support their particular beliefs. Indeed, many children at this stage are ready to help by volunteering for tasks that are appropriate if not earth-shattering. Whether it's stuffing envelopes, visiting nursing homes, helping in a soup kitchen, or collecting used toys or food for the poor, children's organizations such as Scouts and religious youth groups allow ten- to twelve-year-olds to participate in the world in active ways. Nor is it too early to show children how we as citizens are involved in the political process of selecting and electing our leaders. Again, middle-years youngsters can stuff envelopes, hand out flyers, run errands, and find satisfaction in being involved. Children who grow up in homes where issues are discussed are learning meaningful lessons about the responsibilities of citizenship that schools alone cannot teach. They are involved in "social studies" in one of the most meaningful ways possible.

SCIENCE

To teach science, many schools still rely chiefly on science textbooks that essentially dictate the curriculum. In the worst possible scenario the text is read and questions about what has been read are then answered. I say worst because such an approach views science as a body of facts to be memorized and recited rather than a way of looking at the world. Some teachers take the textbook lessons a step further by demonstrating what the book is teaching with related activities. For example, after reading about water, the students are given opportunities to do several experiments with water. While these hands-on experiences may be better than none at all, even this textbook-plus-demonstration approach has a predetermined outcome, a far cry from the spirit or nature of science as a discipline, which involves exploration, trial and error, making hypotheses, discovery. Moreover, this approach tends to be a disjointed series of lessons with little or no connection to children's real-life experiences or what they are studying in other areas. As a result, science becomes a dull, lifeless subject or, for some, a subject in which there are only right and wrong answers instead of a way of discovering causes and effects, of seeing relationships.

Developmentally, the middle-years child has a great appetite for such information. But how that appetite is fed is crucial. Although middle-years children are better able to deal with more abstract ideas, the starting point for understanding still begins with what they can observe and connect to their own firsthand experiences. A rich science program invites students to ask questions rather than memorize answers.

A more desirable science program is very much an integrated part of the curriculum. For example, when children are studying Native Americans in social studies, their science program might examine how Native Americans wove cloth. Indeed, they might actually learn to weave cloth in Native American style from wool they dye from berries and other plants. In making their own dyes students would keep written records of what and how much they used to get the hues they want for their wool. Instead of following a science "recipe" in some book, they are learning at firsthand how scientists test and change formulas to achieve a desired result.

In another classroom I visited where students were beginning a study of the Arctic, they were asked to speculate on what kind of weather they would expect to find there. As a group they hypothesized:

1. Snowy and icy most of the time

2. Rainy

3. Snows a lot

4. Hails

5. Warm in summer (not in the 90s but 50 to 60 degrees)

6. Winter temperature—50 degrees (below)

7. Short summer—plants don't have long to grow

8. Snow melts—it will be wet—there are evergreens

9. Snow never melts—because if it did, it would flood New York City

10. There are no trees

11. There are trees

Judging from statements 8 to 11, not everyone agrees on what they will find out. Rather than confirm or deny, the teacher allows each child's opinion to be tested and explored in the course of future study of the Arctic. She treats all answers with respect and reminds them that for now they are hypothesizing. Only later will they use research to prove or disprove their theories.

Since they cannot go to the Arctic, in this instance they will use a variety of films and books to do their research. However, their inquiry begins with what they know (or think they do) and leads them to test their ideas.

In such classrooms students are learning about the process of thinking in scientific ways. Rather than learning a series of facts or right and wrong answers, they are being encouraged to formulate their own questions, to hypothesize about possible answers, and to test their hypotheses. In the process they must also learn how to observe, keep records, compare what they learn with what they know, and discover what they still need to find out. Such an approach, whatever the specific content of a middle-years science program, teaches children positive attitudes about the way scientists approach problems and search for answers.

If your school is still doing science by the textbook, your parents organization might help bring about change. Interested parents can undertake a study of how science is being taught in other schools around the country. As a group you may be able to compile a list of resource people in your community with science backgrounds who would visit your child's school. In one school, parents and teachers set up a nature trail near the school that became a lab for class field trips. By making their interests and concerns felt, parents can do much to stimulate change or at least some new kinds of thinking.

How Parents Can Help with Science

Parents often feel nervous about helping children with science. For many of us, science was a series of tests with diagrams and facts promptly forgotten. Yet there are many ways parents can encourage children's interests in science.

When children ask questions for which we have no ready answers, there's no reason to be embarrassed. Having the right answer is not nearly as important as your willingness to help a child look for an answer. You, too, can start with some "what do you think" questions that will give children a chance to focus their thinking and use what they know. "Where do you think we can find out?" is not a bad follow-up. In some instances, finding out may involve making observations or, in other cases, using resource books at home or in the library. Without taking over, parents can do a great deal by sharing in children's enthusiasms, puzzlements, and interests.

Parents can also provide children with the raw materials for science investigations in the backyard or in the kitchen. A great deal of science can be learned through informal experiences that happen on a daily basis. For example:

▲ Baking bread with yeast, cakes with whipped eggs, gravy with flour, pickling cucumbers, and turning fruit into jam all provide opportunities for observing how things change when combined with heat, air, or other substances.

• A windowsill can provide the light and space needed for growing plants from seeds, bulbs, or cuttings, or if you have a backyard, why not involve kids in growing a small garden?

▪ Household items such as a thermometer, barometer, or weathervane can help kids become more aware of weather changes.

▲ Magnifying glasses, telescopes, microscopes, and field glasses all give children new ways of looking at the world.

• Collecting becomes more detailed and elaborate at this stage. Providing kids with adequate space, scrapbooks, shelves, and display boxes signals your approval and support of their interests.

▪ Children at this age are ready to take greater responsibility for pets. If space or allergies won't permit the usual cat or dog, you might consider tropical fish, a bird, or a gerbil.

▲ Small science kits are available for building small working models of instruments such as a periscope, a clock, a kaleidoscope, or a birdhouse.

• Trips to natural history museums, aquariums, planetariums, zoos, and botanical gardens can extend subjects they're learning in school or stimulate new interests.

▪ Keep some resource books available for research or just browsing. Field guides for identifying birds, trees, rocks, shells, or bugs can be taken along on camping trips and outings or enjoyed in an armchair.

▲ If encouraged, many children like keeping a life list of birds sighted (or for that matter a list of anything sighted). If possible, a bird feeder in the backyard or on the windowsill offers front-row seats to an ongoing show.

• In the library or bookstore there are many excellent books with science experiments children can do with common household equipment and ingredients. Two of the best are Vicki Cobb's *Science Experiments You Can Eat* and Sara Stein's *The Science Book*.

▪ Your local museum or Y may have an astronomy club for older elementary-age children.

While issues surrounding sex education, drugs, and AIDS are often addressed as "science" by the schools at this stage, it may be that what we need is a less clinical approach with heavier emphasis focused on social and personal responsibility. These are issues children hear about, often worry about, but sometimes find it difficult to broach with adults in the classroom or at home (see drug prevention section, pages 278–82). Given the statistics on teenage and preteen pregnancy, drug and alcohol abuse, and the continuing spread of AIDS, it seems obvious that these are issues parents need to address with children whether your school is doing so or not.

If you feel uncertain about how to discuss such issues, you will find excellent ideas in the following:

How to Talk to Your Child About Sex
How to Talk to Your Teens and Children About AIDS
Your Children and Drugs

These small but well-written brochures list suggested conversation starters as well as further readings for parents and children and are available from

The National PTA
700 North Rush Street
Chicago, Illinois 60611–2571
(312)787-0977

MUSIC

During the intermediate years many schools offer instrumental lessons in addition to the usual singing and music appreciation. For some this is the start of a lifelong interest; for many it is a passing fancy; for a few it's instant pain. Before you invest heavily in purchasing an instrument or dreaming of debuts in Carnegie Hall, give it some time. Renting an instrument for a while is usually a good idea. Indeed, some children play one instrument for a few weeks or months and then want to switch and try another. At this stage both school and home should be open to some exploration.

Developmentally students are better prepared at this stage to deal with mastering notation, which is, in fact, yet another symbol system that requires both math and reading. By grades four to six, children are also better able to take responsibility for practicing and giving the sustained effort that is needed, and it is often at this time that they choose instruments to learn.

How Parents Can Help with Music

Eager as you may be to have your child play an instrument, forcing the issue will rarely succeed. If the child is only taking lessons to please you or because everybody is doing it, the interest is likely to fade quickly.

If your child is studying piano or any other instrument, here are some of the ways you can support those efforts best:

▲ Provide uninterrupted time and space for practicing. That means keeping younger or older siblings out of the young musician's hair.

• If the child needs help and you are knowledgeable, by all means offer the help. But avoid taking over or overdirecting the practice.

▪ Some children find it difficult to set a time for practicing and sticking to it. For some, two short practice sessions are better than one long one. Talk about it and allow for some flexibility. If you find yourself in a daily battle over practicing, it may be that your child is not really ready or interested enough to make the effort. He or she may be better off coming back to this interest six months or a year from now.

▲ Not every music teacher is temperamentally right for your child. If your son or daughter seems to come home from lessons with a steady stream of sad stories, a change of teacher may be appropriate.

• Keep in mind that most of us who took lessons don't end up as great performers. If your child seems to be enjoying the lessons and making slow progress, the investment is still worthwhile. Being the outstanding student in the spring recital should not be your measuring rod.

▪ Children do go through periods when practicing is not on the agenda. Before proclaiming an ultimatum, "Practice or no more lessons!" be sure you've considered the consequences. Taking lessons and playing occasionally has its own value and may be worth supporting. If the teacher can't accept this, you may need to find another teacher.

▲ Whether they're studying an instrument or not, children's

appreciation and pleasure in music should be encouraged in many ways. You can supply a variety of tapes and records to broaden their musical horizons. These can be borrowed from your local library's tape collection rather than bought. Aside from current pop music, introduce them to ethnic music, light classics, show tunes, and folk music. If you listen yourself to such music—as with reading—you will be a model for your child. You will also automatically introduce him to the range of music you like.

• Where possible, this is the time to introduce them to live music performances. For the novice, you'll want to choose programs that are sure to be engaging. A trip to a concert hall, ballet, musical theater, or band concert is quite a different experience from listening to a recording. You don't need the best seats in the house. In fact, you may get a better view up in the balcony. Don't overlook music and dance programs on TV, chiefly on public broadcast stations. Pop some corn and make it a family event.

If no instrumental lessons are available or if you feel it's too soon, consider some of the musical instruments that invite exploration through play. Woodstock Chimes makes a handsome instrument, called the Chimealong, which has good musical tone quality. Also interesting at this age are small electronic synthesizers, made by Texas Instruments, Casio, and others, that kids can improvise on or play with notation and record their own compositions. Formal lessons are a turnoff for some, and many children teach themselves to play the recorder, harmonica, or autoharp. Others enjoy improvising with steel drum or bongos. Any of these informal paths may lead children to more traditional studies in time and are well worth exploring.

ARTS AND CRAFTS

Depending on your school's budget, art may be taught by the classroom teacher or a special art teacher who comes to the classroom once or twice a week. As in the primary grades, the art specialist may have an agenda that bears little relationship to the ongoing curriculum in the room. She may introduce a project or materials that must be completed in the twenty-five to forty minutes scheduled. One week it may be paint, another week clay, or the following week a cut-and-paste collage. Often, too, art lessons are geared to end products and following directions instead of exploring materials and giving expression to individually shaped projects. As a result, the lesson becomes a test of following the leader, with thirty kids reproducing tasks whose end products look very much alike. Students in such classrooms often lose their interest or motivation to do their own thinking or to trust their own vision. This is especially harmful at a moment when children are becoming more critical of their own work and frequently have greater expectations of themselves than their technical skill allows.

Sensitive teachers of this age group are aware of these opposing forces that can inhibit children's artwork. It is at this stage, for instance, that teachers can give more direct instruction in techniques that help children deal with problems in perspective. In contrast to the five-year-old, who is usually satisfied with his loosely drawn representations, eight-, nine-, and ten-year-olds are frequently frustrated with their attempts. However, they are technically better able and therefore willing to learn some of the techniques that artists use, so the art teacher encourages students to take time in observing light, shadow, and lines more closely. She introduces them to basic concepts of perspective and encourages them to try their hand at still-life drawing. Yet even as they are honing such skills, students are encouraged to use more three-dimensional materials, such as clay, collage, and wood, that tend to free students to produce more expressive and abstract creations.

As indicated earlier, art should be very much related to ongoing work in social studies. In addition to group-made murals or models of villages, students frequently study the artifacts of a culture's folk art. They may see slides or visit a museum and then do their own versions of Dutch tiles, kachina dolls, or Egyptian tomb statues. It is in connection with social studies that most work in crafts —such as weaving, dyeing, or woodworking—takes place.

HOW PARENTS CAN HELP WITH ARTS AND CRAFTS

Keep in mind that art is an important avenue for nonverbal expression. For many children art materials offer a wonderful vehicle for ideas that at an earlier age might have been expressed in dramatic play. Remember, too, that many schools give little time or value to such expression. Even schools that have regular art classes rarely

Egyptian drawing. Alex, age 9.

provide time to stay with a task or to explore fully the nature of pastel crayons, paint, or clay.

At home children can have the luxury of experimenting, of making goofs and starting over again, of working on projects that are self-designed and unlimited by the time restraints of a classroom schedule. Parents can encourage this kind of learning by providing space and materials that are easily accessible. At this stage children should be able to take most of the responsibility for setting up and cleaning up their own art projects. A work surface that can be wiped off, stored, or left undisturbed for long-term projects will cut down on hassles.

For special occasions don't overlook gifts of art supplies such as

colored pencils	tape/glue/staples	construction paper
markers	acrylic paints	looms
water paints	collage materials	lanyard
pastel crayons	clay	poster paint
calligraphy pens	woodworking tools (not power tools)	scissors

Essentially these materials are unstructured and invite more exploration than the typical coloring book or paint-by-number kit. Although paper dolls and punch-out activity books are popular at this age, they should not replace the possibilities of more open-ended materials.

Middle-years children also enjoy arts and crafts classes that teach them the techniques of batiking, weaving, puppet making, jewelry making, woodworking, or potting. You may be fortunate enough to live near an art museum or Y that offers such instruction. If you don't, this may be something you can enjoy learning as a family project. Your local library probably has enough craft books with step-by-step instructions to get you started.

Involve children in your own artistic pursuits. Whether it's photography, decorating cakes, needlepoint, arranging flowers, or refinishing furniture, children learn a great deal by observing the way in which you work. Encourage them by answering questions simply and allowing them to assist where possible.

Instead of buying invitations and cards for holidays and birthdays, provide the supplies for child-inspired designer creations. Original art or handcrafted projects can be given a place of honor on an end table or framed and hung. Without pushing for perfection or being harshly critical of their end products, parents can show they value their children's artistic efforts by making use of the handmade potholder or displaying a drawing or sculpture.

PHYSICAL EDUCATION

By the intermediate grades, many children have developed an almost obsessive interest in team sports. It is at this time, too, that some children grow to dread team games, in which teams are chosen and the less able children are often left to be grudgingly placed on one team or the other—to play outfield or to bat last. In meeting the needs and interests of so many in this age group, physical education programs tend to emphasize team effort. Children are increasingly ready to grasp the concept of the rules of the game and willing to struggle with the concept of being one member of a team. A good physical education program will emphasize the social/intellectual aspects of team sports as well as the game itself, helping children to learn how to play cooperatively and fairly, how to lose and win, and how to give everyone—not just the best players—a chance to experience a variety of positions.

Really good gym teachers know how to give a sense of team play without overemphasizing its competitive aspects. Teams can be juggled in mid-game to blur the emphasis on scoring. Parents should know that studies show that pressure to score high actually leads kids to cheat. Although some competition is natural at this age, pressuring children to score high and win should not be the main thrust of the gym program. Along with an emphasis on learning the basics of team sports, other physical activities, such as folk dancing, gymnastics, and fitness activities, should still be very much a part of the program. Care needs to be taken to help motivate children who feel physically inept or self-conscious and to include activities that they can do well. It's at this stage that gym classes are often divided by sex, and the programs offered to each sex may vary significantly. Parents may need to pressure school officials to offer a full and nonsexist program for both boys and girls.

But what can you do if your daughter comes home complaining that girls always get to bat last? What if your son is always the substitute in basketball games and doesn't want to go to school on gym days? Or what if the competitive nature of the gym program is affecting the behavior of your already overly competitive son? As a parent you should not dismiss these issues as less important than academic problems. Indeed, such problems can color children's attitudes about themselves and affect their performance in class both before and after gym. If you feel that the gym program is creating such problems, talk with your child's teacher directly. You may need to talk further with the gym teacher or the school principal. You may be surprised to learn that other students are having similar problems. If that is so, you may be able to push for a rethinking of the school's gym program. Again, you are more likely to succeed if you work with a group of parents who share your concerns.

However, keep in mind that even if you can do nothing to change the school's policy, there are many things you can do to minimize the long-term effect of a poor program.

PARENTS' ROLE IN ENCOURAGING PHYSICAL DEVELOPMENT

Recognizing that team sports are often central to the child's social life, parents can play an active role in supporting developing skills and attitudes. Aside from providing the needed equipment, a bit of one-on-one time in the backyard or park can help in developing pitching and catching skills or in learning to sink a jump shot. Unfortunately, it's at this stage that many families get caught up in heavily organized team sports and competition. Yet children still benefit from informal games where the emphasis is on playing rather than on scoring.

Keep in mind, too, that some children do not enjoy team sports but can be encouraged to play actively. They may prefer riding a bike, skating, skiing, swimming, hiking, dancing, gymnastics, or tennis. In the long run, these individual pursuits that can be pursued solo or with one friend may be of greater value. After all, how many of us play baseball or soccer as adults?

▲ Group sports instruction is often available and not too costly—whether it's swimming lessons at the Y or a one-week "baseball camp" at the park around the corner. This is a good way to "try on" a sport without making a huge investment.

• Some children learn best with a few one-on-one lessons with a pro. Though such lessons are likely to be more costly, these children may be less self-conscious and better able to focus on the instruction without having to keep up with the group.

▪ Avoid sexist mind-sets that limit the kinds of activities your son or daughter participates in. Your daughter may

want a baseball bat and mitt at this age just as much as your
son.

▲ Remember, the model you provide says more than your
words. If you are physically active, children are more apt to
follow your lead.

• Parents can also help by supporting the notion of working
on tasks that demand practice. Children don't always see the
cause-and-effect connections between working at a skill and
becoming skillful. They still need encouragement and someone who can help them see small gains rather than wishful
dreams of overnight triumphs.

▪ Looking at Terry Orlick's *Cooperative Sports and Games
Book* and *Second Cooperative Sports and Games Book* (Pantheon) may give parents some good ideas for ways to play
more cooperative games. These books may also be useful to
introduce to a school whose gym program for this age group
relies too much on a fierce competitiveness.

SOCIAL DEVELOPMENT

While teachers and parents are still the ultimate power brokers
who hold the controls, increasingly a drive for greater independence is felt both in the classroom and at home. As we have seen in
the primary years, children begin shifting from their almost total
dependence on adults to a new and growing dependence on their
peers. This is the stage when finding acceptance among one's agemates takes on even greater importance than before. Indeed, it's in
the company of their peers that children now test and measure
themselves. On the playground they know who is the fastest runner,
the strongest fighter, the best pitcher, the worst catcher, the poorest
sport, and the meanest tease.

In their eagerness to "join up" and belong, this is the age when
cliques and "clubs" are constantly being formed and disbanded.
Since most of these self-made groups are essentially mutual-admiration societies, one of their functions is invariably to exclude more
people than they include. Of course, being left out is painful, and
the usual response is to organize yet another club that excludes
others. Such clubs rarely serve any real purpose beyond belonging.
The "members" may talk about putting on a play, becoming a
musical group, or building a clubhouse, but in fact, it's rare for

kids to even agree on who's going to do what or how it will be done. Kids can spend hours debating the club's rules, the name of the group, or who is entitled to be the president. As a result of this internal squabbling, the longevity of such groups is rare. Social stability is often more easily found in groups where adults guide the rudder through the waves. Ready-made groups such as Boy Scouts, 4-H, Sunday school classes, Little League, and dance school offer children a way of belonging and doing things without the responsibility for holding it all together. Both the informal and the ready-made groups play an important role in learning about group life.

One-to-one friendships are now much stronger and longer lived than earlier. This is the stage when some friendships are forged that will last a lifetime. "Best friends," with whom children share sworn secrets, adventures, and aspirations, fill a real need for new attachments as they reach for ways of becoming more independent in the bigger social world beyond the family. In part, this need for friends helps children in learning the give-and-take that such relationships require and therefore in seeing things from another person's point of view.

Of course, even best friends don't always agree. Nine-year-old Sarah may come home vowing never to talk to Jill ever again because she's such a brat. By the next day the two may be planning their weekend activities. Or Ben may spend Saturday sulking because his pal, Marc, has been playing catch with Jay. It's not easy at this stage to understand that a person can have more than one friend at a time or enough camaraderie to go around.

While the ups and downs of these relationships are frequently resolved with relative ease, not all friendships last for long. Kids may go through a succession of "best" friends. As interests change, children are often attracted to new alliances, and old buddies are left behind, or best friends may be separated when a family moves or kids are assigned to different classrooms. Whatever the reasons, the loss of such relationships can be a heavy weight until children find new ones.

For parents and teachers it's important to recognize that these social issues are of great importance to the middle-years child's sense of himself. While parents often fear that children may be led astray by too much dependence on belonging or by the negative influence of certain friends whom they consider "undesirable," the positive value of agemates should not be overlooked.

It helps to understand, too, that children are sometimes attracted to friendships with children who are quite different from themselves. So, the quiet child may especially enjoy a boisterous and rather flamboyant child or the cautious child may be attracted to one who takes risks. While such friendships can be worrisome to parents, they are usually fascinating to children. Indeed, it's during these years that children are discovering and comparing the amazing range of opinions and life-styles of those they come in contact with outside the confines of home and family.

Parents who provide an open-door policy are often in a better position to give guidance than those who forbid or try to close out "bad" influences. Indeed, by welcoming children to bring friends into their homes, parents will have a better sense of the child's social world and be better able to discuss both negative and positive influences. Without attacking a child's choice of friends, parents can discover for themselves what issues or behavior they find inappropriate or unacceptable. Eager as they are for independence, children of this age group are not apt to be "at war" with parents. In fact, most children's values and attitudes at this stage are essentially a reflection of their parents' view of the world, despite their growing dependence on friends outside the home. Without surrendering their own values *or* shutting the world out, parents can help children to find a balance and retain their independence by encouraging both friendships and the pleasures of family activities. Often an outing to the museum, the mall, or a concert is more pleasing at this age with a friend along. Our daughter's best friend attended her first ballet with our family, while our daughter went on her first camping trip with her friend's family. In a sense their friendship opened new worlds to both of them. Parents can also help children find ready-made groups that satisfy their social, recreational, or intellectual needs.

HOMEWORK IN THE INTERMEDIATE GRADES

Ask most adults what they remember about homework and you're apt to hear words like *boring, hard, awful, tedious,* or *dumb.* They also recall tensions between themselves and their own parents, angry words such as, ''If you paid attention in class, you would know how to do this,'' or ''You're not going to hand in a sloppy-looking paper like this!''

In their eagerness to help, parents often become enmeshed in nightly confrontations. All too often homework becomes an issue between parent and child instead of remaining a part of the school curriculum—something between teacher and child. Does this mean you should have nothing to do with homework? Not at all. However, to avoid turning homework into a nightly police action, there are things you should know. During the intermediate grades homework is likely to be a regular fact of life. Sorting out your role in the scheme of things may be more important than offering the usual advice about establishing routines and an orderly workspace.

Parents sometimes become overly involved in unnecessary ways. For example, when Michelle came home with a project for the Science Fair, her dad became so overly involved in ''winning'' that he virtually took over and produced a model of an earthquake that was obviously not built by a fourth-grader. While his interest was admirable, parents need to guard against overparticipation. For Michelle winning had to be a rather hollow victory, even a fraud. What she may have learned was not to trust herself to do a competent job.

With the best of intentions parents often become overly intrusive in their children's homework. They may fear that unless they check every assignment and oversee every mistake, their child will fail. Yet, correcting every error may have the effect of giving your child's work a false look of competence that can mislead a teacher as to where and how to help. Most homework assignments are designed to reinforce (and check) skills that have been taught in school. If your child is not able to do the task, it's important for the teacher to know that this is an area that needs further work.

Distressing as it may be, when your son dashes off a half-hour assignment in five minutes, it's a safe bet that the teacher will notice the sloppy handwriting or inaccurate answers. Generally, if you have faith in the teacher, it may be best to let the teacher deal with this matter rather than insisting the job be redone. If you are worried about the situation, you can certainly check with the teacher and see if she wants you to do anything. Don't be surprised if the teacher is well aware of the problem or has already taken steps to deal with the situation.

Helping with homework calls for a delicate kind of balancing act. Knowing how many questions you should answer or when to stop and throw it back to the child really depends on multiple factors. In some instances not helping may leave a child feeling abandoned and distraught. On the other hand, helping too much (or in the wrong way) can be hurtful, too.

You really need to know both your child and yourself very well. For example, if you are a stickler for grammar and spelling or if you are bubbling over with ideas for a story, you may be the wrong person to read through your child's writing assignment. Your expectations may be unreasonable. Similarly, your know-how in math may be counterproductive, particularly if it contradicts the approach the teacher is using in class. Parents often fall into the trap of answering simple questions with more than any child ever wanted to know.

Consider, too, that playing the role of teacher not only calls for special skills, it can get in the way of your relationship as a parent. All too often children feel embarrassed or fearful of losing parental approval when they (or you) begin to feel they are not "getting it." Although you may give them all kinds of verbal assurance to the contrary, kids are quick to pick up on negative feeling from your tone of voice, body language, or facial expression. For one child you may be the perfect mentor for getting the spelling list mastered. But the same child may see you as an ogre when it comes to science or math.

No book can tell you exactly how, when, or how much to help. Usually, it's best to respond to your child's requests rather than to initiate or interfere by stepping in too soon. That way you are less likely to be seen as a pushy enforcement officer but rather as an ally your child can turn to when needed.

Keep in mind that children have different styles of approaching their homework. Some prefer to be left alone. They neither need nor want someone hovering or looking over their shoulder. Other children will come to you to talk, complain, or ask for help. One of the benefits of not being someone who polices the situation is that in the long run you can often be more useful. Ideally, your child should think of you as a calming resource rather than as a crutch he may come to depend upon.

Although most children generally take their homework in stride and need only occasional help, some children waste more energy anticipating the job than doing it. Some have trouble adjusting to the inequity of having to work when other members of the family seem to be free to watch TV, play a game, or talk on the phone. They complain that "it's not fair!" To remedy this injustice, your child may look for ways to get you involved, even if it brings negative attention. Rather than giving a long speech about how life is not always fair, you can be a sympathetic listener, recalling how you used to feel yourself. Once the air is cleared, try to help the child focus on the task. "How long do you think it really will take to get done?" "Do you have everything you need to get it done?" Instead of threatening to take away privileges with negative threats, make a positive suggestion to get the wheels rolling. Suggest that "after you finish, maybe we can play a round of Chinese checkers" or read another chapter of a favorite book.

Most teachers give reasonable homework assignments. However, there are those who send home mindless and tedious worksheets or an exasperating overload that turns every night into drudgery. If the child knows how to do the examples, the assignment may simply be boring. If the child doesn't understand it, doing more may only reinforce his feelings of inadequacy. Should that be a regular problem, you may need to contact the teacher and/or discuss this with other parents. You may be able to bring about change or you may have to live with a less than perfect situation. Similarly, you may find the information in a textbook incomplete or inaccurate. Avoid being highly critical of the teacher or text to your child. There's little to be gained by having your child announce in school, "My father says this is a bad history book," or "This was a dumb assignment." There's no reason to put your child into a squeeze play between parent and teacher. If you are concerned about what is being taught or how, by all means take your concerns to the teacher; or in extreme situations, if you are unsatisfied with the response, you may need to take the issues to the principal (see pages 244–48).

With all the hassle over homework, children (and parents) sometimes begin to think of homework as some kind of punishment. Yet the truth is that studies indicate students who develop positive work habits in elementary school have greater success in future years.

On those evenings when the word *homework* evokes negative feelings, keep in mind that homework has positive values. Homework provides opportunities

▲ To reinforce and solidify skills they are learning during the day
• To read and write at greater length than is possible in class
▪ To research information at greater length
▲ To develop greater independence
• To make connections between what a child knows and what she is learning about
▪ To take responsibility for completing tasks

ESTABLISHING HOMEWORK ROUTINES

In addition to the general suggestions that follow, you will find subject-specific ideas in the sections of this book labeled "How You Can Help Your Child in Math, Reading, etc." Strategies for helping with spelling are in the primary chapter but would be applicable for this age group as well (see pages 124–25).

At any grade level when your child begins to have formal homework assignments, establishing routines can help get the job done with less of a hassle.

▲ Establish a quiet place where homework can be done without distractions or interruptions. If the table will be needed at dinnertime, there's no point in starting there. Children in the upper grades may need a workplace where ongoing projects can be left undisturbed and out of the reach of younger siblings (or dogs that eat homework).
• Help organize that workspace so that supplies are easy to find. This gives children an early feeling for the usefulness of keeping things in an orderly fashion.
▪ If it seems appropriate, you could help your child establish a regular time for doing homework. Some children really need free time immediately after school and return to homework refreshed after a play break. Others prefer to get the deed done so that they can enjoy the evening. Trying alternative arrangements may help your child find the best rhythm for his or her needs.
▲ Be aware how long average assignments should take. If you're not sure, ask the teacher to give you an estimate at

your first conference or at Open School Night. In the early grades the expectation may be ten to twenty minutes. Older students may have thirty to sixty minutes of work a night plus a half hour of reading.

• Limit the distractions of TV, loud music, or playful siblings during this work time. Some children may work well with background music. For others it is too distracting.

▪ If your child seems confused or uncertain, check to see if he understands the assignment. If necessary, go over the directions to be sure he understands what is to be done.

▲ If your child seems to be floundering, have her work through one math problem with you or talk through her ideas —or lack of them—for a written assignment. (See appropriate sections on subject areas for specific ideas in each subject.)

• Obviously if the problem is broader and the child does not seem to understand the concept, you need to contact the teacher. Send the teacher a note if the problem is a continuing one or call for an appointment (see pages 233–40 on conferences).

▪ Be sure to praise areas your child is improving in and for work well done.

As a teacher I often had "homework" of my own to do in the early evening. I found that by sitting down at the dining room table together with my children, we all got our work done and enjoyed some quiet time together. Indirectly, I suspect I was also presenting a model for getting a task done. My daughter learned at first hand that sometimes I, too, made mistakes and had to start over or that I needed to use a dictionary or take a break. Indeed, we often took a break together. She also knew I was there or nearby and available for questions that came up. *Without doing homework for her,* I was doing it with her and helping to establish long-term work habits that paid off in greater independence when she reached high school.

WAYS OF EVALUATING AND COMMUNICATING

TESTS, TESTS, AND MORE TESTS

When you think of tests, what comes to mind? Is it a column of spelling words with a star on top? Is it a ditto sheet of math examples with red checks? Or is it a printed booklet filled with page after page of questions with little dots to be filled in? Can you remember how you felt about the tests you took home or the ones that you accidentally "lost" somewhere between school and home? And how come they never gave back those special booklets with all the dots?

Certainly few experiences conjure up such a mixed bag of feelings as those tests we recall taking in our school days. Indeed, some of those feelings are carried over to our responses to our children and the tests they take.

Even before children enter kindergarten, the testing process begins. In the course of their school lives students today are faced with what seems like an endless and confusing glut of tests. For parents it is important to understand what kinds of tests your child is taking, what the purpose of the testing is, how the information from those tests is used, and what you can do to best prepare your child for successful test taking (which also means low-anxiety test taking).

WHAT KINDS OF TESTS DO THEY TAKE?

The great majority of tests children take are those designed by their classroom teacher. Typically, teachers write and administer their own tests in order to evaluate how well their students have mastered what they are teaching. It may be the week's spelling list, reading words, math computation, or any other subject recently covered. The results of such tests can help evaluate what skills need further work and where a student's strengths and weaknesses lie. Often the teacher will use the results of such tests to adjust future lessons. She may also use the test results over a period of time to grade a child's report card or to place a child in appropriate instruction groups. In some instances, the results of such tests are used to motivate students and help them see their own progress (or lack of it). Teachers sometimes reward students' success with stickers or extra time for free-choice activities.

Since parents do not always see tests that get "lost," it's important to have some idea of what tests are given on a regular basis. You should ask about this at a conference early in the year. In that way you can offer your assistance if and when it seems appropriate with preparations for tests before the event, and you can also go over results after the fact. If you keep in touch with the child's teacher on a regular basis, your child is less likely to fall behind for long. If several tests show no signs of improvement, you will know you need to step into the picture and find out what help is needed. If you're not seeing any tests or grades for several weeks running, in a class where you know these to be a regular feature, chances are there is a problem brewing. In a school that sends reports to you only every six, eight, or ten weeks, the problem could be drifting toward a disaster. You're better off asking questions of the teacher earlier, even at the risk of being considered overly concerned. It's your right and responsibility to be concerned.

By contacting the teacher you can find out if there are things you can be doing at home to help. The teacher may give you some materials to work on or perhaps tell you that the situation is being handled in the classroom. If, after several weeks more, you do not see improvement, you may need to discuss alternative plans with the teacher. In some instances the teacher may suggest how you can give the child extra help or that you should find a tutor outside of school. While many teachers dislike the idea of a child needing a different teacher for help in a given subject area, there may be real value in your child's having a fresh or different or individual approach to a given problem or subject. This doesn't mean that the classroom teacher is incompetent but rather that the child and teacher may be at an impasse in one area or that a situation may be emotionally charged with other issues that get in the way of the subject matter. A tutor may be a short-term solution to a situation that might otherwise turn into a long-term problem.

Often teachers themselves recognize this and are willing to recommend tutors or school specialists they feel can help. If the teacher can't suggest someone, you may need to ask the principal or parents whose opinions you respect.

STANDARDIZED TESTS

There are two kinds of standardized tests:

▲ Achievement tests which are designed to measure what children have learned in particular subjects
• Aptitude tests which are designed to predict how children will do in certain skills and abilities

Unlike teacher-made tests, standardized tests are given to thousands and thousands of children in schools all over the country. Since all children tested are given the same questions, the same rules, and the same amount of time, the conditions are said to be "standardized." As a result, it is believed that scores from such tests can be used to measure how your child's work compares to that of all other children in the same grade in his school or in schools all over the country.

In some respects, the results of such testing are more useful to school officials for reasons other than the evaluation of your child's aptitude or achievement. Indeed, the prevalence of testing is often directly related to state policies that fund programs on the basis of test scores in a school district. For example, in order to get funds for a remedial reading teacher a school may have to prove its need for funds by showing that it has x number of students who fall below a certain score. Similarly, standardized tests are used to evaluate how well (or poorly) experimental programs are working. In addition, schools or teachers within a school district are often evaluated on the basis of how their students' scores rate compared to some larger group on standardized tests. Unfortunately, such evaluations often fail to take into account the ratio of students to teacher in a classroom, the quality of the textbooks or programs used there, the teacher's credentials, or the physical state of the classroom itself.

In many instances the tests are given solely because they are required by law or because they are the only way schools can keep a cumulative record of a student's "progress" from grade to grade. The results of such tests may also be used in making placement decisions about students who, based on their test scores, may qualify for special classes or gifted programs.

ACHIEVEMENT TESTS

During the elementary years your child is likely to be given two kinds of standardized tests:

CRITERION-REFERENCED TESTS: At the end of a reading book or math unit your child may take a standardized test that evaluates how well he or she has mastered the work studied. Such tests are usually made by the textbook authors who designed the program. Criterion-referenced tests focus on a student's knowledge rather than how he or she compares with others. As such, they can be useful in helping the teacher evaluate what areas need continued or remedial work.

NORM-REFERENCED TESTS: These tests are usually given at the end of the school year. Such exams have a number of sections meant to test various subjects. It may take a week to administer all the sections of a test that might include reading comprehension, vocabulary, spelling, math computation, math word problems, science, and social studies. Such tests are known as norm-referenced tests, since individual scores are compared to the scores of many students at the same grade or age level who have taken the same test. The ''norm'' group may be within the school district, state, or nation.

Some of the most widely used tests are

SRA (Science Research Associates) Achievements
Iowa Tests of Basic Skills
Stanford Achievement Test
California Achievement Tests
Metropolitan Achievement Tests

Some schools report the results of such tests directly to parents, whereas other schools do not report the results unless you request them or there is a problem. Since achievement scores generally become part of your child's permanent cumulative record, you are entitled by law to review that file and its contents. If you should want to do so, for whatever reason, contact your child's teacher or the school principal. Don't be cowed by the confusing numbers. You can ask whomever you meet with to interpret the scores.

Understanding the scores on achievement tests can be confusing. Such tests do not have one score but several. You'll find the following categories of ratings

PERCENTILE SCORE : This score indicates what percent of the ''norm group'' scored lower than your child. For instance, if Jenny scored in the 70th percentile in reading, you know that 70 percent of the norm group scored below Jenny in reading. It does not mean that she got 70 percent of the answers correct.

RAW SCORE : This score usually refers to the number of questions your child answered correctly. A score of 100 does not, however, mean Jenny got all the answers. There may have been 150 questions, and a perfect score on such a test would be 150. So the raw score refers to the number of possible correct answers. Basically, this is a score that's only useful in terms of the group's raw scores.

STANINE : The stanine score really gives you another

kind of look at the percentile score. Stanine scores range from 1 to 9. Five is the average score for the age and time of year tested. If your child has a stanine of 6–9, she has scored above the average scores of other children who were tested. If she scored with a 1–2 or 3, then her score is below average.

GRADE EQUIVALENTS : This is perhaps the most confusing score. Say your child, at the end of second grade, scores 5.6 in math, which means fifth grade six months. "WOW!" you say. "My kid is a genius!" Not quite. That is a high score, but it does not mean your child is ready to skip ahead to fifth grade. That score reflects the average grade level of other students in second grade who achieved the same score. It does show that your child is well above average in that area. However, a grade equivalent that is below second grade in another subject does not mean your child is necessarily failing. He may need extra help or more attention in that subject, or the subject may not have been taught in his school.

Standardized tests are usually scored by machine. Since these tests are generally given in late spring, this year's teacher may not get the results until the school year is almost over. If your child has been having academic problems all year, the test may help to further document those problems. However, most teachers are well aware of such problems long before the test scores are recorded. The results of this year's testing may help next year's teacher in diagnosing your child's instructional needs and group placements.

WHAT PARENTS SHOULD KNOW ABOUT TEST RESULTS

Before getting overly concerned about test scores, it's important to remember that no single test should be used as an all-purpose measure. On any given day a child may perform poorly because he or she

- ▲ Is not feeling well
- • Did not understand the directions
- ■ Was tired, hungry, or distracted
- ▲ Was overly anxious about the test itself

Often the format of the test and answer sheet is so unlike any test children have taken that they simply lose their place or spend great energy on filling in those little circles. Although tests usually come with sample questions to introduce students to the format, children in the lower grades especially can easily forget what they are to do. Such "mechanical" problems are not uncommon in this age range.

Remember, too, that some children simply tense up in an exam situation. However well the teacher prepares them, there is an air in an exam room that children sense. For some it produces pressure that gets in the way of performance. In testing first-graders one year, I had a child who vomited as I began to read the first question. I've had other students who filled in every circle—in spite of clear directions—and others who cried because they did not finish all the questions in a timed section. Granted, most children take the process more or less in stride. However, it's important to recognize that in the lower grades part of the business involved simply has to do with learning how to take such tests—which is in many respects not the same thing as evaluating children's ability to handle the content of those tests.

Remember, too, that achievement tests do not predict future ability or performance. This is one of the greatest—and most destructive—notions that people often have about school aptitude and achievement tests. Some children get off to a slow start in the early grades and become excellent students. Similarly, some high-achievers in the early grades fizzle out. Achievement tests have no way of determining who these are.

Keep in mind, too, that achievement tests, with their multiple-choice questions, do not measure important skills such as children's writing, thinking, or creative abilities. In other words, they test what the test makers think should be tested but not necessarily the important things children should be learning. Unfortunately, a great deal of time and curriculum is often geared to teaching children what they will be tested on. In my last year of teaching, the school district bought pretest drill and practice booklets that were designed mainly to teach children how to handle testing formats. We actually were required to take valuable classroom time to teach six- and seven-year-olds how to fill in the grids on the covers of test books by darkening in circles that spelled their names, ages, and other information. It is not hard to imagine a better and less torturous introduction to testing than this kind of exercise in futility, nor is it difficult to imagine some of the attitudes that were being shaped and anxieties that were being planted before we even opened the test booklets.

SHOULD YOU PREPARE YOUR CHILD FOR TESTS?

Most schools do (and should) send notices home before tests are administered. Does this mean you should be "preparing" your child for the tests? The answer is yes, no, and maybe.

THINGS NOT TO DO:

▲ Avoid creating extra anxiety by telling your child how important these tests are to his whole school career. The fact is, they will probably have no effect on his college admission or the job he will ultimately have in life.

• There's no point in pushing children to do extra studying before these tests. Basically, there is no way of cramming for such tests and doing so only raises anxiety levels.

▪ Avoid playing the tests down as stupid or insignificant (even if that's what you believe). Some parents tell kids it's like a game with lots of questions they will have fun answering. That's not really true or useful information. One little boy I know decided he didn't like the "game" and simply refused to play.

THINGS TO DO:

▲ Keep your messages low-key. You don't want to pass your own testing anxiety on to your child.

• If your child comes to you and wants to talk about upcoming tests, by all means listen.

▪ Be responsive to your child's concerns. Often children need your reassurance that doing their best is all that anyone expects of them.

▲ On the night before testing you'll want to be sure the child gets a good night's rest and has adequate time for breakfast in the morning.

• Avoid lots of advice or hassling in the morning. There's no point in arguing over trifles that may send him off to school with mixed feelings of anger and guilt.

MAYBE: A good teacher will have prepared your child with a variety of test-taking strategies. If you have reason to doubt that the teacher has done this or that your child has a history of being inattentive, you may need to

▲ Talk to your child about the importance of listening carefully to the teacher's instruction.

• Tell him that if he doesn't understand the directions, he should ask the teacher for help.

▪ Older children should find out from the teacher whether they will lose points for guessing wrong answers and if they are better off skipping a question they don't know. This varies depending on the way different tests are scored.

▲ Children should also know that most achievement tests ask some questions that even the test makers don't expect most children to be able to answer, so they should not be worried or surprised by some of the harder questions.

• If they don't know an answer, they should not give up. They can give it their best guess or skip it and go on to the next questions. This is especially important on timed tests, when kids are working independently and may fixate on one problem. Tell them they can go back and fill in the answer later.

▪ Older students should be reminded to go back and check their answers if they have time left at the end.

Keep in mind that your child's work throughout the year is a better measure of achievement and ability than any single test score. Indeed, if there is a great difference between a test score and a child's usual work, there may be reason to have him or her retested. This would be especially important if decisions about grade placement or possible retention hinged on these scores. It might also be important if your child is competing for entry to a school or program in which his score falls just short of the mark.

If you are not satisfied or feel concerned about your child's scores, make an appointment to meet with his teacher. You may need to review what happened that day. For example, was the child sick the night before or did he seem unusually upset. It may be helpful to compare last year's scores with this year's. Has your child made progress or is he falling behind? How is he doing in comparison with his classmates? Is he weak in all areas or only a few? How can you work on the weak areas?

After a teacher conference, if there are problems, you may need to discuss them with your child. Talk with the teacher first to decide what might and might not be helpful for you to bring up with your child. What you want to avoid is doling out a heap of your misplaced anger or laying on a heavy dose of guilt. Talk about the problem as something that needs work and what solutions you and the teacher have discussed. Keep the focus positive. Instead of shaming the child, assure him that you're going to help him over this hurdle. The plan may mean a regular work time together, a tutor, or a combination of the two. Give your child a sense that this problem is fixable—it's something you're going to help him accomplish.

APTITUDE TESTS

Unlike achievements tests, which measure what children have been taught, aptitude tests are designed to measure abilities linked to learning, such as memory, verbal skills, reasoning, and logic. Kindergartners are frequently given reading-readiness tests, which are thought to help teachers predict if a child has the skills needed to begin formal reading instruction. Some of the most commonly used readiness tests are

Metropolitan Readiness Test
Lee-Clark Reading Readiness Test
Murphy Durrell Reading Readiness Analysis

In my own experience I was required to give such tests to first-graders in September. Frankly, the results rarely gave me information that was not already quite apparent from several weeks of working directly with the children. Indeed, from classroom discussions, children's drawings, their body language, and how they listened and reacted to stories or interacted with peers, adults, and classroom materials, I had a much fuller view than any test could offer. Furthermore, as a parent I learned early how wrong such tests can be.

Indeed, I began writing for children because of a readiness test my eldest child "failed." Although he already had a sight vocabulary, his teacher told me that she had taken him out of his reading group because he scored so poorly on his readiness test. Naturally I asked to see the test and discovered that three of the four "errors" he made were culturally biased. For example, one question asked, "Which of these tools does mother use to clean the porch?" The pictures showed a broom and a mop. The correct answer, of course, was broom. However, to clean our concrete porch I had always used a mop. Another question asked, "Which of these toys do you never use in the living room?" The "correct" answer was a tricycle. However, since we had no furniture to speak of, he had always used the center hall and living room as a regular roadway for his tricycle. In any case, four ""mistaken" answers should not have decided his reading fate in first grade. My solution was to use all the words in his preprimer in a different story and write a new book to prove that he had not merely memorized what he heard. He was not only "ready"—he was reading.

The bottom line here is that no single test should be used to evaluate or lock children in or out of programs.

IQ TESTS

Perhaps the most misunderstood tests of all are the aptitude tests known as the IQ (Intelligence Quotient) test. Such tests are used to measure a child's mental age. Interestingly enough, IQ tests were originally designed to identify those whose mental abilities were below average. Today, they are commonly used to identify children with special needs at either end of the spectrum. In other words, the scores are often used to identify children who might benefit from special classes for the gifted or those who are considered mentally retarded. IQ scores below 70 are considered retarded, 80–90 is considered below average, 90–110 is average, and scores over 110 are considered above average. Many schools require a score of 130 or more for entry to a gifted program.

Some schools administer IQ tests automatically at the end of third or fourth grade. Some IQ tests are designed to be given to whole groups, whereas others must be administered individually by a specialist. The most widely used IQ tests are

Stanford-Binet IQ Test
Lorge-Thorndike Intelligence Test
Wechsler Intelligence Scale for Children

Some educators believe that the IQ test can predict how well children will do in school, but others question its value either as a predictor or as a meaningful measure. Some psychologists say that group testing for IQ is in many instances inadequate. Test results from individually administered tests can be significantly different from tests given to groups. Children who become upset on tests or have problems with reading or following directions may score poorly in a group but do well in a one-to-one situation. Many parents (and teachers) think of an IQ score as a permanent mark and measure of a child's native abilities. The problem for most parents is that these tests make them think that "intelligence" is a concrete entity that's fixed like the color of one's eyes. In fact, it's nearly impossible, no matter what you rationally believe or know, not to feel this way when it comes to your child and such tests. Yet IQ scores do change. Indeed, some of the sections of any IQ exam test things that children have (or have not) been taught. In that respect they are not so different from achievement tests. Like the readiness tests, they have cultural biases—ones that favor white middle-class children, whose environment and experiences are reflected in their higher scores. For example, one question asks children to make the following analogy: "A shoe is to leather as a napkin is to *linen.*" It's not hard to imagine how such questions measure one's class but hardly one's intelligence.

Nor should you assume that a child with an above-average IQ will necessarily do well or better in school (or in life) than a child with an average IQ. As with the achievement tests, parents need to keep in mind that such tests are only one measure of that elusive concept, intelligence. They do not test children's creativity, their curiosity, or their appetite for learning.

GIFTED CHILDREN

For the past decade programs for the gifted have grown in popularity. Although the federal government does not mandate such programs, many states do, and individual school districts have instituted classes for the gifted whether they are mandated or not. There are educators who believe that special attention to the needs of gifted students is the only way to save our "best" minds from being wasted. Others believe that giving certain students extra attention is an elitist and therefore inappropriate approach to education in a democracy.

To further complicate matters, many educators disagree on how to identify the gifted. In many schools a student must score 130 or more on an IQ test. Indeed, in the school where I taught, the original required score was 135. However, when parents of students who scored 130–134 complained bitterly that their children were left out, the required score was lowered to make parents happy. As indicated earlier, IQ scores are only one measure of a child's abilities. Furthermore, they are rather imprecise measures. On any given day a child's score may vary by enough points to qualify or disqualify her for a gifted program. Understand that students' scores may fluctuate as much as ten points from one occasion to the next. Nor should you assume that a student with an IQ of 129 is significantly less gifted than the child who scores 130, 132, or 139. Simply put, wherever the cut-off score is placed, there will be students who will "just miss." Keep in mind, too, that a child who scores 128 in a school district that requires 130 would be gifted in a district that sets its limit at 125.

Parents should also understand that in defining who is gifted many schools fail to identify or provide programs for those who display outstanding artistic or physical abilities. Academic skills tend to outweigh creative talents or demonstrated leadership qualities. Overlooked, too, in such a test-oriented setting, is a student's performance record. As noted elsewhere, a student with a high IQ may not have as much motivation as another student with a lower IQ. While there are those who say that children with high scores and low achievement may need more stimulation, there is no guarantee that high scores will ultimately lead to high achievement nor that enrichment programs would be anything but a benefit for students with lesser scores. Indeed, many of the programs offered to the gifted would probably be of benefit to all students.

Most schools that offer programs for the gifted do so after school hours or in "pull-out" programs, whereby students are pulled out of regular class activities for their special programs. A special teacher or a classroom teacher may have the responsibility for planning activities for the gifted. Ideally such programs are not designed merely to give students more work or to teach them at the next grade level. Although such students may already read or compute at a grade level well beyond that of their classmates, the objective is rarely to hurry them on. Instead, gifted programs provide enrichment activities that encourage students to investigate whatever they are already doing in greater depth. They also bring together a group of students who are more likely to challenge each other and share like interests.

In a program for the gifted, children may be taken on field trips, work on joint projects, meet with guest experts, publish a newspaper, share readings, dramatize original plays, conduct surveys, run a science fair, go to concerts, or visit art and science museums. For some students this kind of enrichment and camaraderie with a group of peers is a welcome change from the classroom, where the teacher needs to go over material the above-average student has grasped the first time around.

However, for some children being "pulled out" is an intrusion. In my own experience, there were first- and second-graders who resented being pulled out of recess or art period. They preferred being with their classmates and disliked being cast as special in any way. Naturally, there were also those who liked to show off and boast that they were in the "gifted program" because they were smarter than others. Within the regular classroom there were also those who suffered from wounded pride at not having been anointed as a gifted one. To say that such students suffered because their parents were disappointed is, I believe, unfair. My experience indicates that children are themselves keenly aware of such labeling or differentiation. Indeed, studies indicate that such early labels can be self-fulfilling prophecies. I have known students who believed that if they were not gifted, then they must be its opposite —which by their definition was dumb.

Recognizing how such labels may affect children's self-esteem, parents will need to exercise some discretion in their own responses to gifted programs. Children should not be made to feel that making it into the gifted program (or not) is of great significance or sets them apart. Those who seem upset about not making it may need assurance that, like many other things, there are simply cutoff scores that the school must apply. It does not mean that they will not do well in school or that they are less smart. Nor should those who are accepted be treated as if they are geniuses. That, too, can backfire. Children don't like being put on a pedestal or having to live up to overblown expectations.

Whether the school rates them as gifted or not, children still need to know how to get along with those who are smarter and less smart than they are. They still need to learn how to follow as well as lead, how to treat people with respect and kindness. Whatever their scores, they still need to learn how to play and work beside people with varying talents and interests. At the same time that they are learning all of these important lessons in life, you as a parent should be helping them to develop whatever talents they have to their fullest. In doing so, you will be focusing on the gifts that make them uniquely special as warm and giving individuals, who know how to live with others as well as themselves.

There are still many fine schools that do not see the need for special programs for the gifted. In such schools instruction is individualized in the lower grades, each child moving along at his or her own speed. At every grade level there are opportunities to work at greater depth in a subject area that holds great interest. While teachers may recognize students with special gifts or talents, the program itself allows for developing each child to the fullest without prematurely labeling children who may come into their own on a slightly different timetable or at a different angle than IQ tests measure.

If you are interested in knowing more about gifted programs or your parent group is eager to see such a program in your school, the following organizations may be able to help you:

American Association for Gifted Children
15 Gramercy Park
New York, New York 10003

National Association for Gifted Children
5100 N. Edgewood Drive
St. Paul, Minnesota 55112

Program for the Education of the Gifted and Talented
U.S. Department of Education
400 Maryland Avenue, S.W.
Washington, D.C. 20202

CONFERENCES

Years ago when parents were called to school to see the teacher, it was a sure sign of trouble. In fact, teachers often used the threat,

"I'll have to call your parents," as a way of keeping children in line. In many schools today, parent-teacher conferences are no longer reserved for problem children but rather for problem solving and even problem prevention.

Conferences are typically scheduled for the parents of every student in a class once or twice a year. In some cases the conference replaces the usual report card; in others parents receive both an oral and a written report. For parents and teachers this chance to talk one-to-one about their common interests and concerns can lead to significant gains for the child.

Unlike a report card, the conference offers opportunities for two-way communication. As a parent you bring with you a kind of history and expertise about your particular child that no teacher can have. You have lived with your child longer than anyone else and will continue to do so when this academic year is done. While teachers have access to your child's academic records, what you have to say about your child's earlier experiences and current concerns can give the teacher valuable insights in working with your child. Academic records won't tell the teacher if your daughter is worried about her grandfather who's in the hospital or that your son's best friend moved away in August. Last year's school records may not indicate that Jason didn't participate in oral discussions until mid-September, nor do Amy's first-grade records show that recently she's been incredibly cranky when she comes home from school and has begun to suck her thumb—as she always does when she's anxious.

As a parent you bring to the conference not just questions but answers that can enhance the teacher's understanding of your child and her needs, fears, and interests. Unfortunately, many parents also bring their old childhood fears of the teacher to the conference room. Parents often worry about revealing too much about themselves. They may worry that the teacher will not understand their child or may be judgmental about a personal problem they're having in the family. For example, in one of my first-grade classes I had a series of conferences with a parent after her child's work took a dramatic slump in mid-winter. This formerly enthusiastic and able child became increasingly sullen and withdrawn. By spring she was not only falling behind academically, she arrived late and stood at the door crying when her mother left. What was happening here? I wondered if somehow she was on academic overload. Maybe we had gone too far too fast. Maybe she needed time to consolidate her skills, to plateau for a while without more pressure. Discussions with her mother led nowhere. Mom insisted she couldn't understand what was wrong or why there was such a change. When testing was suggested, the mother refused. It was not long after school closed that I discovered that the parents were in the process of getting divorced.

Would my knowing that have changed the previous months? In some ways, yes, I believe so. As a teacher I could not have saved the child from the unhappiness of her world at home coming apart, but I could have helped perhaps by providing a better support system. The school psychologist might have been called on to play a role in helping the child through the crisis. Whatever else I might have done, I would have been better able to understand that the daily tears had little to do with what was going on in the classroom.

Parents are often afraid that the teacher will disapprove of their life-style or their abilities as parents. What parents forget is the fact that when the school day is over, teachers are not so different from parents. In fact, many of them have sat at the other side of the conference table as parents.

As a working parent your hours may conflict with the conference schedule. Schools that value parent involvement have more flexible conference hours. Some arrange evening meetings and even provide child care services in the school library. If your school does not make such provisions, your parents organization may be able to press for such an arrangement. Short of that, you as an individual parent may need to contact the teacher and find a mutually agreeable time. You may have to settle for a telephone or early-morning conference. In most instances you will find that teachers are eager to meet with parents and will adapt to time constraints.

PREPARING FOR CONFERENCE TIME

Your child's teacher will be preparing for the conference, and so should you. She will probably have a folder with some examples of your child's work. You, too, may have some questions about assignments, grades, or papers that were brought home. If so, this is your time to ask about them.

▲ Since time is limited, you should make a list of the questions that have been on your mind. Put them in order of importance, since you may not have enough time to cover everything.

• Be prompt about arriving at the appointed hour. Teachers usually have several conferences in a row arranged. If you have a younger child, try to have a friend or sitter take over for you. Having a toddler running around the room can be distracting, to say the least. If you have no option, bring along a snack and toy that may keep the younger child busy.

▪ If both parents can make it, great. If not, before the conference ask your spouse if there are any questions or issues he or she would like you to raise.

▲ Give your child the same courtesy. Ask her what she thinks the teacher will tell you. This will clue you in on her concerns. Ask, too, if there are any problems she would like you to discuss with the teacher.

• Think of something positive to say to break the ice. You don't need to take a lot of time with it, but where possible it's nice to start out by mentioning something your child seems to be enjoying in school.

▪ Try to relax. Don't go in with preconceived notions or worry about making the ''right'' impression. Approach the teacher as another caring adult who shares in the responsibility for your child's development. Be prepared to listen as well as speak.

▲ In some instances, children in the upper grades participate in part or all of a conference. This is especially true when there is a continuing problem. It gives everyone a chance to talk about what's going on. It's a good way of saying, ''Are we all hearing the same thing? And what can we do about it?'' This should not be an occasion for putting kids on the hot seat or for the child to have to defend herself against everyone's frustration or annoyance. Even when a child has misbehaved, it's important for her to feel that the people at the conference are a potential support system, not her judges or enemies.

POSSIBLE QUESTIONS
FOR THE CONFERENCE

A good conference is a two-way opportunity and should cover your child's academic and social development. After the teacher has given you a general report, she is likely to zoom in on the areas that are problematic. You yourself may be concerned about your child's performance in certain subjects or behavior in certain areas. In either case, this is the time to ask for specific information.

The questions that follow are by no means intended as a script. Your child's individual needs will dictate the questions you'll want to raise. Here, however, are some issues you may want to discuss:

▲ I've been concerned about (penmanship, spelling, math, etc.). He doesn't seem to be improving much. Am I expecting too much or missing something you're seeing? Remember, the teacher may see positive activity in an area that looks negative from the point of view of home. For instance, a child who refuses to do any reading of significance at home may nonetheless be doing perfectly adequate reading in the classroom. One thing a parent should be doing in a conference is not just bringing up problem areas but *checking* to see if, from the school's point of view, an area is a problem area at all. On this issue, parents can sometimes be in for surprises.

• Does my child need extra help with (reading, math, writing, other areas)?

■ Are there any specific ways I can help at home? Are there books or activities you can suggest?

▲ How does he get along with other children? Does he have any special friends? Does he have problems with particular kids? What kind?

• Does my child participate in group discussions? Does he volunteer or do you have to draw him out?

■ I notice he has (a lot of/almost no) homework. Will this be true all year, or will it change? Should he need help with it? What, if any, role should I have in the homework process?

▲ I notice he brings home papers with (spelling/math/reading/good grades), but I hardly see any with (spelling/math/reading/poor grades).

• I don't always understand the grades you give. Can you explain the grading system to me?

▪ Is there any way I can help you? I have a flexible/tight schedule but you can call on me for trips, parties, meetings occasionally.

At the end of your conference you'll want to sum up what you've learned or what you've agreed to do. If there is a plan of action or specific problem ask, ''When do you think we should talk again? I'd like an update on how things are going.'' If for some reason you feel you need to talk further and the next parent is at the door, ask when you can return. Keep in mind that the teacher's afterschool hours are often scheduled with faculty meetings and preparations for the following day. Some teachers may suggest a follow-up conference by phone. Most teachers are quite willing to maintain contact. However, they should not be expected to discuss issues at length at the classroom door while children are arriving or leaving, nor should they be called at home unless there is a real emergency or they've invited you to do so.

What if you feel unhappy about the tone or outcome of a conference?

There are times when you as a parent may feel that a conference was especially unsatisfying or that a situation is not being productively handled and the conference in no way reassured you. In my own experience as a teacher, I occasionally suggested that a parent speak with the school principal or perhaps with the school psychologist. If the teacher doesn't suggest it, you as a parent certainly have that right. Without making a bad situation worse, you can let the teacher know that you'd like another opinion or other suggestions and feel you would like to meet with the principal. This need not be said in anger or as a threat. Most teachers will respect your concern and welcome your interest. At least, you will have been forthright about what you are doing instead of giving the impression of ''going over her head.''

FOLLOWING UP
AFTER THE CONFERENCE

Your child is definitely going to want to know, ''What did the teacher say?'' That's fair. After all, that's what the conference was about. Share what you feel is appropriate. Give him the good news as well as the other kind. Of course, not everything at the conference between parent and teacher is necessarily to be shared with the child. In most instances the positive should be emphasized over the negative.

Discuss what the teacher suggested and how you can work on those suggestions. Set up a game plan and act on it. If you know there should be spelling words coming home on Monday night, put it on the calendar to remind both of you. If you know there's math homework that's not being handed in, talk about it and make it your business to check if work has been done before the evening wears on.

As a temporary plan you may be asked to date and sign homework or test results and return them to the school. This kind of checking up sometimes helps students establish more consistent work patterns. Ultimately, of course, the objective should be for the child to take responsibility for handing in assignments or bringing home papers.

WHEN YOU SHOULD REQUEST A CONFERENCE

▲ Any dramatic change in behavior and/or performance that continues for an extended period of time needs your attention. An occasional paper with poor work or a sad story about a falling out with a friend is to be expected. However, when such events happen repeatedly, a conference—or at least a phone conversation with the teacher—may provide clarification and a course of action.

• Your child seems to be having repeated problems with assignments or tells you he has none (and you suspect otherwise). Better to check this out with the teacher. The child may be telling the truth or covering up. Together you and the teacher can come up with a joint strategy for handling the situation.

▪ If there is an extraordinary family problem, such as a death, serious illness, or marital strife, it may be important to let the teacher know about the situation.

▲ Your child comes home and tells you the teacher said or did something of which you totally disapprove. Make an appointment but don't assume the worst. Kids are not always entirely accurate reporters. If the report was true, discuss your point of view openly. There's nothing to be gained by getting into a shouting match.

• If your child is going to be out of school for a week or more, it's important to contact the teacher. She may want to send work home and even give you guidelines on how to help. This can make a big difference when your child is ill or has to go out of town with you.

REPORT CARDS

In my teaching experience the subject of report card revisions surfaced on a regular basis. Over the years, despite the efforts of one committee after another and several new forms, no perfect report card was ever designed.

At best, a report card can only give you a general notion of how your child is doing. It cannot answer questions about why your daughter is having trouble with math or what you can do to help. It does not explain whether your son's grade in spelling reflects a comparison with that of his classmates or his own previous work. In some instances, the card may indicate that a child is doing excellent work in reading but neglect to tell you that the child is working with the slowest reading group and is a year behind most second-graders.

Elementary school report cards use a variety of codes for grading. In one school the highest grade may be an S for satisfactory, whereas in others it may be an A. How the grades are arrived at may be on the basis of test scores, evaluation of participation, or a combination of the two. Often the most informative part of a report card is the written comment, if space is provided or the teacher takes the trouble to use such space. Unfortunately, in my own experience, the provision for such comments was limited to two sentences at best.

While most schools continue to depend on traditional report cards, many use written reports and parent conferences. In such schools, parents and teachers have at least two conferences a year, and teachers write two anecdotal reports a year. These reports include a description of the child as a member of the group; observations about her social and emotional growth and her study skills (if she is an older child); descriptions of her work in art, music, woodworking, and physical education, and examples of her thinking; as well as progress reports on academic subjects. This kind of report is obviously a much fuller description of a child than letter grades can convey.

Whether you get a graded or written report, you can, if it seems appropriate, use this occasion for discussing your child's schoolwork with her. Remember, even a poor report usually has some positive notes. Try to start off with some of the good news. Talk about what's going on in the bad news department. Get your child's point of view and talk together about possible steps for improvement. Where possible, give praise for grades or comments that indicate progress.

If you are concerned about any of the grades or comments, call for an appointment with the teacher. Discuss the matter and ask if the teacher has any suggestions about how you can help. Although you may feel justifiably upset about your child's lack of progress, there's no reason to go into the conference feeling ashamed or apologetic. Nor should you let the matter drift and hope for a better report card next time. Acting promptly can keep a problem from growing out of neglect. It also shows your child that this is a matter of concern and that you are interested enough to become involved in the remedy.

Should children be punished or rewarded for their grades? Most experts agree that the carrot-and-stick approach seldom works effectively. They also feel that children should find their own rewards in doing well. Indeed, many educators believe that bribes are counterproductive and promote extrinsic motivation at the expense of building intrinsic values. Does that mean one should never reward good grades? Not at all. Like all of us, children enjoy a pat on the back. There's nothing wrong with celebrating success in small but appropriate ways that say, "Well done!" The thing to avoid is getting locked into an "if you do this, I'll do that" mentality. In my own experience I've found that the motivation to do well could rarely be achieved by bribes alone. No matter how well resolved a child may be to "do better," if he needs help with division or with organizing work habits, his best intentions or the biggest bribe will not suffice. First, he needs help getting to the root of the problem and solving that.

Often parents respond to poor grades by taking away children's privileges or limiting their social life. If your child is spending too much time with friends or TV, he undoubtedly needs help in using his time more wisely. That's the important message. The object is not so much to punish the child but rather to help him shape his priorities and to help him see the connections between his efforts and their outcome. Linking these steps directly to the arrival of a report card and a set of bad grades may not be the most effective way of going about this.

DEALING WITH THE HIERARCHY

Five-year-old Sarah comes off the bus with wet pants and tears. "The teacher wouldn't let me go to the bathroom!" she cries. "That's the rule!"

Next door, six-year-old Matthew is telling his mom how the teacher let him scratch her back because he did such good writing today. "Scratch her back?" his mom wonders. Is that the way she rewards good work? Talking with other parents from the same class, she discovers that Matt's teacher not only has a strange way of doling out rewards, her punishment routines involve tying kids to their seats.

What do you do when kids come home with tales that make your hair stand on end? Do you call the teacher or do you go directly to the principal? In fact, there is no blanket rule that can cover all situations.

Sarah's mom called the principal. I know, because I was the teacher. The truth was that there was no rule that prevented Sarah from going to the bathroom. Indeed, Sarah's mom should have guessed as much, since Sarah was a terrific storyteller. On the very first day of school she had told me that her mother had died and she had to take care of herself and make her own dinner. After school that day I called her home to see if there was anything I could do to help. You can imagine my reaction when her mom answered the phone. The point is, Sarah's mom should have called me directly instead of the principal. I did, of course, make a point of explaining again to the class that anyone could go to the bathroom whenever they needed to. I also allowed more time at the end of the day for getting ready for the bus and reminded kids that this was a good time for going to the bathroom.

On the other hand, after speaking with several parents and verifying the stories, Matt's mom went with a group of parents directly to the principal. Clearly, this was a situation that required supervision, attention, and action. After observation the teacher was replaced.

As suggested earlier, in most instances a problem in the classroom should be addressed first with the teacher. There's no point in getting children needlessly caught in the crossfire of a war between parent and teacher. Unfortunately, some teachers pay back parental complaints to the principal by taking aim at the children. While there are situations that are worth that risk, whenever possible start by making your concerns known to the teacher. If you are still unsatisfied, move on to the next level of authority.

In most instances the principal will listen to your problem and help decide on the next step. Sometimes a three-way meeting with parents, teacher, and principal can iron things out, or the principal may suggest that other specialists in the school need to evaluate the situation.

But what if the problem you're having is not addressed to your satisfaction? Where do you go next? Your next step is to make an appointment with the authority over the principal. In a public school this is generally the superintendent of your school district. In a private school you may need to take your problem to your school board representative. In a large school district there may be several assistants to the superintendent who deal with various kinds of problems. You may need to explain your dilemma in order to reach the right person. Try to keep your cool but be persistent. If phone calls don't work, put your story on paper, make a copy, and mail it. If you do not receive a prompt reply, you may need to take your problem on to the school board or, in some cases, even hire an attorney to represent your child's interests. Of course, that would be a scenario for only the most extreme kinds of problem. For example, if the school is not providing an appropriate program for a child with a handicapping condition, you might need an advocate to press the issue, or if your child's civil liberties are being breached, again you might need a lawyer to articulate the child's rights.

Keep in mind that in acting as an advocate for your child's rights for an education, you will generally do best by enlisting others' goodwill rather than stirring up their ire. Most administrators are eager to please parents, if only because it's easier to help than to have you on their back (or their phone) or in their office.

This is not to say that they have no real concerns about children. Many are genuinely concerned—even dedicated—and can be enlisted as allies.

In addressing an ongoing problem with teachers or administration, parents must also remember to use judgment in what they share with children. Annoyed or angry as you may be with the "rules" or inefficiency of school personnel, calling the teacher an idiot or the rules "ridiculous" can only give your child the impression that he need not respect the teacher or the rules. By all means, work toward changing what you can, but avoid giving your child the idea that you have no respect for the system or the school's authority. All too often children caught up in such struggles make matters worse for themselves. By following parental example they take it upon themselves to talk back or challenge the teacher's authority, and the original problem snowballs into a much bigger one.

On the one hand, you want your child to know that you appreciate his situation and are doing what you can to straighten it out. On the other hand, you need to temper what you say and do so that the child can function in what you and he may consider a less than perfect situation. Keep in mind that you may not be able to get him transferred to another class or change the school's rules about detention and tardiness. If you make sweeping proclamations about what you're going to demand and then find yourself powerless, chances are your child is going to mistrust both your authority and the school's.

WHAT ARE THEY TEACHING MY CHILD?

Situations may sometimes arise in which you disagree with what the teacher is teaching your child, or there may be a school policy that you feel is inappropriate or even illegal. In either case you need to evaluate the best course of action.

Let's take a farfetched example. Suppose your child's teacher believes that the world is flat, and that is what she is teaching her class. Clearly, she has the right to her personal beliefs. However, she does not have the right to inculcate her personal views upon children. As a parent you can insist that she stop giving children misinformation. However, let's suppose you believe the earth is flat and you are annoyed that the teacher is teaching your child that the earth is round. As a parent you are free to share your private views with your child, but you cannot insist that the teacher alter the curriculum to fit your view of the world. You can try, but you are unlikely to succeed with this kind of issue.

In the event that you are in conflict either with the teacher or the school's policy, you have the right to question or challenge that policy. But doing so does not necessarily mean you will succeed. Many people confuse the right to object with the right to win. Before rushing into a confrontation, in each case, you will need to know as much about an issue as possible. The better informed you are, the more likely you are to succeed. It can also help you decide whether or not you want to proceed and how to do so.

To begin with, you need to know who made the particular rule or policy to which you are objecting. In many instances schools are governed by federal and state laws. As a result, for example, the schools in your state may require that all kindergartners have proof of immunization shots. If you object on religious grounds, you may succeed in having your child exempted from this rule, but you are not likely to change the statewide policy. Indeed, a parent who objects for other reasons may not even succeed in getting an exemption.

Although you may object to the Supreme Court decision under the Constitution that prohibits organized prayer in schools, you are unlikely to succeed in changing a public school's policy, nor can students in the public schools be required to say the pledge of allegiance to the flag, although their teacher and class may do so. Indeed, although some schools have ignored the Court's decision, if a parent objects to his child's saying prayers or the pledge and that parent brings an action to stop such practices, he is likely to win. Unless the Supreme Court's rulings are changed, public schools cannot overstep the law. As a parent, you can pray with your child before he leaves for school or you can tell him to say a silent prayer before he begins his work, but you cannot insist that everyone else do so. You also have the option of enrolling your child in a private school that reflects your values, but you cannot impose those beliefs in the public schools.

Similarly, let's suppose you find the language in a library book or textbook offensive. Can you insist that the book be removed? Not really. You can voice your concern, and the school is likely to review your objections. However, by and large, the selection of books for the classroom is not left to parents. In most states that power is invested in the hands of schools and state departments of education. Does this mean there's no point in objecting? Not at all. If you know that a book is outdated or contains incorrect information, you should bring this to the attention of the teacher and/or principal. However, if your concerns center on what you consider inappropriate language or ideas, you are stepping into a gray area. School officials are more likely to override your objections on the grounds that removing the book would condone censorship and give parents control of the curriculum.

In most instances schools review parental objections to books on a case-by-case basis. Often they have a book review policy. Parents are asked to write their complaints on a form that is then reviewed by a committee. Obviously, the success of your case will depend on who's listening. In a liberal community, for instance, you are more likely to get a sympathetic finding to your objection that a book is racist. Keep in mind, too, that often the book review policy is not designed to get books removed but rather to make parents feel they have exercised their rights and aired their views. This can be a tactic to defuse an issue without bringing about any real change. Once parents have expressed their opinions, the committee is probably going to review the book with the same criteria that put the book into the school to begin with. Even where a book review group is organized, the hope is that the problem will go away. From the school's point of view the review procedure may also be a way of dealing with one parent, which is preferable to dealing with a hundred at a school board meeting.

In part, this defensive stance is understandable. Once an issue over school books flairs, groups sometimes get caught up in the heat of the debate and what they perceive as a good cause. No matter how well-meaning they may be, such committees can pose a real threat to what children will learn and even what publishers choose to print. As a writer I recently did an adaptation for a textbook of Mark Twain's *Connecticut Yankee in King Arthur's Court*. In it I included a scene from the book that denounces slavery. You may be surprised to learn that the editor wanted to delete that part of the story on the grounds that in some communities parents would object and the book would be unsalable. It may be hard to believe, but out of fear of not satisfying everyone, publishers may sanitize their texts, diluting their content to make it more palatable to an articulate and noisy minority.

Public furor can also lead some parents to take sides with the best talkers. Those who participate in the process should not take someone else's word or opinion about any book. Intellectual honesty requires that you take the time to read the whole text for yourself. Those who fail to do so are almost certain to lose their case. Keep in mind that the easiest way for school officers to deal with you is if you don't know what you're talking about. Parents who don't bother to read the questionable material are also making a mistake in terms of the example they set for their own children.

In the long run, whether you win or lose, it behooves you to read the material, not so much to censor it but so that you can deal with it via-à-vis your own child. In the event your child is expected to read what you consider inappropriate material, you at least will have an informed position that can help you to balance the picture in your own home. There, you also have the right to control what is read. You can forbid certain reading, but often at the risk of making forbidden fruit more desirable. By censoring less and being better informed you will be better able to discuss and convey your own point of view. Remember, too, that children do not, in fact, receive the ideas in books uncritically. Some people believe that books and ideas can't harm. Others are less sure how a book will be received. As a parent you have an opportunity to help children become critical readers and thinkers. This cannot be done in a vacuum. Indeed, learning to evaluate and deal with multiple points of view is one of the goals of becoming an educated person.

But the problem does not arise solely with regard to books. You may object to the school's dress code, their approach to drug or sex education, or any number of other issues and ideas that are different from your own. In each instance you will need to evaluate whether you want to act or not. Remember that not every right needs to be asserted to its limit. Parents also need to consider the social and cultural implications of objecting. Pursuing an issue may have a serious effect on your child, which may or may not be worth the struggle. If, for example, your child is in a private school and you object to the way they celebrate holidays or teach math, you may have few options short of withdrawing from that school; or you might be prepared to live with that policy while explaining to your child that "It's not what we do in our home."

In dealing with such decisions you will also need to know when to get in and when to stay out. For example, when our daughter was in fifth grade, the school had a policy that said girls could only wear slacks on Fridays. Oddly enough, in other schools in the same district both students and teachers could wear slacks any day of the week. Why was that? she wanted to know. We suggested that she ask the principal. A few hours later the principal called my husband's law office to find out what he intended to do. We knew, as did the principal, that the policy was illegal in the public school.

We all learned a great deal from that experience. Rather than doing it for her, we encouraged her to take the issue to the right person. We were prepared to back her up if necessary, and the principal knew we would do so. He also knew that the policy could not be enforced. Faced with an issue, you need to evaluate how best to approach it. Sometimes it is possible for the child to handle a problem without the need for a major confrontation. Of course, you need to ask yourself, can your child handle it? The younger the child, the less likely he is to be able to do so.

In almost every instance the procedure you follow will be the same :

▲ Begin by being well informed.

• Start small rather than igniting an emotional fire.

▪ Ask questions of those most directly involved. If you are objecting to something the teacher reportedly said, go to the teacher first and be prepared to listen. Remember, children don't always report accurately and may misinterpret information.

▲ If for some reason you feel you cannot go directly to the teacher, go up the ladder to the next level. In most instances this will be the principal.

• Know from the start that you may assert your objections and still not succeed in bringing about the desired change.

▪ Evaluate the issue to determine its importance to you and your child in order to decide how far you are willing to carry your objectives.

• ▪ ▲

ELEMENTARY-AGE CHILDREN AND COMPUTERS

In the early eighties, when the computer revolution was coming alive, articles in newspapers and magazines speculated endlessly about how technology would change education. The time would come, some said, when every student would have a desktop terminal and an individualized software program. As with earlier innovations, from calculators to educational TV, promises of better teaching and new kinds of learning were in the air. Overnight many schools launched programs to train teachers. Those with large enough budgets bought expensive computer labs. In less affluent communities, parents groups baked cakes and ran fundraisers for new equipment. No one wanted to be left behind.

From kindergarten to the workplace, the buzzword of the day was *computer literacy*—although the definition of this term meant different things to different people. More often than not, *computer literacy* was translated to mean "learning to program"—that is, learning a computer language such as BASIC or Pascal. Such literacy often also included deadly lessons on the history of computers. Given the high cost of equipment and staffing, some schools offered minicourses to "expose" kids, as if one could actually learn a new language from a six-week course or from twenty minutes of instruction once a week.

There is still no universal approach to computers in the classroom. Educators today have strong doubts about the value of teaching all children to program. Those who are now more familiar with computers know that programming is a rather specialized discipline that calls for more abstract thinking than most young children are developmentally prepared to do. Although some schools do introduce children to the use of the computer language known as LOGO, others put more emphasis on using the computer as a tool for other skills. During fourth and fifth grades many students begin to use child-oriented word processing programs for writing. The ease of making corrections and editing sometimes has great appeal to young writers. Other schools put more emphasis on using computer software and computer "games" for drill and practice lessons in math, spelling, and other areas that lend themselves to right and wrong answers. Although the latter is the most limited

January 3, 1777

Dear Lauren,

I have persued my promise to you when I said I was coming to America. I have become a printer. I make all of the newspapers for the town. I studied how to do this ever since I came to Jamestown. Despite the way it seems this job is quite a bloody challenge.

I have a very small one room log cabin. It is very quaint with just the mere assets like a fire place a bed, a table and so on. All of that is fit into one room. Never the less every thing I need is available and it doesn't get too cold in the winter. I still sit up on my bed even though it doesn't get that cold I still would rather be healthey than ill.

Now back to my job. The job of making the newspaper is harder then I expected it would be. It usually takes me a month to finish one newspaper! The hardest thing I think about making the newspaper is copying it. It takes me a whole day to make 200 copies. To make the newspaper I have to first place every letter into place on a metal board. I have memorize were all of the letters are places since I have been doing it for so long.

There are a lot of very nice stores here. There is even a broom shop. Imagin a whole shop just for brooms. At the broom shop there are two diffrent kinds of brooms. One broom is very little and the other broom is regular size. We have many other stores like a drug store, a toy store for the little children and of course we have a blacksmith. I almost forgot we have a print shop but I sort of figured you knew that since I told you I was a printer.

There are a few farmers here so therefore some of the space is taken up from there land and there barns. There is a school house here for all grades. The school is very strict and I think that has some thing to do with that the teacher is depressed because she is not allowed to do most things that everyone else does. You know she isn't allowed to ride off in a carrige or see any man that is not her father or brother.

Lauren I hope you come visit this lovely town, but till then I say goodby. But one more thing that you might of thought I forgot. Happy Birthday!

Your brother,
Peter S. Ellman

This letter combines social studies, writing, and word-processing skills. Age 12.

kind of computer use, for many youngsters the impersonal computer is a good drillmaster. It is a potentially less judgmental experience than having a teacher or a classmate quizzing them. It allows students to work at their own pace and get as much repetition as they need.

Like all the new technology introduced into the schools, the arrival of computers was linked to exaggerated expectations. They have not replaced teachers, nor have they changed the way children think or learn. While some schools try to push computers as a special feature to attract parents, your child will not be "left behind" if he doesn't have computers in kindergarten or even in the primary grades. By fourth grade your school will probably offer some form of computer use. To evaluate that program, it's important to understand how computers are being used—that is, the way humans are organizing the technology.

▲ Are there enough terminals so that all the children in the room have adequate opportunities to use the equipment on a regular basis?

• How much time does each student actually get at the keyboard? Is there a schedule, or do only the most assertive kids get their turn?

■ Is there a variety of software? Is it all drill and practice? Are there any open-ended programs that allow kids to explore drawing, writing, or music?

▲ Are children learning to use the computer for word processing to develop writing skills?

• Do the children see the teacher use the computer for her own needs? Teachers who feel at home with the computer are more apt to give that sense of competence to their students.

The main thing to remember here is that no matter how organized or how much the hype, computers are still a minor issue in schooling and not an issue in itself that should be crucial in the various decisions you make about schooling for your child.

If you have a personal computer at home, chances are your son or daughter will enjoy exploring it. Children as young as five or six like to play simple games and use music and art software programs. By seven or eight many enjoy using word processing programs to write stories or make posters. Older children will use it for homework, game playing, and some math. They may even be interested in exploring simple programming. Keep in mind that many children find written assignments much easier to accomplish (and especially to correct) when they have access to a computer. For many who simply hate writing, the opportunity to use the machine often makes the prospect of writing less distasteful. You will find specific software suggestions in the primary and intermediate chapters.

Should you go out and buy a computer as soon as your child enters school? Not really. There's no reason to fear that your child will miss the boat if you don't have a personal computer and lots of software. In fact, once the novelty wears off, kids don't generally use so-called ''educational'' software voluntarily, nor does such software teach lessons kids can't learn without an electronic quizmaster.

CHILDREN WITH HANDICAPPING CONDITIONS

Most children who come to school learn the basic skills on a fairly predictable timetable. Although some blossom earlier than others, the vast majority of children master beginning skills in reading, writing, and math during the primary years. Of course, there are some children who do not. There are children who are born with mental or physical handicaps that evidence themselves at birth or during the early years. Other disabilities may not show up until a child reaches school age.

By law parents should know that public schools are required to identify and provide programs for all children, whatever handicaps they may have. Schools must not only provide a plan for dealing with handicaps, they must involve you in the decisions they are making.

In some instances a child's physical, emotional, or mental handicap may require a special program outside the scope of a regular classroom. In many instances, the school may design a schedule that combines instruction for part of the day with a specialist along with time in a regular mainstream classroom. Instead of isolating children in special classes, educators now believe that a great many handicapping conditions are better handled by enabling children to work alongside their agemates most of the day, while still providing individual instruction for short periods of time. Such pull-out programs give all children opportunities to learn about living in a world that includes people with and without handicaps.

Until the early 1970s, however, schools either turned away children with handicaps or isolated them in special classrooms. In the school I attended as a child, there was a class known as the opportunity grade. It did not take any of us "regular" kids long to know that entry to that class represented anything but an opportunity. Except for their annual sale of Christmas cards and crafts, the opportunity class and its inhabitants were to be avoided. They were "different."

Today, educators believe that such isolation is frequently unnecessary and even inappropriate. Instead of viewing children in terms of their handicaps, a more holistic approach recognizes the importance of looking at children in terms of their total development. For example, a child who gets about in a wheelchair may need ramps instead of steps, but socially, emotionally, and intellectually he is more like his agemates than not. Similarly, a mildly retarded child or one with a hearing impairment or visual problems may need a special program and extra teaching time, but he or she can function in and benefit from spending part of the day in a regular mainstream classroom.

Indeed, advocates of "mainstreaming" believe that the benefits are real for all children, handicapped or not. In a sense, the mainstream classroom then better reflects the real world, where people with and without handicaps work and live together.

With the enactment of the Rehabilitation Act of 1973 and the Education of All Handicapped Children Act of 1975, the federal government mandated that public schools are required to provide

▲ A free and appropriate education to all children, regardless of their handicaps
• That children be placed in the "least restrictive environment" possible
▪ That the school design an Individualized Education Program (IEP) to meet the specific needs of each handicapped child

Of course, children with severe physical or emotional handicaps may still need more full-time individualized programs than the regular classroom can provide. For such students a regular class would be inappropriate. However, for thousands of children the mainstream approach coupled with "pull-out" sessions with specialists has provided a richer and fuller educational experience. Federal law and funds are available for children who may have handicapping conditions such as autism, emotional disturbances, hearing impairment or deafness, learning disabilities, long-term or chronic ailments, mental retardation, or physical impairment. To know your rights you may find the following publications useful:

94-142 and 504: Numbers That Add Up to Educational Rights for Handicapped Children
Children's Defense Fund
122 C Street, N.W.
Washington, D.C. 20001

Special Ed Checkup: What Federal Law Requires in Educating Your Child
National Committee for Citizens in Education
410 Wilde Lake Village Green
Columbia, Maryland 21044

LEARNING DISABILITIES

Quite apart from severe physical or mental handicaps, some children suffer from handicapping conditions known loosely as learning disabilities. Studies indicate that 15 percent of all children have some kind of learning or language disabilities, and that is considered a conservative estimate. However, part of the problem in counting heads is built into the definition of *learning disabilities*. According to the U.S. Department of Education, the definition is as follows:

> *"Specific learning disability" means a disorder in one or more of the basic psychological processes involved in understanding or in using language, spoken or written, which may manifest itself in an imperfect ability to listen, think, speak, read, write, spell, or do mathematical calculations. The term includes such conditions as perceptual handicaps, brain injury, minimal brain disfunction, dyslexia, and developmental aphasia. The term does not include children who have learning problems which are primarily the result of visual, hearing, or motor handicaps, of mental retardation, of emotional*

disturbances, or of environmental, cultural or economic dis-advantage.

Of course, the definition is so broad and undefined that it is small wonder it is of little use to educators or parents. Indeed, there are many children who under this definition would at some stage or other be labeled as learning disabled. In part, that is exactly what has been going on. It's almost as if any problem a child may be having is easier to cope with once it has a label. As a result, a lot of teachers and parents use the words *learning disabled* as a catchall to explain away otherwise unexplainable lags in learning or even children who, at a given stage, seem troublesome to the teachers or "disruptive" in the classroom. Frequently, too, one hears people saying, "I'm sure she has dyslexia! Look at how she writes her letters backward."

While writing letters backward is one symptom of dyslexia, the truth is most children of five, six, or even seven do occasionally reverse letters and numbers. They do not necessarily have dyslexia or any other learning disorder. The symptoms of dyslexia are far more complex than letter reversals. Identifying those who suffer from dyslexia and other learning disabilities requires exams administered by specialists.

Avoid trying to diagnose your child's problems. If you have concerns, by all means speak to the teacher and ask her if she feels your child should be tested. If you cannot get the school to respond or act promptly, talk to your child's pediatrician or ask the doctor or school to refer you for private testing.

Keep in mind that learning disabilities show themselves in a variety of behaviors.

SYMPTOMS OF LEARNING DISABILITIES

True learning or language disabilities need professional intervention. They can affect a child's academic, social, and emotional life. All too often such children are accused of being lazy or told they could do better if only they tried. As a result, the learning-disabled child has to deal not only with his or her disorder but with negative feelings that eat away at self-esteem and motivation. If you're an adult who can't hit a tennis ball, you don't volunteer to play tennis. However, when you're a child, you often get shoved onto the "tennis court" whether you're ready, willing, and able or not.

Living with a child with learning disorders calls for sensitive attention to his emotional as well as his intellectual needs. Parents need to focus on the child's abilities as well as his disabilities. Remember, the underlying disorder is not going to disappear overnight. Learning to compensate and find viable strategies takes time and a support system of caring and knowledgeable adults. Children with learning disabilities can and do make progress, but they also need assurance that they are not dumb and that the struggle is worth the effort. It may help to know that the majority of learning/language-disabled children have average to above-average IQs. Indeed, one of the symptoms of a learning disorder is a marked discrepancy between a child's potential and his or her performance.

Typically, young children with learning disabilities have difficulties in remembering names of objects, learning the alphabet, understanding directions, processing and producing language, and consequently learning to read, write, spell, or do math.

Identifying learning disabilities is difficult and calls for careful diagnosis. Children (and adults) with learning disorders may have problems with

- Focusing their attention
- Verbal communication
- Processing visual information
- Memory
- Fine motor coordination
- Sequencing ideas or ordinary time and events

These are just a few of the most typical disorders, and one child may suffer from a combination of such problems that affect performance in school, on the playground, and for years to come.

Recognizing such multiple problems is not easy. Almost all children at one time or another may exhibit some of these behaviors. Those with true learning disorders will differ in the degree to which such behaviors are displayed. Here are some patterns that in combination over a prolonged period may indicate the need for intervention:

- Poor academic performance by a child who seems capable of much better work
- Poor performance despite great efforts to do otherwise
- Impulsive behavior

▲ Depression and loss of motivation to keep trying
● Inability to make or keep friends or feel at ease communicating with peers
■ Inconsistent performance in academic work—big swings from great work to disasters
▲ Difficulty following oral directions
● Knows how to shape letters and/or has ideas for stories but can't control pencil and get ideas from head to paper
■ Problems recalling information
▲ Difficulty with tasks that involve several steps or organizing one's time

Identifying a learning disability is just the beginning. More important perhaps is how to treat such problems. Children with learning disabilities can learn techniques that may not take the disability away but that do allow them to cope with the problem in productive ways. For example, a child who has difficulty with writing skills because of fine motor problems may be able to dictate a story on tape or learn to type it on the word processor or typewriter. In most instances, learning disabilities are not "cured"; rather, children are given strategies for functioning around them.

If you are dealing with a learning disability, it may be useful for you to know about the following organizations:

Association for Children and Adults with Learning Disabilities
4156 Library Road
Pittsburgh, Pennsylvania 15234

The Council for Exceptional Children
1920 Association Drive
Reston, Virginia 22091

Office of Special Education and Rehabilitation Services
U.S. Department of Education
Washington, D.C. 20202

Remember, too, that children who are having difficulty with learning may respond by venting their frustration through misbehaving or drawing back from group activities. Once the root of the problem is recognized and treated, some of the other behaviors may disappear.

PSYCHOLOGICAL SERVICES

If a student is having consistent learning and/or behavior problems, the teacher may suggest that the child be evaluated by the school psychologist. Teachers are not trained to diagnose learning or emotional problems. Indeed, the two are often intertwined. A child who is having an emotional crisis may have problems with academic work, while failures in academics may trigger behavior problems. Although a teacher (or parent) often recognizes that a student is having difficulty, the job of identifying the cause of such problems usually requires a different kind of expertise.

Parents often become distraught at the suggestion that their child should see the psychologist. Many react with anger. Typically parents respond, "So, you think my child is crazy!" "My child does not need a shrink!" or "I don't believe in that kind of mumbo jumbo!" Others become defensive, fearing that the child's problems are a reflection of their failures as parents. Still others are afraid that in allowing the child to be tested they will have left a permanent mark on their child's school records that will mar his or her entire school career. For all of these reasons, many parents resist or refuse to allow the school to do any testing.

Although it is understandable that parents have such feelings, the fact that psychological evaluation is suggested does not mean that the teacher thinks your child is in any way mentally ill, nor does it mean that you are a rotten parent. A referral often simply indicates that the teacher wants and needs extra guidance in doing a better job with your child. Such testing is not generally done without first discussing the reasons with parents. In fact, in many instances, legally the school must have parental approval before it can administer such tests. The fact that the psychologist's report may be in your child's file does not mean he will be labeled for life. Indeed, legally you are entitled to read and challenge any objectional material in that file (see pages 265–67). Parents fear that such records will affect their child's future academic career. However, the lack of appropriate intervention, if needed, will do far more long-term damage than a record that indicates the child was tested. Nor can schools legally release such records to other schools without your written consent.

Having said all that, if you still feel uncomfortable about allowing the school to proceed, you should at least consider going to a psychologist in private practice or seeking a consultation at a community mental health agency. Some parents may feel more comfortable consulting first with their family doctor or pediatrician. Others prefer to seek counseling from their family minister, priest, or rabbi, many of whom have specific training in family counseling.

How Do You Know When Your Child Needs Help?

Anyone who lives with children knows that problems are a normal part of life in the classroom or the family. Yet all problems do not need professional intervention. So how do you know when a child needs help? What are the signs that a problem is more than a passing phase? Here are some signals that can help you know:

▲ If an experienced teacher recommends that your child is having learning or behavior problems, that is certainly a signal for attention. Keep in mind that the key word here is *experienced*. Teachers who have worked with dozens of children over the years are usually able to recognize problems that need intervention.

• When a child who has been relatively cooperative and easy to get along with becomes very hostile or rebellious and things keep getting more and more difficult, this, too, may be a signal. Of course, most children do test limits and are occasionally argumentative. The difference here is in degree and persistence. If no one can say a word to him without his flying off the handle and all the things you try aren't working, you should recognize the need for help. Even if the school isn't calling and saying this child is in trouble, you as a parent should know you're seeing a signal.

▪ Prolonged sleep disturbances are another signal. An occasional nightmare is not unusual. However, a child who has persistent "night terrors," who has difficulty coming out of the sleeping state when you try to awaken or comfort him, and for whom the terrors persist may need professional intervention.

▲ Prolonged eating disturbances are another signal. Children as young as ten and eleven sometimes become obsessed with their weight and overly involved with dieting and being thin. This is a situation that needs immediate attention.

• A child who has been a good student but suddenly, without a clear pattern, has a dramatic change in school performance is revealing a trouble signal. Of course, some fluctuation in grades is normal and no cause for alarm. However, a marked shift in competence or a real plunge that persists should be a matter for concern.

▪ Marked mood changes are another signal. Again, all of us have our ups and downs. However, a child who has been reasonably stable but becomes depressed for more than just a few days may need professional intervention. Sometimes even though the child may be able to say it's because "my friend moved" or "my dog died," she can't break out of it. She may limit her social contacts and/or show signs of eating or sleeping problems. If the mood doesn't begin to change, certainly within a month, you should seek counseling.

▲ Regressing to behavior that is no longer age-appropriate is another signal of trouble. Children as old as seven or eight may have an occasional accident and lose bladder or bowel control. However, when this happens consistently for several weeks, it is another matter. Similarly, a significant loss of cognitive function can signal trouble. For example, an eight-year-old who has no trouble making himself understood but suddenly displays a notable lack of speech is signaling the need for help.

• Keep in mind that in some instances there are traumas in our own adult lives that have serious repercussions on our children. Rather than waiting for a child to fall apart, it may be helpful to both parents and children to seek expert advice as a preventive measure. Professional intervention or simply advice may help you in handling the predictable but often painful realities that come with the death of a sibling or parent, severe prolonged illness, divorce, severe losses, accidents, and other catastrophic situations. In such circumstances parents themselves may need support with their own grief as well as guidance in helping their children.

DEALING WITH SCHOOL PHOBIA

At one time or another most children will balk about going to school. They may come up with mysterious aches and pains or other complaints to avoid going. Most of us can recall phony stomachaches or sore throats when our homework was due or a dreaded test was scheduled. On an occasional basis such behavior is to be expected. However, for some children such behavior becomes a pattern that is symptomatic of school phobia. Although the temptation is to be firm or ride it out, often the best solution is to seek help from the school psychologist.

With young children the underlying problem frequently begins with difficulty in separating from home and family. Often, bringing the child to school and spending an extra few minutes with him in the classroom helps the child cross the first hurdle from one world to the other (see pages 64–67). Many children need a few days or weeks to make a smooth transition between the two worlds. However, some children not only find it difficult to make the break, they are unable to stay in school once they arrive. In such instances professional help is needed.

Older children who suffer from school phobia more typically are struggling with specific school-related problems rather than separation issues. They may be fearful of criticism by peers or teachers or having difficulty performing in class or gym.

In some instances a three-way conference with the child, parent, and teacher will improve matters. This is particularly true with older students, who are better able to articulate what they are feeling. However, with children of any age, once the problem has become a pattern that recurs over a period of weeks (or months), professional intervention is needed. Unfortunately, such problems are unlikely to solve themselves.

WHAT THE SCHOOL PSYCHOLOGIST DOES

In most schools the psychologist begins by observing your child in a variety of ways. She will visit your child's classroom and observe his behavior with the teacher and his classmates. She may also want to interview both you and your spouse. She will talk with your child informally and in some schools may give him or her a variety of tests. Your child may be given IQ and personality tests.

On the basis of both her observations and the testing, the psychologist will then give you a report of her findings. She will also make recommendations about how the school can best help your child. She may work directly with the classroom teacher on a strategy for handling your child's needs or indicate that your child would benefit from a special education program. She may advise that you contact a therapist for counseling. In most cases the school psychologist refers students to other specialists. Few schools can afford to provide therapy to individual students or their families. Keep in mind that parents are not obliged to take the psychologist's evaluations as the final word on the child. These are aptly called recommendations, not orders.

Although the request for psychological evaluation usually comes from the classroom teacher, most schools will respond to parental requests for services. Indeed, in some schools, such as Bank Street, parents can call upon the school psychologist directly. They may see her individually or at a regular monthly "rap" session, when parents are welcome to discuss problems that range from sibling rivalry, discipline, sexuality, and responsibility to dealing with death, illness, or other issues.

According to Dr. Bernice Berk, psychologist at Bank Street's School for Children, working with teachers and parents is often more effective in the prevention of more serious problems than working directly with children at this age. Although she does observe and occasionally work with a child on a short-term basis, she believes that much can be achieved by supporting the significant adults in the child's life. Together they examine strategies not only for dealing with ongoing problems but for developing necessary long-term parenting skills in otherwise stressful situations. If more intensive "long-term" intervention is needed, this usually comes after the parents, with the help of the psychologist, have tried to effect necessary changes themselves.

Many schools do a great deal of testing in their psychological evaluations. In part this is because they haven't the time or budget for a more in-depth process of observation and discussion. Ideally, the psychologist, teacher, and parent should be involved in a mutual process. They need the give-and-take of sharing what they see. Together they can plan and try different strategies and meet again to evaluate how they're working out. Time is needed for trial and error.

This is not to say that testing is not important. According to Berk, testing is used if the process of collaboration has not led to a successful conclusion. In other words, if the way the child functions has not improved, testing can give the psychologist clues about what's happening under the surface. Or if at the outset the cause of difficulty is very unclear, the psychologist may feel that testing will help in choosing the best path of intervention. But testing in and of itself is not a remedy.

SHOULD CHILDREN BE RETAINED?

Educators are by no means in agreement over the issue of holding children back. Those who oppose retention point to studies indicating that the gains on test scores after an added year in the same grade are insignificant, nor do they believe that whatever gains there are balance out the sense of loss children and their families tend to carry away from the experience. Opponents of retention claim that even if the family casts no shame or blame on the child and the situation is handled sensitively, children who repeat a grade frequently see themselves as less smart or even as failures. Studies also show that this early perception of oneself is likely to cast a lasting shadow for years to come.

In some schools young children and their families would not need to face such a dilemma. Instead of retaining children or pushing them on to the level of their own incompetence, schools that address all children's needs are less locked into such age and grade grouping. Their solution is to have mixed-age groups. A five-year-old may be placed in the four-to-fives classroom or in the five-to-sixes classroom. Similarly, there are classes for six-to-sevens and seven-to-eights, eight-to-nines, and nine-to-tens. In such a situation, staying another year with your same teacher carries little hint of "being left behind," since many children have the experience.

However, flexible age grouping is not yet a widespread practice. While parents may work toward changing the lock-step patterns of grouping in their schools, there is still the problem of what to do until such changes come.

Essentially, the question about your child's situation needs to be addressed on an individual basis. No book can give you a blanket rule. To say that no child should ever be retained because he or she will feel like a failure does not address the fact that going ahead may also reinforce a sense of failure. This is especially true in

263

traditional classrooms, where the teacher assumes that all children who arrive are prepared to go on with the next level of work. A child who is just getting a grasp on addition and subtraction may lose it all if the teacher is going to move right on to multiplication and division. Similarly, the child who has just gotten a handle on decoding words may drown in a classroom where students are reading chapter books and developing comprehension skills. For such students, if instruction cannot be adjusted to meet individual needs and differences, retention may, in fact, be a better alternative.

There are also borderline cases, where neither teacher nor parent is quite sure. Occasionally, the decision is better delayed until fall. This is especially true in schools that offer a summer program. For some children a smaller group or more individual attention gives them the extra boost they need. In my own experience I have had students who made significant gains over the summer as well as those who might have been better off playing outdoors. There are borderline children who do a lot of growing up from June to September and those who seem to forget so much that they need more than the few weeks provided for review. I recall one child who was promoted to second grade in spite of her first-grade teacher's recommendation for retention. Emily was not just physically small, she had difficulty relating to her classmates and did not participate on the playground or in classroom discussions. She had no phonic skills but had memorized, and forgotten, most of the first-grade reading vocabulary. After several weeks I urged her parents to come and observe for themselves. Once they did so, it was apparent that this was not an appropriate placement, since I was teaching in a school with a rigid set of curriculum expectations. In fact, both the principal and the reading coordinator considered individualized reading instruction a waste of teaching time and told me to stop it. Given such attitudes, the gap between the child's needs and the administrator's demands were too broad to overcome. Until schools change, it may be that children like Emily will have more success taking that extra year than they would in having to spend their early school years playing catch-up.

Again, these are individual issues that cannot be addressed with a simple yea or nay. Before any final decision is made about promotion or retention, you will want to discuss the choices with your child's teacher, principal, and others who are involved in the decision making. Indeed, you should be involved in the process. You should have a full explanation of how your child has been evaluated.

▲ Is the recommendation being made solely on the basis of the teacher's observations?

• Have any other specialists observed? The principal? School psychologist? Reading consultant? Other?

▪ Has your child been tested and, if so, by whom, with what tests, and what were the results?

▲ Is the reason for retention solely an academic problem?

• If not, what other problems are being reported?

If you are not satisfied with the answers to any of these questions, feel free to discuss them at this meeting or make an appointment for a fuller discussion. For instance, if only the teacher has observed, you may want to have the principal or school psychologist visit the classroom and do an evaluation. If your child's test scores are heavily coloring the issue, you may want him to be retested individually, either in the school or privately.

Keep in mind that retention should not be treated as a penalty or punishment for "not doing what the teacher said" or "not acting like a big boy." Heaping shame or guilt on your child is not going to help now or in the year ahead. Children usually want to succeed as much as we want them to succeed. Your attitudes are going to color your child's feelings about himself, school, and your long-term relationship as a family. Of course, it may be disappointing to you and to the child. However, in sharing that disappointment children need to feel your unqualified love, confidence, and support.

PERMANENT RECORDS

From the time your child enters school, records begin to accumulate in his or her permanent record file. Usually such a file will include grades from report cards, achievement and IQ tests, health records, and reports written by teachers or specialists who have worked with your child. This cumulative record can be useful in evaluating your child's progress and can give a new teacher insight in planning for your child's individual needs. In the event that you move, it will give the new school an overview of your child's achievements and help in making an appropriate placement.

As a parent or legal guardian of a public school student, you are entitled to read and review your child's file. Under the Family Educational Rights and Privacy Act you have the right to prohibit the release of that information to anyone except school personnel. You also have the right to challenge information that you consider "inaccurate, misleading or otherwise in violation of privacy or other rights of students." In examining your child's files you should feel free to question and challenge any information that you consider harmful or inappropriate. If you have such concerns, the first step is to make an appointment with the school principal. Before writing a formal complaint or rushing off to hire a lawyer, talk openly with the principal about your objections or concerns. You may be able to have the objectionable or inaccurate information removed. If not, you may need to contact an attorney and/or the organization listed below.

Your child's file is likely to include the following:

▲ Enrollment date: legal name, address, birth place, date of birth, parents' names
• Health information: name of family physician, person to contact in an emergency, special health conditions
▪ Cumulative records: report card grades, scores from standardized tests, health and attendance records
▲ Disclosure records: these are records that you would have signed giving your consent for anyone except school personnel to see your child's personal records
• Special services: reports from specialists, such as the school psychologist, nurse, social worker, speech therapist, special education teacher

You should not find informal notes or unsigned reports about your family life or political views. Nor should there be records about your child's behavior or learning problems of which you have not been notified.

In the event that you have problems in gaining access to the file or problems with what you read in the file and you find your school officials resistant, you may need to contact your state's commissioner of education or the U.S. Department of Education.

Keep in mind that these laws govern the public schools but not necessarily the records kept by private schools. Unless a private school receives some funding from the federal government, it does not need to comply with the Family Educational Rights and Privacy Act. If it is not covered by this act, you will need to check with your school to see what its policies are on parental reading of records.

If you are having problems with school records, here are two addresses you may need:

FERPA Office
U.S. Department of Education
HEW Building (North)
330 Independence Avenue, S.W.
Washington, D.C. 20201

National Committee for Citizens in Education
410 Wilde Lake Village Green
Columbia, Maryland 21044

DEALING WITH COMMON PROBLEMS

"I HATE THAT TEACHER!"

During the early weeks of school it is not at all unusual for children to complain about the new teacher. Before jumping to conclusions, keep in mind that such complaints in September are often short-lived. Although most elementary-age children are generally fond of their teachers, the bond may not form instantaneously. For some children the transition from one teacher to the next can be bumpy. The affection and trust built during the previous year is hard to relinquish. This is especially true in the early grades, where children are most dependent on their teachers. It's almost as if liking the new teacher is a breach of loyalty. Besides, this new person doesn't do things "right"—right, in this case, meaning like last year's teacher.

It takes time to get to know this new person, how she responds, and what she expects. These opening weeks of school are a time for getting acquainted. As in any relationship, a sense of ease and trust are usually built gradually. Children don't automatically transfer their trust. So, parents need to listen to mild complaints with a wait-and-see attitude. If the negative feelings persist, become intense, or a specific incident arouses your concern, you'll need to contact the teacher directly. But avoid jumping to conclusions.

Parents can help children through this transition if they

▲ Listen to complaints with patience and understanding.

• Talk about the differences between two people the child may like. Discuss the idea that this year's teacher may be different in her ways but no less likable.

▪ Discuss whatever the specific problem or problems the child may raise and ways of handling them rather than talking in generalities. Instead of discussing how bad the teacher is, talk about the incident in order to clarify the issues.

▲ Last year's teacher may have accepted homework done in pencil, whereas this year's teacher expects work done with pen. Talk about the fact that each teacher has different expectations and that one of the secrets of success in school comes with knowing what the teacher wants and delivering it.

• Ask leading questions that may help children look at a problem from other perspectives. For example, ''Why do you think she asked you to . . . ?''

▪ Agree upon a course of action. Sometimes a parent conference is called for. Older children often prefer (and are able) to handle a specific problem themselves once they have a plan of action. For example, say your child is being distracted regularly by the person who sits next to him. He might ask to have his seat changed and/or talk with the teacher about the situation.

▲ If your child is going to ''handle it,'' follow up. Ask about how a situation is going.

• If the problem warrants your involvement, make an appointment with the teacher promptly. But avoid overreacting before you have all the facts.

▪ Keep in mind that you've only heard one perspective. Much

as we love them, children are not always accurate reporters and may be contributing to the problem.

Certainly, during the course of our own school years, all of us had some teachers who remain all-time favorites. But sometimes we need to remind ourselves that even those memorable teachers were once strangers. We also need to remember that not every teacher will be a favorite.

This is not to say that when a child and teacher seem to be mismatched there is nothing that can or should be done. However, keep in mind that we can't always make everything perfect for our children, nor can we pick and choose the "right" teachers or tell them how to run their classrooms. Even if we could, doing so would give children false expectations of how the world works.

Although the teacher may not match your ideal (or your child's), saying things like "She's nuts" or "I'm going to get her fired!" only reinforces your child's problem. Indeed, when parents are openly critical of a teacher, children often follow suit and end up making matters worse by misbehaving in school.

Does this mean you grin and bear it? Not at all. There are circumstances when parents need to step into the picture and negotiate appropriate changes. In extreme cases the change may be a totally new class assignment. In most instances the change will be more moderate.

In my own experience with teachers I still recall my preconceived notions of the "old witch" who was to be my fifth-grade teacher. According to everyone she was "strict, mean, and hollered constantly." After shedding tears and fearing my fate all summer, I was amazed to discover that this wicked teacher did not devour children. Indeed, she turned out to be, if not a favorite, one of the best.

WHEN YOU HAVE TO MOVE

Moving from one community to another puts a strain on the entire family, not just the children. While it is not always possible to choose the time of year for a move, most kids find it easier to make the shift at the beginning of the school year rather than after they have settled into one class and have to go through the entire process again. Keep in mind, too, that in the beginning of the year they are less apt to be the only new kids entering a class.

Whether it's September or not, take the time to visit the new school before entry day. This gives you and your child a chance to gather some firsthand information. You can get a preview of the school's physical plant and location. It helps children to know the answers to ''Where is my classroom?'' ''How far is the school from home?'' ''How do I get there and back?'' ''How much does lunch cost?'' They may get to meet their new principal, the school secretary, even their teacher. You can also get an idea of how students dress so that your child doesn't go to a jeans-and-sweatshirt school dressed in a tie and shirt.

This preentry visit is also usually the time for required paperwork. Most schools will expect you to bring proof of your child's age and health records. The district you are leaving should be asked to send copies of your child's permanent records.

There may be choices between schools in the community to which you are moving. Often the neighborhood you choose to live in will affect those choices. Before you make the big move, it's a good idea to talk with parents who are already living in that community. Real estate agents are often knowledgeable about the schools, but remember they're in the business of selling houses, not education. You can write to the chamber of commerce to find out the names of school districts within a convenient radius of your job before you rent or buy a home. Where possible, it makes sense to visit the various schools and gather your own firsthand impressions before settling in. Parents who have enough lead time to investigate also find it useful to subscribe to the local papers and follow school events for several months. In comparing schools the question posed in chapter one should be considered.

"I Don't Know Anyone!"

If you've just moved to a new school district or your child has been shuffled into a class with mostly new faces, the early weeks of school are apt to be bumpy. Besides assuring him that they will make new friends, there are more active and positive steps you can take to help the process along.

Your child's teacher can help you make contact with parents of classmates. Afterschool or weekend ''play dates'' give kids a chance to get together one-to-one. Unlike their time in school, where the day is structured, these out-of-school experiences give children a chance to establish friendships. Older students can usually make such arrangements themselves. However, younger children often need parental help and encouragement.

Afterschool organizations and activities also provide ready-made groups that fit the child's needs to be with agemates. Whether it's dancing school, Scouts, art classes, Little League, or whatever, such groups bring children with a common interest together and involve them in building new skills and social connections.

While some parents may feel these issues are of less importance than schoolwork, the fact is they can impact on the child's performance in school. At an age when belonging is so central, the child who feels disconnected socially is also likely to feel disconnected in the classroom.

Helping children through the temporary state of being the "new kid" can be demanding. They may need more of your time and attention until they establish a new network of friends. Making visitors welcome during afterschool hours or on weekends can hasten the process. So can family outings to social events where you and your child may meet new people.

Eager as you may be to get your house in order or break into the new job, it can be helpful not to postpone your child's social life. His new acquaintances won't care if the drapes are hung or the dishes are unpacked. Sandwiches or a slice of pizza on paper plates are probably more fun anyway.

Children may also need assurances that their unsettled feelings are in fact normal but temporary. Young children with limited experiences in change don't always understand that they won't always feel so new or lonely. They may focus on what's different. Parents can help them see the plus side of some of those differences and help them see the positive possibilities of change. If your own attitude about the move is enthusiastic, chances are they'll share your view.

WHEN YOUR CHILD IS ABSENT

Even the healthiest child is apt to miss a few days of school. This is especially true during the early years. Kindergartners who have never before lived in a group situation sometimes catch every bug they're exposed to in school. In most instances, a day or two out remedies the situation. However, occasionally more serious ailments call for longer absences.

If your child is going to be out of school for a week or more, you should contact the teacher. Give her an estimate of how long your child will be at home. If you feel your child is up to it and the teacher feels it appropriate, she may want to send home some current assignments. While a week may not seem like such a long time to you, for a child it can feel like an eternity.

With your help, doing current assignments can keep your child from falling behind. Furthermore, when he returns to school, he will be less overwhelmed by the work that needs to be made up. In extreme cases, when a prolonged absence of several weeks or months is needed, the school may make provision for at-home instruction. Since this kind of arrangement varies from state to state, you will need to contact the principal or superintendent's office in your district.

Whether your child is going to be out for a few days, weeks, or months, making the most of that time is important. Children in such situations don't need to turn into passive lumps spending their day glued to the tube. Nor should they be expected to work as if they were in school for the day.

▲ Limit their TV time.

• Provide other activities for involvement, such as arts and crafts, books, games, and puzzles.

■ If homework is to be done, set a time and be there to provide support and guidance. Don't let it drag on and on or turn it into a hassle.

▲ If they are having great difficulty with some assignment, assure them that you will talk with the teacher about it.

• Follow up on such work when your child returns to school, or contact the teacher for suggestions on how to help if your child is to be at home for several weeks.

■ Keep in mind that children are apt to feel cut off and lonely. Just spending time together without schoolwork or some other agenda has its own value. Talking, playing a game, reading aloud, or just resting together has its own rewards.

▲ Older children may also enjoy talking with friends by phone. It helps them stay connected and probably makes reentry easier.

When children return to school, it often takes a few days for them to readjust to the old schedule and demands. They may come home tired or irritable about some event they missed or work they need to do. They may also miss the less-demanding ambiance and extra attention of home. If you can picture yourself the day after you return from a vacation, then perhaps you will have a sense of how they're feeling. Those first days back call for an extra dose of patience and understanding. Indeed, for some children it's like starting school all over again.

DISCIPLINE

When we think of discipline, what usually comes to mind is punishment. Yet discipline should be more than a negative response to unacceptable behavior. In positive terms, experienced teachers rely less on punishment and more on classroom management. Instead of reacting after the event, they set the stage by establishing realistic expectations for behavior. Indeed, in such classrooms teachers involve their students in making the rules and therefore build an understanding of the need for living within those rules. Does that mean students never misbehave? Of course not. However, when a group of children has been involved in making the "social contract," the commitment to those rules comes from the peer group rather than just the teacher alone.

While it may seem that there's more movement and talk in your child's classroom than you remember, the changes do not necessarily mean that there is no discipline there. When children are walking in the hall, the fact that they are not silent does not mean they are undisciplined. Today's teachers seldom require or expect the kind of automaton behavior that was demanded a generation ago. Teachers who value the sorts of learning that come out of students working together do not demand silence. In fact, they provide activities that encourage cooperative work. They value interaction and the hum of industry that comes with the territory. Children who are engaged in learning and living with each other are rarely likely to sit still for long periods of time or to be absolutely silent.

Having said that, even in the most ideal setting there are times when students go out of bounds. They may get silly or forget that what they are doing is disturbing others. For a variety of reasons they may test the boundary lines of what is acceptable and try to discover exactly how far they can go. In classrooms that set reasonable expectations a firm reminder is usually enough to help children remember the rules. On occasion, a teacher may need to separate a child from others. And there are occasions when misbehavior snowballs and the teacher and class need to address what's going on and look for solutions together.

While there are still teachers who control their classrooms with a stern system of punishments and rewards, the real objective of discipline should be to help children discover self-control.

CORPORAL PUNISHMENT

Unfortunately, many schools have returned to (or never left behind) the philosophy of "spare the rod and spoil the child." Only nine states have outlawed corporal punishment. The fact is that parents would be convicted of child abuse if they did to children what some schools do. There are still school personnel who use paddles, twist ears, pinch, pull hair, or force children to stand or squat in one position for long periods of time. Although most districts have laws or special codes for administering such punishment, the logic of physically punishing children is hard to understand.

Studies consistently show that the use of corporal punishment is ineffective. In fact, excessive use of corporal punishment has been shown to decrease learning. Basically, corporal punishment serves only as a temporary solution. It does not teach children new behavior and it may actually provoke more aggressive or worse behavior. What it does teach is the very poor model of using violence to solve problems.

Schools that have outlawed corporal punishment have discovered that they have no worse discipline problems than before. Actually, some have fewer problems. Nevertheless, the practice of hitting children persists. In part, this may be due to the way we ourselves were brought up. We know that teachers who were hit frequently as children are more apt to do the same to their students. Studies also show that teachers who hit frequently tend to be impulsive, neurotic, and/or relatively inexperienced. More often than not, those most apt to be hit are boys in the primary and intermediate grades. Further, they are apt to be boys from minority groups or white children from poor families.

You may be surprised to learn that many countries have outlawed corporal punishment in their schools. According to the National Center for the Study of Corporal Punishment at Temple

University, the following countries prohibit the use of corporal punishment:

1. All Continental Europe

2. All Socialist-Communist countries

3. Japan

4. England

5. Ireland

6. Israel

7. Qatar

8. Mauritania

In our own country most major cities have local codes outlawing corporal punishment.

If corporal punishment is still being used in your school, you should demand a copy of your school's discipline code. You can also work with other parents to bring change about.

There are now nine states where corporal punishment is outlawed: Maine, Vermont, New Hampshire, Rhode Island, New York, California, Hawaii, New Jersey, and Massachusetts. (Ohio and Maryland are expected to do so soon.) The ten states that most frequently use corporal punishment are Arkansas, Alabama, Mississippi, Oklahoma, Florida, Georgia, Texas, Missouri, Tennessee, and Kentucky.

If this is an issue you are concerned about, you can contact the following organization. They can help you find other people in your area who are working for change.

National Center for the Study of Corporal Punishment and Alternatives in the Schools
Temple University
Philadelphia, Pennsylvania 19122

DEALING WITH RACISM

Chances are that at some point in his school years your child will experience racism. This is true whether you are a member of a minority or not. Your child may be on the receiving end, he may be an observer, or he may be a party to it. Whatever the scenario, the problem should not be ignored.

Nonminority parents are often shocked when children come home from school using language laced with racial slurs or make disparaging remarks about a classmate's race or religion. Young children often relish trying out words they do not fully understand but know may have shock appeal. Indeed, they may be looking for a reaction and they should have one. Let your children know that calling people names is unacceptable to you and hurtful to others. Remember, too, that children learn a great deal from the model you present. If they hear you telling jokes with racial overtones, they are not going to see why they shouldn't do so, too. If you're really serious about teaching children to respect others, then your first line of action must be in your own behavior.

If your child comes home from school with reports about the teacher's behavior that strike you as racist, encourage the child to tell you about what happened and why he thinks it happened. Assure your child that you disapprove of such behavior and you are going to do something about if. Follow through. Make it your business to see the teacher as soon as possible and discuss what your child has told you. Avoid jumping to conclusions. Your child may have misunderstood, and the teacher is entitled to the benefit of the doubt. After speaking with the teacher, if, for some reason, you are not satisfied with her answer or attitudes, make an appointment with her immediate superior. But before you go over her head, be sure you have your facts straight.

Disappointing as it may be, your child may also go along with others who are scapegoating a classmate with racial slurs. "Nobody plays with ———," he may say. Or he may generalize by saying, "All ——— are dumb (or dirty or liars)." Middle-years children have a penchant for excluding others for any number of reasons, and racism may seem to them as good as any. Some children are so eager to belong that they are willing to join forces with others, even when they know they are doing something mean-spirited. The fact that they do it does not make it acceptable. Parents need to make a point of discussing such behavior with children and helping them understand how their actions affect others.

If it is your child who is the butt of racial taunts, you may need to contact the teacher and ask her to deal with those who are participating. She may deal directly with those responsible or she may use a situation to discuss attitudes and behavior with the whole group. In some cases a child may be able to take the problem to the teacher without a call from you. However, not all children can or will. If the situation warrants it, don't stay out of it. Although you are not likely to be able to insulate your child from bigotry, you should certainly be able to call on the teacher or principal to act on such behavior in the school.

As citizens of a democracy children need to learn early on that differences are not something to fear, nor is it acceptable to subject others to ridicule and name-calling for those differences. Both home and school have to actively help children discover how much more we all have in common.

DRUG PREVENTION EDUCATION

Until recently, drug education programs were the province of the middle and high school years. Today state and local boards of education are increasingly mandating drug prevention programs for students from kindergarten up. As you might expect, the approach of such programs varies tremendously. Since these programs are relatively new, it is difficult to say how effective they will be.

Traditionally, drug education has focused on giving students the facts about drugs and what they do to you. They have often relied on scare tactics. Usually the information is delivered with outside help from a no-nonsense police officer or a rehabilitated drug user, such as an athlete or an entertainer. You may be surprised to know that such programs have generally failed. Indeed, some educators believe that such programs may even be harmful!

Directed at first- or second-graders, the scare tactics are merely frightening. Although young children believe what they are told, this is not an age group that experiments with drugs, so the long-term importance of the message may be lost in the sea of "thou shalt nots" children are grappling with at five, six, or seven. Experts say that by the time children reach fourth or fifth grade, the scare tactics become less believable. Many students know older kids who may be experimenting with drugs, and what they see often doesn't mesh with what they're being told. Indeed, when celebrities come into the schools to talk about their drug experiences, kids may twist what they see as evidence that people can survive drugs and still be a celebrity with lots of money and fame.

Although many programs continue to use straightforward informational approaches, current thought indicates that this is only a small part of drug prevention education. Newer programs focus on a wider range of goals. Researchers believe that effective prevention begins with giving children a variety of life skills that can help them cope with the drug scene as well as with other problems. Such programs give students various opportunities for learning about the step-by-step process of making decisions. Learning these steps comes with experience in dealing with many kinds of problems, not just drug-related issues. Similarly, newer programs also provide training in how to cope with stress. For example, before exam time, when pressure builds, students are taught techniques for breathing and relaxation exercises along with the value of physical activity and fitness. From the early grades on, students are also given resistance training. Through role playing they are taught not only to say no but how to do it. Newer programs also focus on building children's self-esteem by reinforcing their positive images of themselves. Students who feel good about themselves and their future are more likely to stand up against the inevitable negative intrusions they encounter.

Unlike the drug information programs, the goals of drug prevention education today call for a broad as well as a deeper approach. It is not one thing, but many. It cannot be slotted into a fifteen- or twenty-minute period once a week. You cannot give kids self-esteem the way you can a lesson on equilateral triangles. Nor is learning to make decisions a mechanical skill that can be mastered before math or after gym. Rather than teaching about drugs in isolation, the goals and skills need to be integrated into the total learning experience. Indeed, many issues and skills that relate to drug prevention can fit into their English, social studies, science, art, math, and gym classes.

It is too soon to know how widespread or successful these broader and newer approaches to drug prevention will be. There are still some educators (and parents) who feel the school is the least effective place for such programs. Some believe that drug abuse is a symptom of a deeper societal problem that can't be solved by prevention programs in school. Others feel that subjects such as drugs and sex are moral and ethical issues that should be left for the

home to handle. They feel that the schools tread on parental territory and do a poor job in dealing with underlying values. Still
others insist that if the school does not address such issues, some
parents will fail to do so. For better or worse, whatever your view,
schools are increasingly stepping into this area.

PARENTS' ROLE IN DRUG PREVENTION— MORE THAN JUST THE FACTS

Whatever your school is doing, keep in mind that as a parent you
play a vital role in shaping your child's attitudes about himself
and drugs. What you say may have less of a long-term effect than
what you actually do. If at the end of the day you need a drink to
unwind or a pill to relax, you are sending a more powerful message
than words can deliver. Children learn much more from our model
for coping with stress than from what we say. Within the family
children can also learn about the business of decision making. This
is not to say that parents should shift the burden of decision making to children, but rather that, wherever possible, children should
be included in the process. By giving children opportunities to
make choices (even less than perfect ones), we strengthen their
problem-solving abilities and prepare them for greater independence. Kids who have all their decisions made for them by well-
meaning parents are ill prepared to take on conflicting issues as
they inevitably arise outside the home.

It is also from their parents that children learn lasting lessons
about their own self-worth. If kids are constantly bombarded by
messages that eat away at their confidence or they are compared
unfavorably to others, their basic sense of themselves can be
eroded. During their preadolescent years, when the powerful tug
of peer pressure mounts, kids especially need the secure base of
home and family, where they can find both acceptance and guidance. It's not just drugs but a whole range of group issues and
values that come home from school. By talking with your children
rather than at them, you can help them take responsibility for their
own actions rather than blaming them or making them depend on
the approval of their peers. Long before they reach adolescence,
they need to learn about making choices that are important to them
as individuals. When communication lines are open, parents stand
a better chance of helping kids sort out their own values from the
conflicting values in the peer group.

Parents sometimes fear that talking about issues such as drugs or sex may actually lead kids to more curiosity and experimentation. Yet talking about such issues can help kids clarify the information (and misinformation) they receive from movies, TV, and friends. Listening to what they say can be as vital as delivering your own message. Indeed, children's questions often reveal their feelings, thoughts, and confusions. Don't worry about getting all of your message across in one important lecture. Attitudes and values are learned through ongoing dialogues between parents and kids that continue over the years.

You don't need to be an expert to convey your views. As the subject of drugs, alcohol, or tobacco arises, the opportunity for commentary is ready-made. Kids may not always seem to listen. They may even argue with your opinions. Despite protests to the contrary, most kids care deeply and want to know what their parents believe. Your attitudes and values are central and are often borrowed as whole cloth until children are able to integrate and shape their own personal value system. In my own family the telephone calls from anguished parents to my husband (who is a lawyer) helped deliver to our children the message that students who were "busted" ended up with legal problems that might affect their career choices in the future. While I suspect that had real impact, the more central message we tried to convey had to do with the positive power of being in control of one's own life rather than being controlled by peers or chemicals.

During these years when children begin to compare other values and life-styles with those of their family, parents are often pressured by those often-quoted experts known as "everybody"—as in "Everybody else gets that much allowance" or "Everybody else can go to the party." What parents sometimes forget is that everybody else is also quoting the everybodies. Parents still need to set and enforce firm but reasonable limits and expectations. Although they may balk and complain, studies show that children actually feel that parental limits are an assuring way of knowing you do care about them. While your long-range goal is to develop and motivate their own self-control, children at this stage still need parents who are not afraid to say no or, "That's not acceptable in our family."

In our everyday exchanges we can help children learn about themselves and their self-worth. They not only need to feel good about themselves and optimistic about their future, they need to learn how to cope with inevitable doubts and even failure. Parents can't protect kids from disappointments, but they can give them strategies for coping with frustrations in healthy and constructive ways. They need encouragement to develop their individual talents and interests. You may need to remind them that no one learns to play the piano well, read a book, or master other solo endeavors if they need constant companionship. The object is not to isolate them. You can't raise your child in a hermetically sealed capsule. Even if you could, when would you release him? Parents can help children balance their dependence on peers by supporting and encouraging their individual interests and aspirations.

When you talk directly about drugs, be sure that the information you're giving is up-to-date. For example, if you considered pot a safe drug while you were in college, you may be surprised to know that the marijuana that's being grown today is much stronger and far more hazardous. According to some experts, articles and books written about marijuana just a few years ago are out-of-date because the drug is now so different. In talking about drugs, your stance should be clear and not negotiable. Don't equivocate! Avoid statements that convey the notion that if your child is going to do something, you'd rather he drank, or you'd rather he smoked pot. Such statements are likely to backfire and be misinterpreted.

Some experts suggest teaching your child how to say no. They recommend role-playing in hypothetical situations, teaching kids how to answer those who are trying to get him to "just try it." There are no guarantees that this will work, but it may give children the confidence to say, "Forget it! Drugs are dumb! I'm surprised that you would do something that dumb!"—or something similar.

Yet giving children all the facts is not enough. Parents need to give their children a positive sense of themselves as individuals. Children who feel good about themselves and about the excitement of life, even with its ups and downs, are less likely to become drug-dependent. They will not need the artificial highs and lows that drug users need to get instantaneous thrills or to dull the inevitable painful moments of real life.

STAYING CONNECTED

MAKING THE TRANSITION TO MIDDLE SCHOOL

Your child's elementary school years will end at either fifth or sixth grade. At this stage students generally enter the middle school, or what you may have called junior high. Although some schools, such as Bank Street, continue through eighth grade, the tempo, style of instruction, and structure of the day represent significant changes. In most instances students will no longer attend a self-contained classroom with a single teacher. More typically they will have departmentalized instruction from a variety of teachers, each of whom teaches a different subject. During these years students are also more likely to be grouped by ability. A child who excels in math may be in an accelerated math group but in a regular or remedial English class. Placement is usually based on past performance, standardized tests, and teacher recommendations. Classes are apt to be larger than in elementary school, and more emphasis is placed on whole-group instruction.

Although most students are excited and ready for this new experience, making the transition can be stressful. Moving from the school they have attended for five or six years represents another kind of separation. They leave behind the familiar routines and people they have come to know and trust. Instead of being one of the "big kids," once again they are the youngest or little guys. Just the physical business of finding the way around the new building and remembering the schedule and locker combination can be confusing. Instead of having one constant "parental"-type teacher, suddenly the child must adjust to multiple adults with different personalities and expectations. The demands for greater independence and work after school hours are increased. More time in class is spent on direct instruction with follow-up work assigned as homework. Individual teachers may give heavy assignments without knowing or caring what other teachers are also assigning.

Suddenly the child has more work than he has ever had before, and it can be overwhelming for a while. Faced with new and accelerated demands, students often panic, and parents follow their lead. Rather than falling apart, parents would do best by seeing this transition as a normal if somewhat trying time. In other words, knowing that this may be a bumpy transition period should help you understand that there's nothing seriously wrong with your child.

To ease the transition, many schools take their elementary students to visit the school they will attend the following fall. Like the kindergarten visitation programs, this can alleviate some anxiety. If your school does not do this, you should be able to walk through the building with your child or suggest to the principal or parent organization that they institute such visits.

Keep in mind that after a few days or weeks most children know their way around the new school and soon enjoy a new sense of independence. However, students at this stage often have difficulty with their work load. They are not ready yet for total independence. Parents will still be needed to help children organize their workspace, time, and approach to their out-of-school assignments.

Although you may have been doing this earlier, you can expect that you will have to do more of the same. Without policing or getting overly involved in teaching, you can give your child organizational strategies for dealing with multiple demands. For example, if they have not needed an assignment book, they will need one now, along with a pleasant workspace. Parents may need to help children settle in and look at what must be done and how long it should take and should try to remain available as the need for help arises. Many of the suggestions in chapter six will still be appropriate.

If, after the first four to six weeks, your child seems to be floundering, you may need to make contact with the school. Although your child has many teachers, most schools assign each student to one teacher, who is responsible for looking at the overall picture of what's happening. This ''core'' teacher or adviser will get reports from each of the teachers and will be able to access whether a problem is general or specific to one subject. Ideally, the child's multiple teachers will plan as a team so that their content has some overlap and students do not get four heavy assignments at one time. For example, the written report in social studies may be read by the English teacher; or the literature assignment may reflect the content they are studying in social studies. In other words, there is still an integrated curriculum underlying the departmentalized program.

Some families may have the luxury of choosing from several middle schools in their community. At this age students are often ready to travel a greater distance, and doing so may open more options. In some urban areas a voucher system allows students to enroll in schools outside their neighborhood. If there are choices, you will want to visit the schools while they are in session and evaluate what you see. Many of the questions in the first chapter will still apply in helping you select a school that fits your child's needs best.

Whether your child attends the most perfect school or not, your continuing interest and involvement will still be needed during these important years. As your child enters puberty, there are new physical, emotional, and intellectual changes that will call for understanding, patience, discipline, love, and a good sense of humor.

Often parents assume that the need for involvement ends by the time children enter the upper grades. Yet studies indicate that parental involvement and expectations have a direct effect on students' behavior, learning, and success. Although their roles change over the years, parents must stay actively connected to their children's learning throughout the school years.

Drawing from Egyptian studies. Age 9.

AFTER SCHOOL, BEFORE SCHOOL, AND IN-BETWEEN TIME

For working parents, the afterschool hours represent a worrisome problem. Where can children go during that gap in the day when school is out but parents are still at work? Who will supervise and see that children's needs for safety are met? Essentially, what parents want and need is child care. In many communities the school is filling that void, not just after school, but before school and in between times, such as vacation days and the summer months when school is closed but parents must be at work. Although in some communities other organizations, such as the Y or Parks Department, may sponsor such programs, increasingly schools are taking that responsibility. And it makes sense. Schools have gyms, playgrounds, instruments, art rooms, computers, science equipment, and libraries that get locked up when the last bell of the day rings. For too many years the best facilities in the neighborhood have been off-limits to those who needed them most. Now, instead of turning kids out on the streets or sending them home to empty houses, loneliness, and wasted time, schools (often with the help of parents organizations) are providing free or relatively inexpensive programs that benefit children and their families. National surveys indicate that both teachers and principals believe that student performance could be improved if kids weren't left without supervision for so many hours every day.

If your school has no such program as yet, this is a project your parents organization could work toward. To evaluate or plan such programs, you should know that the best programs provide much more than baby-sitting or a roof over kids' heads. Despite the fact that children remain in a school building, afterschool programs should not be a continuation of academic work. These afternoon hours should be a real change of pace that replicate, in a way, the kind of experiences children used to have when they went home and played with a friend or in the neighborhood.

After a full day in the classroom, kids need programs that provide for a lot of physical activity. They need real offerings, such as gymnastics, tumbling, dance, ball games, and freewheeling active play with supervision. There should be choices, and some of those would include some low-key activities that still involve active doing, such as art activities, board games, music, crafts, and even cooking (where possible). The best programs, those that have the fewest behavior problems and that children look forward to, provide real activities. They don't expect children to be passive or to plug kids into watching videotapes to keep them quiet. Solid programs require a reasonable ratio of children to adults. A trained teacher should not be running an activity with twenty-two children. A group that large should have an aide to assist. Sometimes parents or grandparents volunteer their time or high school students participate as members of community service organizations or for limited wages.

Such programs not only provide needed child care and peace of mind for parents, they give children a ready-made circle of caring adults they can depend upon, agemates they can enjoy, and enrichment activities that add new learning experiences to their lives.

In communities where parents work beyond the dinner hour, some schools also offer a meal and supervised work time for homework. Such programs are more typically in urban settings and provide a valuable service to families. Teachers as well as trained aides can give students the help they need, help that parents may not have the time or teaching skills to offer. However, such programs should not constitute the entire afternoon and evening. Homework in the elementary years simply shouldn't require that many hours.

If you are looking for ways to get such a program started, contact:

School-Age Child Care Project
Wellesley College
Center for Research on Women
Wellesley, Massachusetts 02181

PARENT VOLUNTEERS AND PARENTS' ORGANIZATIONS

Although the focus of this book is largely on helping your own children at home and school, there is no doubt that joining forces with others can do much to affect the quality of education for all children in your school district. Despite the fact that more than 50 percent of women with school-age children are employed outside the home, parent involvement is on the rise. Increasingly, schools are coming to understand how connections between home and school promote achievement and success.

For many parents, involvement goes no further than paying their annual PTA dues or contributing cookies for the bake sale. Others play a more active role in planning parent-teacher organization meetings; running science, art, or book fairs; volunteering to go on field trips; assisting at classroom parties; or making phone calls for special events.

In many schools, parents and grandparents are being recruited to serve as volunteers or paid aides in the library or classroom. They may read stories with children or help individual students with work laid out by the classroom teachers. In my own teaching experience such parents made a real contribution to the quality of classroom life, not just for their own child but for others as well. Not only did they help those children who needed some extra one-on-one time, their own children took pride in their parents' or grandparents' participation. In fact, the model they presented set the scene for students helping students.

Of course, only a small percentage of parents have the time or inclination to volunteer on a regular basis. Yet there are other ways that parents can make a real contribution. Some schools keep a file on which parents have special interests or talents they can share directly in a classroom. For example, a parent or grandparent with a background in geology might bring a wonderful show-and-tell collection to a classroom that is studying rocks; or a person who has been to China might bring a slide show or artifacts into a classroom that is studying that part of the world. Similarly, such a file might yield an interesting visit to a bakery, a factory, or a newspaper where a parent works. In my own experience, one of our best field trips involved a trip to the local racetrack, where we saw horses being curried by the mother of one of my second-graders. We not only visited her at the stables, she came to the classroom with some of her tools and answered the children's questions.

On other occasions, parents of students contributed to classroom life by preparing ethnic foods, welcoming the class to the local greenhouse, talking about piloting a tugboat, playing musical instruments, or demonstrating origami, the Japanese art of paper folding, to mention but a few. Each of these occasions added yet another meaningful dimension to otherwise insular school days.

Since studies consistently show that parent participation greatly influences children's motivation, behavior, and success, schools are increasingly wooing parents into becoming involved. This is particularly true of school districts with low-income families, who tend to feel apprehensive about coming into a school. Recognizing that families of the poor often suffer from a sense of being powerless or unequal to those with more formal education, new programs are being designed to meet their needs. For example, in Memphis, the Parent Training Program offers a series of workshops that focus on discipline, time management, planning and monitoring home study, building parental self-esteem, communication skills, drug and alcohol abuse, and nutrition.

In other parts of the country there are programs that involve parents and children learning together in computer classes. Some schools offer services, such as the Dial-A-Teacher hot line to assist children and parents who are stumped with homework assignments they don't understand. Still other organizations have instituted home-visiting teams, who go to students' homes and provide positive support systems by suggesting places where students can work quietly and management ideas for establishing a good climate to promote effective work habits. In California's Positive Parenting

Program visiting teachers make it their business to emphasize the students' academic strengths and cue parents in on their children's progress. For adults who may have a history of negative feelings about school, such programs can build bridges that foster success. Indeed, reports indicate that some adults return to complete their own education or job-training programs as a result of such experiences. Many also learn to feel more competent about their role in helping their own children.

Through cooperative efforts parents can also influence decisions that shape the philosophy and direction of their schools. For example, in a school in Maryland where kindergartners had a pressured academic program, parents banded together and applied pressure of their own. They invited early-childhood experts to a meeting to talk about what an appropriate kindergarten program looks like. Parents formed a study group and took their suggestions to the administration. Together they managed to change the direction and quality of their school district's kindergarten program.

In another school, where parent-teacher conferences were scheduled during business hours that working parents could not attend, the parents group pressured for evening conferences and supplied baby-sitting services for those who needed them. Other working parents had problems finding good child care during the after-school hours when they were still at work. As a group they organized an afterschool program with the cooperation of the school staff. Instead of worrying about their children being at home alone (or who knows where), they now have peace of mind and their children have the benefits of a safe and stimulating program.

In yet another school, parents were confused by the lack of math homework in the primary grades. To address those concerns, they asked the administration for a program that would clarify what the children were learning and how they could help without confusing their children. A series of workshops run by several teachers gave parents reassurance and helpful tips on how they could reinforce, in informal games at home, what the children were learning.

Parents' organizations have the power to question current policies, prod for change, and support quality education. Working together, parents can do much more than run bake sales or act as a rubber stamp for the school administration and the status quo. Parental participation in school affairs is often a source of pride to children, another link between home and school, and a model for active service in the community. By working in your parent-teacher organization or attending meetings of or serving on the school board, parents can bring about school reforms that shape the quality of education for their own children as well as others. In a sense, becoming an activist in school affairs enables parents to influence outcomes more directly than voting on most other political issues. Activist parents can work to support (or defeat) school budgets as well as the policies they fund. In effect, the school may be the last frontier where citizens can make their views so immediately felt by active participation.

If you are interested in finding out more about parent volunteers and parents' organizations, you may want to contact the following:

The National School Volunteer Program, Inc.
Suite 320
701 North Fairfax Street
Alexandria, Virginia 22314

The National PTA
700 Rush Street
Chicago, Illinois 60611-2571

The National Committee for Citizens in Education
410 Wilde Lake Village Green
Columbia, Maryland 21044

WHOSE JOB IS IT?

As a first-grade teacher I can remember feeling upset when second-grade teachers complained about some of their new students' reading or math skills. Similarly, on those rare occasions when primary teachers met with those who taught the intermediate grades, one would hear the same complaints. This business of pointing fingers and shifting blame is not unusual within the school. It is even more prevalent vis-à-vis school and parent.

"If parents taught children values and instilled discipline, I'd be free to do my job," teachers complain. Bring a group of educators together and you're likely to hear someone say, "Schools can't correct all the ills of society!" Yet, from the parents' point of view, all too often there is a feeling that schools today are failing to do their job. Indeed, some may feel that the multitude of suggestions in this book present an onerous task. "If the schools were any good," some will say, "I wouldn't need to do any of these things!"

Yet the simple truth is that neither home nor school can do the whole job alone. School does not last the whole day, and everything that is learned is not taught in the classroom. At its best, education is a cooperative venture that involves all the players. For the child, who lives in both worlds, the need for appropriate support from parents and teachers is basic to these formative years, when skills and attitudes are being forged.

INDEX

About the Author

Joanne Oppenheim is a senior editor for the Media Group at the Bank Street College of Education in New York. The author of *Buy Me! Buy Me!* and (with Barbara Brenner and Betty D. Boegehold) *Choosing Books for Kids,* among other works, she writes regularly for the major parenting and family magazines. A first- and second-grade teacher for close to a decade, she is also the working parent of three.

WHAT IS BANK STREET?

The Bank Street School for Children is a laboratory school for Bank Street College of Education and a working model of the college's approach to learning and teaching. The school offers a rich learning environment for 450 children from the ages of three to thirteen, and it provides the college with a setting for teacher training, research, and the development of curriculum materials. This collaborative effort between the college staff and school faculty focuses on the *developmental interaction* approach to learning.

Developmental refers to the patterns discernible as children grow physically, mentally, emotionally, and socially. *Interaction* includes not only the child's relationship with his or her physical environment, and with other children and adults, but also the internal interactions between the intellect and the emotions.

This approach can be applied in home life just as well as in school life. For of all the child's teachers the first and most enduring ones are the parents. Bank Street's philosophy concretely supports parents and other caregivers by helping children explore and better understand their world; by sharing interests and ideas with children while allowing them to develop their own curiosity; and by establishing a value system as a framework for and a guide to children's growing independence.

This approach to learning puts great emphasis on child development and individual learning styles, the importance of experiential learning, and the understanding that the emotional life of children is inseparable from their learning, interests, and motivation.

It is perhaps a misnomer to call the Bank Street approach experimental or nontraditional. For more than sixty years Bank Street has influenced educational theory and practice in both private and public schools. It has trained teachers, administrators, and other children's advocates, who in turn have played a vital role in shaping policies and practice in schools, museums, hospitals, and child care settings. Unlike some private schools, at Bank Street the students are not all drawn from middle- and upper-class families. Thirty-five percent of the children attend the School for Children on a full or partial scholarship. Furthermore, through its Follow-Through program, the Bank Street model has been carried to schools in the inner cities and rural settings all over the United States.

Bank Street has always considered the best teaching/learning situation to include three partners—teacher, parent, and child.